WHITE QUEEN

White Queen

*May French-Sheldon
and the Imperial Origins of
American Feminist Identity*

TRACEY JEAN BOISSEAU

Indiana University Press
Bloomington and Indianapolis

This book is a publication of

Indiana University Press
601 North Morton Street
Bloomington, IN 47404-3797 USA

http://iupress.indiana.edu

Telephone orders   800-842-6796
Fax orders   812-855-7931
Orders by e-mail   iuporder@indiana.edu

© 2004 by Tracey Jean Boisseau

The paper used in this publication meets the minimum requirements of
American National Standard for Information Sciences—Permanence of
Paper for Printed Library Materials, ANSI Z39.48-1984.

MANUFACTURED IN THE UNITED STATES OF AMERICA

Library of Congress Cataloging-in-Publication Data

Library of Congress Cataloging-in-Publication Data

Boisseau, Tracey Jean.
  White queen : May French-Sheldon and the imperial origins of
American feminist identity / Tracey Jean Boisseau.
    p. cm.
Includes bibliographical references (p.) and index.
  ISBN 0-253-34389-5 (cloth : alk. paper) — ISBN 0-253-21669-9
(pbk. : alk. paper)
  1. Sheldon, Mary French, 1847–1936. 2. Feminists—United States—
Biography. 3. Women explorers—Africa—Biography. 4. Nationalism
and feminism—United States. 5. Feminism—United States—History.
6. Imperialism. I. Title.
  HQ1413.S43B65 2004
  305.42'092—dc22

                                                        2003023181

1 2 3 4 5 09 08 07 06 05 04

For the first feminist I ever knew,
my mother.

An individual "emancipated" woman is an amusing incongruity, a titillating commodity, easily consumed.

—Sheila Rowbotham,
Women, Resistance, Revolution, 1972

CONTENTS

LIST OF ILLUSTRATIONS

ACKNOWLEDGMENTS

I have accumulated many debts in the writing, and rewriting, of this book. Undoubtedly, my oldest debt lies with my advisor at Binghamton University, Sarah Elbert, without whose shepherding I could not have begun this project. Other senior scholars encouraged me along the way with specific advice and the benefit of consultation. They include Kelvin Santiago, Anna Davin, Helen Callaway, Dorothy Helly, Grey Osterud, and Sara Mills. I also wish to thank my editors at Indiana University Press, Marilyn Grobschmidt and Richard Higgins; my assistant at the University of Akron's Pierce Library, Ann Evans; as well as the copyeditor, Angela Burton, and the anonymous reviewers who have contributed so much to this work. Foremost among those who have guided this work through publication is Louise Newman whose model of intellectual analysis of early-twentieth-century feminism is one I admire and whose encouragement and specific advice I have benefited from greatly. A fellowship at the Five Colleges Women's Studies Research Center in South Hadley, Massachusetts, gave me my first opportunity to reflect upon and present my findings related to this project. I would like to thank all the women who helped make that year such a productive one for me at an early moment in the history of this project. Of more recent note, I'd like to thank all the members of the Department of History at the University of Akron for the comradeship and intellectual vibrancy they have provided in the final stages of my work.

Debt-making is endemic to research and my debts are spread over three continents. On Zanzibar, administrators of the national archives patiently helped me comb through nearly every scrap of evidence from the early 1890s in a fruitless search for traces of French-Sheldon. Dominique Hoppe, conveniently posted with the Peace Corps in Dar es Salaam the very year my work took me to Africa, supplied the transportation (and picnic items) for a trip along the approximate route French-Sheldon took to Lake Chala in the Kilimanjaro region of northern Tanzania. Her willingness to share her workspace and her table also made writing the first version of this work convenient and even pleasurable. In Britain, the Wellcome Institute and the staff at the Archives of the London Royal Geographical Society were efficient and thorough and pointed me in investigative directions I would not otherwise have followed. In Belgium, the archivists at the *Archives de Palais Royale* and the curators at the *Koninklijk Museum voor Midden-Africa* at

Tervuren provided materials and new insight into the relationship between French-Sheldon, Henry Stanley, and King Leopold II. In the United States, the staff of the manuscript division at the Library of Congress and the National Archives in Washington, D.C., were helpful and patient with me as were staff at the Armstrong Browning Library at Baylor University in Waco, Texas.

Most recently, dear friends have helped with my refining the manuscript into a readable whole. Dearest of these are Karen Flynn whose editorial knowledge and skills are only slightly less remarkable than the sincerity and loyalty of her heart. Only Martha Butler's early and rigorous editing assistance and friendship compares. Sarah Wilcox and Julie Drew also kindly made time in their busy schedules to read portions and to give advice and encouragement in the last year in ways that kept me moving towards my goal. Ever supportive have been Anna Creadick and Kevin Dunn whose intersecting academic interests and political fervor keep me motivated and inspired and whose love and support I could not do without. Along with my parents, in-laws, and brother and sister, these friends have often bolstered my spirits and my confidence in the value of my work.

Finally, like most of us involved in long research and writing projects, I need to thank my life partner, Kirk Hoppe, but hardly feel capable of finding words sufficient to characterize the enormity of the role he has played or to communicate the bond I feel with him. His beauty, his intelligence, and his humanity sustain me.

WHITE QUEEN

Introduction:
A Tale of Imperial Feminism

I wish to be remembered not as Madame Sheldon
but as an unknown, unnamed potentiality
in the great throbbing world.
—May French-Sheldon, as reported in the
Waco News-Tribune, February 27, 1925

In June 1891, upon her return from a three-month trek that had led her
and her retinue of nearly 150 African porters from the coast of East
Africa to the base of Mount Kilimanjaro and back, an American woman
named May French-Sheldon (1847–1936) successfully laid claim to the sobriquet "first woman explorer of Africa."[1] The region had seen much European activity of late as British colonial officers and German soldiers wran-
gled with each other and with African armies for control of the area that lay
between the great lakes of the interior and the coast of East Africa. However, in spite of the recent influx of white soldiers and military scouts, by
1891 there were still very few white women who had visited this part of the
African continent. The few who had done so came as nurses or missionaries and were usually the wives of missionaries or colonial officers to boot.
Such women exhibited little ambition to compete with white men in their
pretensions about their roles as "discoverers" of Africa.[2] As a rule, they rarely
published accounts of their travels, and even more rarely demanded the
public stature associated with male explorers and discoverers once back in
their homelands.[3]

Infusing the tales of her experiences in Africa with a pronounced grandiosity as well as definite scientific and social purpose, the American woman
French-Sheldon stands out sharply from the mostly European colonial wives
and missionaries who were her contemporaries. French-Sheldon led her

Fig. 1. White Queen
French-Sheldon posing in
the White Queen costume
she wore to meet African
headmen in East Africa in
1891.

own sizeable expedition of 150 or so African porters; she traveled at her own
expense, unaccompanied by the husband she had left back in London or by
any white man for that matter, and as she would claim in the end, purely for
the twinned purposes of anthropological exploration and geographic discovery. She returned from what she presented to the public as an ethnographic study of Africans' "inner lives" with a definite blueprint for further
colonial intervention in Africa. Her ambition to be grouped with those influential male explorers whose opinions and information gathering had
made them central authorities in Britain and elsewhere led her to refer to
herself often in accounts of her trip variously as a "Lady Stanley" (referring
to the more famous explorer Henry Morton Stanley who was a friend and
mentor to her), a "White Queen," and a "Bebe Bwana" (translated from the
Swahili by her as "Woman Man").[4] Expressive of the gender hybridity and
sexual tension that lay at the base of French-Sheldon's efforts to represent
her race, nation, and class in Africa, such extraordinary titles disclose more

than a straightforward assertion of scientific authority or a desire to influence governmental policy. I argue that French-Sheldon's self-aggrandizement expressed itself in a pronounced performance of femininity that did not just set her apart from most women even of her own race and class —it also crystallized a model of American feminist identity ascendant in the popular culture of the turn of the century.

Examining French-Sheldon's career as a public figure in the decades that followed her 1891 expedition reveals the extent to which colonialist imagery and frontier ideology played an increasingly critical role in the shaping of popular thinking about what American feminism was or should be all about, as well as how feminist ideology related to American national identity and racial politics. My concern is to detail how the ideal of emancipated womanhood publicly introduced in the 1890s by French-Sheldon and other "adventuresses" like her came to occupy a central place in mass media presentations of American womanhood. By the 1920s French-Sheldon's colonialist activities that had once made her a curious example of new womanhood had catapulted her to the position of exemplar of her race and nation's modern spirit.[5] As the United States embraced a broader imperial agenda, colonialist ideology jelled around such performances of liberated frontier womanhood as French-Sheldon's, giving rise to the iconographic figure of the White Queen and yoking twentieth-century American feminist identity to a colonialist imaginary in the process.

FEMINISM, MODERNITY, IMPERIALISM: THE MAKING OF A WHITE QUEEN

I offer in this book a reading of the arc of French-Sheldon's career as a public feminist from the 1890s through the 1920s that exposes the intertwined nature of the relationship between the origins of popular notions of American feminism, the development of American national identity, and the reorientation of Euro-American imperialism at the turn of the century. French-Sheldon's performances owed their efficacy to the racial backdrop French-Sheldon was able to erect in light of her experiences in Africa, but their enduring relevance depended on the particular gendered spin that French-Sheldon and the press of the time habitually gave to the colonialist import of her message. With the help of a mainstream press eager to baptize her and other "pioneering" women like her as exemplary models of what modernity and America constituted, French-Sheldon parlayed her brief foray in African exploration into a lesson on national identity and feminist deportment. Thus her career provides a lens through which we can perceive the discursive politics of empire at an early moment in the inauguration of a new set of mass cultural ideals for American women. In this study of

French-Sheldon's tactical positioning of herself at the confluence of feminist and imperial discourses, I intend to illuminate this relationship in an attempt to gain a better grasp of how it is that "Western" feminism—and American feminism as the imagined paradigmatic ideal of such—became dependent upon a colonialist imaginary both at the level of rhetoric and at the level of subjectivity.

My adoption of *White Queen* as shorthand for the imperial feminist figure that I argue became central to popular understandings of American feminism in the early twentieth century is prompted by the American press's eager adoption of the title to capture the nature of French-Sheldon's racialized relationship to Africans.[6] A comprehensive analysis of French-Sheldon's performance as a White Queen in Africa awaits readers in the succeeding chapters of this study, but it is important to convey at the outset the literal as well as figurative forms this performance took that made the title such an apt one to describe her. French-Sheldon carried with her to Africa an elaborate court dress made of bright white silk and satin, edged with sparkling jewels made of glass and paste, and designed by the House of Worth in Paris. She wore this dress on ceremonial occasions, especially to greet headmen, or "sultans," as such military and political leaders were known in East Africa in this period. To further enhance the effect of her costume on those she would meet in Africa, she donned a waist-length platinum blonde wig and accented it with a glittering tiara. In addition to hip pistols, a ceremonial sword, and a leather whip, she completed her outfit with a walking staff from which flew a banner emblazoned with the Latin phrase *Noli me tangere* or "Touch me not." With such a toilette, French-Sheldon augmented her class standing, amplified her whiteness, and hyperbolized her gender as a way of signifying her mastery of self and others. She reported that Africans interpreted her costume and her manner in conformance with her intentions—though we have little way of verifying the claim.

Perhaps the more meaningful targets of French-Sheldon's strategic self-fashioning were her American audiences before whom she also appeared dressed in her White Queen costume at times to deliver lectures on the "inner lives" of Africans and the "proper method" of colonizing them. The most prominent among all of the occasions that French-Sheldon appeared so attired represents a watershed event in nineteenth-century America. At the Chicago World's Fair of 1893, French-Sheldon won two awards for her achievements and a special reception for her was held in the Transportation Building to celebrate her exploratory achievements.[7] A reporter for the widely read *Chautauquan,* in an article entitled "A 'White Queen' at the World's Fair," enshrined French-Sheldon as a White Queen and celebrated her supposedly successful exercising of racial authority in Africa. The article attributed French-Sheldon's success as a civilizer to her "prestige" as "a white woman," one "who seemed like a supernatural being sent from the heavens" and whose deliberately racialized performance as a "white queen" aided her in achieving "an unconscious influence over these rude savages." The article cemented this image of French-Sheldon in the minds of its readers with imagistic language, reporting for instance that when Africans "had heard that she had arrived at their borderland, . . . would crowd around to see her, calling her 'Bebe Bwana,' the 'white queen,' and entreating her to remain and rule over them."[8]

As I have argued elsewhere, the use of queenly imagery was ubiquitous at the 1893 Chicago World's Fair, particularly in and around the Woman's Building.[9] More than a rhetorical flourish, at the fair queenliness served as a class and racial marker and, ironically, even as a nationalist symbol signaling the rise of a new kind of woman who did not need to be shielded from public notice and, more, deserved to be put in positions of public authority. French-Sheldon's success in the very male and very public field of colonization and exploration as well as her explicit arrogation of the term *white queen* coincided with the needs of fair organizers to champion a new sort of respectable woman who was capable of representing her race, class, and nation on a global stage in a way that connoted sovereignty, authoritarian power, and racial prestige. The hyper-racialized fantasy of white womanhood that French-Sheldon represented provided a new rationale for the colonial relationships being forged in this period. It is this colonialist fantasy, and its correlations with the development of popular ideas of feminist liberation, that my study of French-Sheldon attempts to deconstruct.

"New women" rarely went to such extremes as French-Sheldon to prove they deserved public roles. Much of what constituted new-woman ideology in the 1890s addressed social issues closer to home. The phrase *new woman* in this period tended to call to the minds of many a woman devoted to reform campaigns advocating temperance, social purity, women's suffrage, or even socialism. Others pictured new women as free-spirited bicyclists and tennis players who smoked and dressed in clothing reminiscent of men's. Still others thought a new woman was any woman who had eschewed marriage and motherhood to pursue education and a career. New womanhood in the 1890s was not a monolithic affair; it was a subject of intense debate and negotiation with colonialist ideology and frontier imagery comprising only a small part of the range of notions associated with the phrase.[10] However, French-Sheldon's White Queen performance was an idealization of a version of new womanhood whose popularity increased rather than lessened in the years that followed. As political reform faded from depictions of new women, vague notions of the triumph of a modern way of life that included feminine liberation from patriarchal restrictions on mobility and public achievement distilled new womanhood into a symbolic form more easily assimilable as a nationalist ideal. The idealization of a new woman that French-Sheldon had so perfectly embodied in the 1890s involved no political reformist platforms or overt organizing on behalf of women. Instead it relied on a portrayal of womanhood empowered solely by dint of the superiority of her race's and nation's propensity toward (literal or metaphorical) conquest. Thus it was that French-Sheldon's White Queen version of emancipated womanhood grew in currency in years when her age and the datedness of her African experiences more logically would have doomed her to irrelevancy and obscurity.

The "modern gal" of the 1910s and 1920s drew on elements of 1890s new womanhood but went further to embrace a radical individualism that contained little room for social reform or political campaigning.[11] By the mid-1920s, young women were pronouncing their generation to be free of the sexual constraints and the cult of domesticity that they viewed as having confined their foremothers. They also rejected a combativeness they associated with past generations of new womanhood, assuming there was no longer any need for struggle against structural barriers to equality with men in a post-suffrage era. Marketers and admen portrayed the modern gal as reveling in a newfound sexual expressiveness in her role as a pleasure-seeking consumer. Even as mother and wife, the modern gal of the 1920s was so adept at the scientific management of the home that she had plenty of time to enjoy the heretofore unknown leisures and freedoms of the "Jazz Age."[12] Most germane to this study is the impression popular cultural texts gave that modern women were liberated not so much from particular men or men as a group as they were from the general contours of a past imagined as particularly repressive and confining in a myriad of ways. The essential difference between modern women and non-modern ones seemed to be best captured by expressions of mobility, whether metaphorically signaled by new fashions in women's clothing that provided for a greater range of movement or whether rendered in mass media images of women accessing new forms of transportation and technology such as airplanes and automobiles. The period saw a revitalization of popular interest in "pioneering" women —women who appeared to be expanding Woman's sphere and opening up masculine fields of employment, achievement, or just pure pleasure to women. This idea turned on the metaphors of empire and discovery, rendering literal acts of empire-building and exploration uniquely resonant with feminist meanings. In such an atmosphere, French-Sheldon's thirty-year-old figuring of American womanhood blazing new trails in geographic exploration for women and taming African savagery along the way gained renewed force and took on new significance.

Although there was little hint of the fun-loving flapper in the eminently respectable seventy-year-old French-Sheldon, her exploration of Africa and interrogation of the "white man's" influence on the frontiers of Western civilization spoke directly to the more substantial of distinctions the media in the 1920s attempted to draw between the modern and all that had gone before. French-Sheldon's frontier experiences went to the heart of the question of women's suitability in the public sphere of masculine authority and accomplishment. Her contribution to the "civilizing mission" was, as she claimed, one of modernizing the process of colonization along with the "primitives" themselves.[13] This was the central message of her written works and lectures in the 1890s, and innumerable commentators and reporters praised French-Sheldon all over again in the 1920s for the stance she adopted as quintessential modernizer of the colonial project as well as liberator of American women. Public pundits and reviewers commended her heartily for helping to bring modern, enlightened rule to Africa while portraying her as the apotheosis of the modern woman "blaz[ing] the way for women in the fields of geology, geography, exploration, and science."[14]

Although the most extraordinary moments of French-Sheldon's life surely take place in Africa, this book is only partially about French-Sheldon and her semi-successful attempts to intervene in the colonization of Africa as an explorer in East Africa and, later, as a colonial spy and ambitious commercial investor in Central and West Africa. Beyond the significance of the relatively minor parts she played in the histories of Africans lies the resonance that her particular embodiment of American womanhood held for American audiences in the years following her 1891 trek. French-Sheldon's ability to carve out a career in the public eye depended not on the lasting significance of her geographic "discoveries"—discoveries that had never amounted to much in the first place. Instead, intermittent popularity she enjoyed with the press and especially with young female admirers even when she was in her seventies (with her researches of Africa by then three decades old) involved a complex performance of femininity that, however flamboyant in nature, scholars of feminism and American women's history should not brush aside as mere idiosyncrasy.

THE PROBLEMATICS OF BIOGRAPHY:
A PUBLIC LIFE IN REVIEW

White Queen is less a biography than a microhistory.[15] The purpose of this study is not to rescue a historical female figure from undeserved obscurity. Nor is it to flesh out the unknown aspects of a dramatic individual's existence or inner psychological reality. I do not mean to provide the details of a life, coherently reconstructed and valued for the intrinsic interest the story might stir in certain readers. To do so would be to resuscitate or augment a story that has circulated in the public realm rather than to deconstruct that story's meaning and the discursive relations it has advanced. In fact, twentieth-century popular interest inspired by stories of the numerous (however often presented as radically unique) exploratresses, adventuresses, and other such female frontier pioneers that date not coincidentally from this period is precisely that which this study interrogates and seeks to problematize. Often overlooked in the celebration of such figures is the fact that these tales are all of white women either literally or metaphorically in the act of colonization.[16] However noteworthy French-Sheldon's life at certain points unquestionably was, the point of focusing attention on her is to throw open our understanding of particular moments in a collective history of American womanhood that have produced metanarratives within which biographical stories of American women have tended to be written. *White Queen* concentrates on the stories French-Sheldon told of herself that became publicly disseminated, repeated, and retold in the press and by onlookers and fans. I am not interested so much in establishing the literal truth or falsity of these stories as I am in discerning the patterns in their features—the constants and discontinuities evidenced in the telling of them and in their relation to the material and ideological context in which they were produced.

While this study does not claim to be a complete or even definitive history of an individual's life, such an approach does not belie the verity or usefulness of providing some simple facts about French-Sheldon at the outset. However inadequate a repetition of these facts may be to explain the histories in which French-Sheldon played a role, a brief outline of the major events of her life may provide coherent scaffolding for my analysis.

The circumstances of French-Sheldon's early life evince a privileged middle-class background but do not foretell the public role she would play in later years. May, born Mary French in 1847 outside Pittsburgh in rural Beaver, Pennsylvania, enjoyed an eventful childhood but not an atypical or public life prior to her departure for Africa in 1891 when she was in her mid-forties. Her travels as an adult were partially sparked by a love of adventure and mobility harbored by her father, with whom she traveled widely throughout the United States as an adolescent in the 1850s and then as a teenager in Europe during the American Civil War. Her father was Colonel Joseph French, a civil engineer and mathematician whose family had made its fortune as planters of sugar, cotton, and tobacco. She was exposed to literature and female professionalism by her mother, Elizabeth J. Poorman—a well-known and successful practicing medical doctor, spiritualist, and specialist in holistic fads of the day such as water-cure therapy and electro-cranial diagnosis.[17] Both May and her two sisters received informal medical training at their mother's knee, and though she never made a living as one, French-Sheldon would often list "doctor" among her accomplishments as an adult.

Fig. 2. A Social Gathering
A social gathering of friends and travel aficionados at the Sheldon's London home
in the 1880s. Upper left is the famed explorer, Henry M. Stanley (leaning). Far left
in doorway is French-Sheldon's husband, Eli Lemon Sheldon. Far right in doorway
is patron and pharmaceutical magnate Henry S. Wellcome. French-Sheldon is
bottom row, far right. Courtesy of Koninklijk Museum voor Midden-Afrika, Tervuren.

The decade following the Civil War was a difficult one for the French
family, as its fortunes declined severely with the changes the war brought to
the economy. Elizabeth Poorman French separated from her husband to
strike out professionally on her own. May also entered a turbulent period of
her life. Though there is little to document the fact and the incident disap-
peared entirely from public notice, it appears that she entered into a hasty
marriage at age nineteen only to divorce within the year.[18] A far more favorable match for her was found in the slightly younger Eli Lemon Sheldon
(1849–1892), a lawyer and investment banker who married May in 1870.
Immediately following the marriage, Sheldon took a job with Conklin and
Jarvis, an investment company that hired him to help secure British investment in American companies and sent him to their office in London to facilitate the firm's relationship with its investors.

With no children and a comfortable income, Eli and May enjoyed a so-
ciable life in London, often collaborating on writing projects and opening
their own publishing house called Saxon and Company in the 1880s. The

company saw a modicum of success, particularly with the series of pocket encyclopedias authored by Eli. The couple also translated a volume on Japanese art and culture for Putnam and Sons.[19] May had a novel published with the respectable Boston publishing house Arena Press. *Herbert Severance* enjoyed moderately favorable reviews and won her the Bookman Prize in 1889.[20] Well-heeled and well-connected individuals were attracted to the enterprising and vivacious couple. Their home became a kind of salon for travelers and explorers and those interested in the increasingly fashionable subjects of geographic research and travel writing. The ground for May's 1891 adventure was laid during raucous parties and lively lectures given by the many guests with whom May and Eli socialized. Included among the most frequent guests were the very successful inventor and entrepreneur of pharmaceuticals, Henry S. Wellcome, as well as the most famous explorer of Africa of the era, Henry Morton Stanley, with whom Eli enjoyed a particularly close relationship.[21]

May's life changed dramatically and abruptly in the year following her return from her expedition in 1891. She found herself an eagerly sought-after expert on Africa and colonialist ventures in venues that included the Columbian Exposition held in Chicago in 1893.[22] However dazzled French-Sheldon may have been by her new life as a public pundit, this was a difficult time for her as well. May and Eli's congenial marriage ended abruptly in 1892 when he died while she was away in the United States finishing writing *Sultan to Sultan,* a narrative of her expedition. Eli's premature death at the age of forty-eight, from what doctors at the time vaguely termed pleurisy, left May saddened and almost entirely bereft of income or a place in London society.[23] In the decade following her husband's death, she relied heavily on her good friend Henry S. Wellcome, who aided her with gifts of money and encouragement.[24] In the 1930s when she was in her eighties, he even listed her among the employees of the his medical museum devoted to pharmaceutical innovation based on tropical medicines garnered largely from colonial Africa. Despite his sincere desire to help his widowed friend, however, Wellcome alone was unable to keep May afloat economically or socially. Luckily, Wellcome was not May's only or even closest friend and supporter in the second half of her life. Within two years of Eli's death, May moved into the house of a woman named Nellie Butler. Although not wealthy, Butler, who had never married, owned a London townhouse and was able to maintain the bare rudiments of respectable middle-class life. Extant photos confirm that their friendship was a close and affectionate one and give the impression that this relationship amounted to as much of a marriage as French-Sheldon's earlier one with Eli Sheldon. Though French-Sheldon was never to enjoy the luxury of extravagant travel, the glamour of high society, or the frills of truly gracious living again, in Butler she found a life partner and economic foundation for the next forty years.

Though frustrated and hampered by her inability to access significant funds in her later life, French-Sheldon's ability to play an international role did not end with her husband's death. French-Sheldon's second major intervention in the colonization of Africa came in the first few years of the new century and was financed not by her or her close friends but by a British-based reformist organization, the Congo Reform Association. In 1903 William E. Stead, a co-founder with E. D. Morel of that organization, hired French-Sheldon as an undercover spy to obtain information about conditions in the Congo Free State that would damage the reputation of King Leopold II of Belgium and help orchestrate the release of his military and economic grip on the region. However, unbeknownst to Stead and Morel, French-Sheldon's sympathies lay with the beleaguered Belgian king and her actions in the Free State and in Britain upon her return seem to have been those of a double agent. The story of this episode in her life is complicated further by her ambitions to found her own plantation and colonization company in Liberia in 1905–1907. Although briefly retraining light onto French-Sheldon, neither of these ventures accrued monetary benefit nor reinvigorated her speaking career.

Such reinvigoration came from an unexpected quarter during her visit to the United States during World War I. During the next decade, French-Sheldon would successfully learn to tailor her public presentation of self to fit the explosion of interest in the heroines that American newspapers began touting as the embodiment of the Jazz Age of the 1910s and 1920s. In the late 1920s, when her age began to seriously restrict her ability to travel and appear in public, French-Sheldon finally retired permanently from the public eye. She lived out the last few years of her life in quiet in London with Nellie Butler until her death just prior to her eighty-ninth birthday in the spring of 1936. The *New York Times, London Times,* and most other major newspapers on both sides of the Atlantic carried glowing obituaries of French-Sheldon that recalled the unique features of her 1891 expedition. However, despite infrequent mentions of French-Sheldon that appeared in chronicles of African travelers and in a few scattered scholarly discussions of the relative brutality or humanitarianism of the "scramble" for Africa, for the most part French-Sheldon's reputation as the "first woman explorer of Africa" faded into obscurity rather quickly following her retirement from the stages of the public-speaking halls of the 1920s. In the 1940s a relative of Nellie Butler, Ann Butler, deposited with the Library of Congress in Washington, D.C., a cache of papers and photographs as well as the fantastic dress and accoutrements French-Sheldon had worn in Africa and to deliver her speech on African colonization to the Women's Congress at the 1893 World's Fair. This cache of papers, her published writings, and archival evidence culled from the papers of Henry Morton Stanley, Henry S. Wellcome, and the Royal Archives in Brussels, set against public reports, interviews, and reviews of French-Sheldon form the basis for my historical assessment of her public interventions in the construction of popular ideas about feminism and imperialism in the period from 1891 to 1928.

FRAMING THE *WHITE QUEEN:* AN OVERVIEW

This study is not a biography, but its analyses loosely chronicle the major events of French-Sheldon's life as a public figure. Part 1 focuses on French-Sheldon's most important public achievement—her caravan trek in the Kilimanjaro region and her representations of that experience. In this part, I take a close look at *Sultan to Sultan: Adventures among the Masai and Other Tribes of East Africa* (1892), the ethnographic narrative she wrote to publicize and commemorate her trek. I mine the text for clues to the strategic manipulation of class, race, and gender ideologies engaged in by French-Sheldon to establish herself as a public authority on Africa and colonization. My dissection of French-Sheldon's travel narrative aims to reveal the commercial aims and colonizing effects of travel writing in this time period. I also intend to demonstrate how, through an orientalization of East Africa that included the emasculinization of its men and the dehumanization of its women, French-Sheldon presented an empowered model of new womanhood whose integrity depended upon a racist imaginary. By manipulating progressive discourses of civilization and uplift, French-Sheldon carved out a space within colonial projects for bourgeois white women to imagine themselves as political actors and authorized Subjects that leaned heavily upon racial hierarchy. Taking a hard look at the multiple agendas underlying French-Sheldon's narrative, part 1 demonstrates that *Sultan to Sultan* is more than a travelogue and perhaps less than an ethnography. More than anything, it is an epic autobiographical tale of hardship and heroism put to the service of what French-Sheldon wanted readers to see as an innovative blueprint for a more humane colonization of Africa. The genteel narrator of this experimental form of new-woman literature constitutes an early manifestation of a feminist on the world stage. That this ideal type was destined to become a ubiquitous feminine archetype in twentieth-century American popular narratives justifies an in-depth analysis of the literary strategies that went into its textual construction.

Chapter 1, "The Caravan Trek to Kilimanjaro," lays out the facts of her expedition and the circumstances surrounding her foray into the fields of African exploration and colonization. In chapter 2, "Self-Discovery," I discuss the knottier of social contradictions surrounding French-Sheldon's representation of herself as a scientist-explorer as well as a respectable woman and national heroine in her recounting of her expedition. My goal in chapter 3, "Forging a Feminine Colonial Method," is to demonstrate French-Sheldon's particular interweaving of commercial interests with scientific altruism and national interests in ways that echo the sorts of "anti" or "new" imperialist rhetoric on the rise in the United States in the 1890s. I also examine in this chapter French-Sheldon's self-image as a global social reformer and explain how she employed new-womanhood ideology and ideas related to racial uplift to craft her White Queen persona. Chapter 4, "Sex and the Sultans," highlights the sexual politics of French-Sheldon's textual self-representation, exposing the erotic elements of her text as subtle strategies aimed at elevating the narrator of *Sultan to Sultan* to the level of a Subject. Chapter 5, "Confessions of a White Queen," concludes my discussion of *Sultan to Sultan* by reflecting upon the internal contradictions of the text, the slippages and fissures that point to the not quite resolvable tensions between the many discourses French-Sheldon strove to turn to her purposes in the writing of her accounts of her expedition.

Part 2 probes French-Sheldon's second overt intervention in the colonizing of Africa—her activities as an undercover agent in the Congo Free State from 1903 and her attempts to establish her own plantation and colonization company in Liberia in 1905–1907. This section of the book dealing with French-Sheldon in a more active role as a colonial entrepreneur and agent of state power substantiates the material links between the liberal political ideas that animated French-Sheldon, the dependence of those ideas upon a racist imaginary, and the logical result of those ideas when expressed as colonial practice. Chapter 6, "An Imperial Spy in the Congo," details the Congo Reform Association's recruitment of French-Sheldon as a "neutral" observer of Belgian King Leopold's administration of the Congo Free State and offers evidence in support of the view that, while in Africa and upon her return, French-Sheldon acted as a double agent for Leopold. French-Sheldon's central involvement in this controversy gave her access to a network of colonial rubber plantation entrepreneurs and positioned her to negotiate a concession from Liberia for a plantation encompassing twelve hundred square miles of territory. Chapter 7, "A Plantation Mistress in Liberia," details the struggle French-Sheldon unsuccessfully waged to execute her plan in Liberia to "repatriate" landless black Americans from the American South to work on the massive plantation she envisioned constructing in West Africa. A worldview that embraced racial uplift as a primary justification for white middle-class women's participation in global politics and colonial conquest facilitated French-Sheldon's rise to prominence in both these situations.

Part 3 describes the new interest in French-Sheldon as a figure for emulation among young women in the 1910s and 1920s. Chapter 8, "Taking

Feminism on the Road," explains how French-Sheldon in her seventies, instead of finding herself utterly eclipsed by the youth-oriented "new woman" of these years, discovered that her experiences as a White Queen in Africa provided her with an even more secure base from which to promote herself as a representative modern woman—now that being "modern" was deemed more unambiguously positive and being a woman who had "liberated" herself from the private sphere was imagined as definitively illustrative of being American. Rather than justifying her colonial activities as an outgrowth of her status as a veritable "true" woman as she had in the 1890s, French-Sheldon now justified her status as a model woman on the basis of her experiences on the colonial frontier as a modernizer of Africa.[25]

This subtle reorienting of priorities and purposes is evident in the kinds of stories French-Sheldon told in these years and in the ways she chose to tell them. To the young girls who made up the bulk of her audiences, French-Sheldon played down the more scientific and practical-minded of her views on colonization to redirect light onto herself as an emblem of the modern era and her nation's unrivaled progress toward the modern ideal of woman's emancipation. The acclaim French-Sheldon enjoyed as a professional feminist illumines a popularized and ostensibly depoliticized understanding of American feminism whose hegemony depended almost solely upon a set of (often erotic) comparisons with colonized society and non-whites for its ideological power. Chapters 9 and 10 of part 3 ask readers to consider the adoration with which young women showered French-Sheldon in the 1910s and 1920s in light of feminist film and psychoanalytic theories of the Subject and fetishism. In chapter 9, "Masquerading as the Subject of Feminism," I argue that psychoanalytically inflected theories of subjectivity that hinge on the notion of the fetish are critical to understanding French-Sheldon's appeal to young women in these years and to the construction of a media-friendly ideal of American feminism. In chapter 10, "The Queen, the Sheik, the Sultana, and the Female Spectator," I take a look at the erotic excitement generated by French-Sheldon and read this excitement against a context of emergent popular narratives such as the desert romance films of Rudolph Valentino. This juxtapositioning points to the features of French-Sheldon's performance that most closely relate to those of more widely known White Queens in the mass media of the time, such as Mae West or Marlene Dietrich. The colonial and race contexts within which these feminine idols were often placed in order to backlight the agency and empowerment of the heroines they portrayed discloses the degree to which the White Queen emerged in these years as a widely accepted heroic persona through a phallic sexualization of the feminist ideal and an accompanying displacement of feminized subjugation onto orientalized Others.

THEORIZING THE WHITE QUEEN

Clearly, French-Sheldon's was not the only or even among the most well-known of performances of feminism in the period of accelerated mass cultural media that stretched from the 1890s through the 1920s, but her stature as a minor popular heroine of the time permits us to see how ordinary public discourse came to thicken around such individuals. Her career spanned an era that included the introduction of the term *feminist* into the English language, one that saw debates over feminism become central to the fashioning of an American national identity at home and abroad.[26] A comparative analysis of the public discussions of French-Sheldon in the 1890s and later in the 1920s permits an appreciation of how perceptions become cemented in public discourse and new symbols condensing and conveying complex ideological convictions form. Her long, yet inconstant, career in the public eye provides historians of feminism with a valuable opportunity to assess the period as a whole specifically with regard to the emergence and consolidation of public understandings of feminism. By focusing on one woman as a clear example of an archetype in the making, I demonstrate in detail how individuals simultaneously can contribute to the construction of ideology even as those ideologies give rise to subjectivities and subject positions from which they as individuals (are compelled to) speak. Rather than asserting this idea purely as an abstract maxim, I intend to demonstrate this in historical specificity to shed light on the implications that the particular construction of popular understandings of feminism early in the twentieth century has had for feminist identity formation since its inception.

Scholarship on feminist subjectivity incorporating the works of Michel Foucault, Louis Althusser, and Jacques Lacan has facilitated new interpretations of the relationship between individuals and ideology that have shaped my thinking about the emergence of feminism as a central motif in the stories that Americans have chosen to tell about themselves. Such scholarship suggests that we examine the White Queen as a subject position in popular culture and not simply as a role or stereotype.[27] I recognize the awkwardness of much of this theory for those of us trained as social historians and in particular as feminist historians of women, given the often convoluted nature and consistent male-centeredness of such theorizing. The question may arise for historians of feminism, why do we need such complex and seemingly ahistorical theories to answer our need to know what happened and why it happened? I see social historians' frustrated attempts to come to terms with the decline of "first-wave" feminism and its aftermath in the 1920s as a prime example demonstrating our need for more intricate frameworks of analyses than those traditional social history provides. While social history has produced abundant documentary evidence of changes in popular discourses on feminism in the Progressive Era, murkiness about why these changes occurred remains, and often, questions of how individuals experienced them and what this experiential dimension holds for feminism as a set of identities fall outside most social histories of American women. Although no microhistorical study is possible without the benefit of more traditional social histories that provide large aggregates of data about broad groups of women and institutions, as Joan Scott has argued forcefully, "to pursue meaning, we need to deal with the individual subject as well as social organization."[28] I hope this study will convince readers there is room within feminist historiography for microhistories that pull in close to individuals, allowing historians to better assess the possible ways that broad patterns of change were experienced and meaning produced in the past.

Sophisticated understandings of identity formation, popular culture, subjectivity, and agency are crucial to our understanding of what has been often noted simply as a deterioration of feminism in the 1910s and 1920s. The more pessimistic of these studies view this period as one of usurpation by commercial interests producing a commodified culture that refused women any sense of themselves as agents in ways that did not conform to industrial needs or male heterosexuality. The more optimistic studies depict the era simply as a holding pattern wherein feminism, imagined in these accounts as a social force somewhat akin to a transhistorical notion of progress for women, goes fallow for a period only to reemerge under new circumstances as the unavoidable outcome of the ongoing human striving for justice. Recent critiques of mass culture as relentlessly totalitarian and the rejection of enlightenment-style teleologies have dimmed the rhetoric of women's history in both regards without necessarily producing new explanations to account for the contradictions of the 1920s.[29]

The analytical frameworks typically applied to this historical riddle are part of the reason our explanations fall short. Let us return to the concept of role modeling, for instance. Many women's historians have relied on the concept of role modeling to explain how, in the words of Susan Ware, popular culture "kept feminism alive" via a celebration of "women-firsts"— mainly of aviatrixes and sports heroines—in the 1920s and 1930s, so that it might be revived later in the century.[30] While I do not entirely overlook the degree to which role modeling was the primary way in which a popular understanding of feminism was performed and conveyed to mass audiences in these years (indeed, my reading of French-Sheldon's public career confirms the basic evidentiary foundations of this argument), the concept of role modeling does not afford adequate explanatory power as an analytic framework for historians trying to understand *why* role modeling displaced all other ways of performing feminism publicly nor why *certain sorts of role models* became hegemonic national ideals while others languished. If a focus on commercial advertisements in this period can blur our thinking about the degree to which feminist ideas were commodified and appropriated (obscuring the possibilities of individual agency entirely), studies of feminist heroines that rely on an unexamined conceptualization of role modeling attribute an enormous degree of power to individual women without permitting us to explain, for example, how particular models of feminism related to the social context of their time, how they relied on other axes of power to operate, precisely how they were experienced, or why and how they changed. Worse, this way of investigating the history of feminism, in the end, often demands that we reinstate, even celebrate, these same models of feminism as heroines all over again rather than use our knowledge about them as tools to better understand feminism in its historical specificity as particular women's complex way of accessing power, organizing identity, and aspiring to subjectivity.

Viewing the psycho-dynamic relationships young women formed in relation to the popular heroines of the 1920s with the aid of theories of the Subject provides some guidelines for determining why and how different groups of women became positioned differently in twentieth-century feminist discourse and permits us to begin to understand the vicissitudes of feminist activism and the myriad forms that resistance to it has assumed. In other words, using theories of the Subject to understanding the operations of feminist identity formation through role modeling permits us to evaluate the operations of power that were enacted in the name (or while avoiding the name) of feminism.

While a Subject is constituted in language (rather than speaking, it is spoken), a Subject position is an ideological location from which a (seemingly) unified subject speaks. *Subjectification* for my purposes refers to the empowerment of a self through discursive positioning. Within the terms of Lacanian theory, a feminine subject is an impossibility as a result of Woman's negation relative to a phallocentric order. Nevertheless, without disregarding the imperatives of phallocentrism, feminist theorists informed by Jacques Lacan (as well as by Louis Althusser) consider the possibilities of (a somewhat compromised) female subjectification through discursive repositioning in ideology.[31] Part of the goal of this inquiry into French-Sheldon's interventions in culture is to understand the construction and assumption of a feminine identity whose allure was a result of the illusion or promise of subjectification. My dual concern is the degree to which imperial relationships fostered this identity and the material and ideological ramifications of constructing such an identity at a particular historical moment. In short, I seek to understand how and why an individual such as May French-Sheldon was able to reject or take up an ideological position, and how she and others were interpellated (repositioned and redefined in ways that compelled their participation in the constructs at hand) by the effects of the discourse that resulted from these decisions.

To answer the question I have posed, I turn the insights of psychoanalytic theory, both Freudian and Lacanian, to feminist and historicist purposes. Like Anne McClintock, whose *Imperial Leather* has contributed a masterful rendering of Freudian and Lacanian theory into a form of "situated psychoanalysis" that she defines as "a culturally contextualized psychoanalysis that is simultaneously a psychoanalytically informed history," I refuse the embedded assumptions concerning universality and timelessness that psychoanalysts traditionally have asserted as their terrain.[32] Retraining the historian's eye back onto psychoanalysis as a theoretical articulation of a particular set of relationships of power specific to their historic moment permits what I hope readers will agree is a more nuanced and layered argument about identity formation in the period this study encompasses than could otherwise be accomplished.

CONCLUSION

My interest in French-Sheldon's public career lies in the ways that French-Sheldon personified an ascendant archetype of American feminism that predetermined and limited who it is that can constitute the feminist and can access the subjectivity that this label proffers. With a deconstruction of French-Sheldon as "pioneer for feminism," I elucidate how such language and promotion constrain what feminist liberation is and can be for women not advantageously located at a twentieth-century nexus of colonial, racial, and class privilege and how certain patterns in American mass culture have positioned feminism as a set of discourses that constitute an imperial threat to colonized or post-colonized people. I hope this investigation contributes to explanations of why it is that feminism does not just *appear* to the colonized often as a rarified form of Western imperialism but actually *functions* that way at times, in the exclusions that it perpetuates at the level of the Subject as a consequence of its acute reliance upon an orientalist and racist imaginary.

Finally, while this study is predicated on an assumption that a line between the civilized and the uncivilized is a cultural construction, it nevertheless postulates that American myths of the frontier produced as well as reflected the material relations of empire at the turn of the century. As an identity as much or more than a bounded set of principles or policy positions, twentieth-century feminism has been an arena for discursive struggle with very real and material consequences and applications. I hope to show how French-Sheldon's popular appeal as a feminist on the basis of her role as an agent and symbol of American imperialism reveals a process whereby feminism became linked with imperialist practices and effects as well as ideologies. In the conclusion to this work, I assert that White Queenliness is not unique to French-Sheldon but forms a key trope in twentieth-century American popular culture that has oriented American feminism towards imperial ends and has helped to shape an ontological conundrum for feminist identity formation. The development and proliferation of White Queen mass cultural narratives have added a level of complexity to postcolonial relationships that is often oversimplified as a conflict between a feminist and generally liberatory West and the hopelessly patriarchal rest. French-Sheldon may not have lived on in the imaginations of most Americans past her own lifetime, but the figure of the White Queen that she so eminently personified is with us still in this easy and poisonous bromide framing much of the geopolitics of our day.

Part I

FIRST WOMAN
EXPLORER OF AFRICA:
THE 1891 EXPEDITION

ONE

The Caravan Trek to Kilimanjaro

Find out the place where you may stand
Beneath some burden bow
Take up the task with willing hand
Be something, somewhere, Now![1]

HO! FOR EAST AFRICA!

"How I wish I could go with you!" whispered the "lovely girl friends, sentimental hero-worshippers," pressed around May French-Sheldon, "who set the seal of admiration upon [her] lips by their farewell kisses" as she prepared to depart from London's Charing Cross Station for Dover and, from there, on to East Africa. In her travel narrative *Sultan to Sultan,* French-Sheldon recalled that the scene at the railway station was a dramatic one, with "a hundred or more" crowded around the American traveler in "a pea-soup fog, thick, black, damp, and chilly," to send her off with "cheers, pelting of flowers, and the usual half-hysterical, frantic commotion attending a departure where a friend's life seemed at stake." Intermingled among the inspiring words were, apparently, only a few "gruesome remarks" prefaced with phrases like, "If you return alive . . ." (*SS: 67*).[2]

Alongside her husband, Eli Lemon Sheldon, and interspersed among the sympathetic friends and acquaintances gathered to see May French-Sheldon off in the cold of an English February 1891 were several London personalities notable for their personal connections and influence in the field of African exploration. Fellow traveler and well-known surgeon T. H. Parke distributed a few last words of advice. "Be cautious, vigilant, ready for any surprise, careful of your health, and you'll win," admonished the doctor. In a gesture suggesting the passing on of a legacy and a mandate A. Bruce —described by French-Sheldon as "the sturdy son-in-law of the great Livingstone—thrust into [her] hands a long-range field glass, as if to bid [her]

Fig. 3. May French-Sheldon in Walking Suit
In addition to her fancy court dress, French-Sheldon wore a plain walking suit on trek making travel by caravan a simpler affair on days when she was not scheduled to meet with African headmen.

be far-sighted" (*SS:* 67). The man present at French-Sheldon's departure who may have been most critical to the success of her upcoming endeavor was a fellow American ex-patriate named Henry S. Wellcome. He had helped French-Sheldon design the *palanquin,* or elaborate litter, with which African porters were to carry her on trek. He also helped arrange the scene at her departure for the benefit of the press, and served as her publicist while she was abroad.[3]

Wellcome, one half of the prosperous pharmaceutical partnership of Burroughs-Wellcome, devoted many of his skills as a promoter and publicist to the cause of African exploration. His patronage of explorers was no mere philanthropic affair, however. The growing pharmaceutical industry of which he was a pioneer depended heavily upon the African agricultural commodities explorers and travelers to Africa identified, the medical knowledge they collected from Africans, and the often coercive relationships they helped to forge between Africans and Western commercial interests. The prestigious School of Tropical Medicine and Medical Museum that Wellcome would go on to establish in London acknowledged the centrality of Africa and African exploration to modern pharmacology, though the exhibits tended to obscure the political and military factors that underpinned the relationship. Wellcome's patronage of French-Sheldon and other even more renowned explorers of the period stemmed from his entrepreneurial interests in Africa as a source of valuable pharmaceutical ingredients as well as from his general predilection toward the excitement and glory associated with African exploration. His help in planning French-Sheldon's expedition and his efforts to shape public opinion of her while she was gone would prove crucial to her success as a public authority on Africa. The aid and acquaintanceship of such a man as Wellcome hint at the many purposes that lay behind the seemingly spontaneous, non-governmental and non-commercial acts of exploration upon which French-Sheldon was about to venture.

Central to Wellcome's strategy to publicize French-Sheldon as the first woman explorer of Africa was his grouping of her in the public mind with the more famous Henry Morton Stanley. By placing ads and announcements in major London newspapers, Wellcome made sure the London press did not forget about the woman he dubbed the "Lady Stanley" as she made her way along caravan routes to Mount Kilimanjaro. Later that year the London satirical newspaper *Punch* solidified the moniker with a mocking limerick that spoofed the odd combination of womanliness and manliness that such a title communicated. "Were she only a man," the limerick mused, "we should hail her as manly! / As it is, there are some who, in wishing to laud / Are accustomed to call her the feminine STANLEY." Solidifying rather than diluting the parallel Wellcome strove to establish between her and the more well-known and admired explorer, it is likely that the weekly newspaper's send-up stung Stanley more than it did French-Sheldon. The limerick ended by conjecturing, "In time that's to come Mr. STANLEY may be / Merely known to us all as the male Mrs. SHELDON!"[4]

In addition to aiding his friend in her pursuit of public recognition, Wellcome intended to capitalize on the notice he attracted to French-Sheldon. As part of a clever marketing campaign for his pharmaceutical company, Wellcome donated a sample "Burroughs-Wellcome Travel Kit" to French-Sheldon's expedition.[5] The kit came complete with the innovation that would help make travel more convenient and Wellcome's name a household word—medicine that came in the form of easily transportable tablets or "pills." With the innovative travel devices that Wellcome supplied in stow, and the attention he had helped bring to bear upon her endeavors in place, French-Sheldon set out for the adventures that awaited.

Fig. 4. The *Madura*
This mail ship was the only regular ferry for European passengers who wished to travel from Southern Europe to East Africa in the late nineteenth century.

French-Sheldon and her husband parted from Wellcome and Parke at Dover and crossed Europe by train to meet a mail ship called the *Madura* in Naples. *Sultan to Sultan* records a tearful goodbye to Eli in the Italian port as French-Sheldon boarded the steamship on one of its regular journeys across the Mediterranean through the Suez Canal and the Red Sea and finally into the Indian Ocean. With only two other first-class passengers on board, both men, French-Sheldon maintained that the steamship soon "assumed the aspect of a private steam yacht" as it set sail for Mombasa and then to the island of Zanzibar that lay a few miles off Africa's eastern coast.[6] The ship itself represented for French-Sheldon her initiation into a world of great men, public events, and History—a world on which she was about to leave a figurative mark, if her telling of it was any indication.

IN THE COMPANY OF GREAT MEN

The *Madura* has its own history, is most famous, every timber athrill with the recollection of the tread of celebrated travellers and explorers. . . . The reminiscences of this vessel would . . . give a history of startling events and tell of leaders who have acted as great discoverers and civilizers. . . . [Y]et with all, she floats on serenely, unruffled, steadfast to her course, making no visible sign of her invested greatness or reflected honors, unstained, excepting possibly the ink splashes with which I carelessly defaced her spotless decks.)

French-Sheldon, *Sultan to Sultan,* 1892

May French-Sheldon was eager to establish her claim to greatness and to her rightful inclusion in the company of great men. With the "ink stains" she left in her travel diaries aboard ship, she strove to document the strength of mind and will that she believed qualified her to such inclusion. Publication of her African experiences in the year following her return helped to convince the British and American publics to accept her expedition as evidence of her heroic worth. To ensure that they would, she sprinkled *Sultan to Sultan* with frequent allusions to well-respected men of authority and public standing. French-Sheldon represented these figures to her readers as alarmed at the dangers she would face in Africa, yet admiring of her determination to embrace a challenge that few men had met.

Male acceptance of French-Sheldon was a tricky affair, however, requiring a few convoluted turns in logic. In the very first scene of the text of *Sultan to Sultan,* French-Sheldon referenced her husband's endorsement of her expedition in order to preempt readers' disaffection or their conclusion that her desire to explore Africa issued from an erratic nature or some hysterical feminine impulse. She admitted to having advertised her husband's support of her intentions widely "as evidence that when he sanctioned my undertaking, it was not irrational" (*SS:* 67). Eli Sheldon's approval was crucial to the public persona that French-Sheldon desired to cultivate. It helped authorize and legitimate her actions and served to protect her reputation as a woman of untarnished respectability. Conversely, evidence of male *dis*approval would prove just as important to this tale of Victorian new womanhood.[7] Throughout *Sultan to Sultan,* to give her narrative a dramatic boost and to foreground her own heroism, French-Sheldon tended to pair her husband's support for her expedition with the skepticism she claimed to have endured generally from men overly attached to conventional ideas about women as unsuited for adventure. Such discouragement remained vague and unsubstantiated in any of her accounts, however. She took it for granted that male hostility in general did not need substantiating. She was much more likely to provide supportive quotes from men such as Sir Edwin Arnold, who drew on his acquaintance with "all the modern explorers of the Dark continent from the illustrious Livingstone down to the honored line of Speke and Grant, Burton, Moffat, Cameron, Stanley and Johnson" to claim that "the authoress of 'Sultan to Sultan' has bravely and plainly earned the right" to have her "charming volume" placed "side by side with theirs" in his library.[8]

French-Sheldon was immensely pleased by praise linking her with the most prestigious male explorers of the century lavished upon her by Sir Edwin Arnold, a respected member of the London Royal Geographical Association. She actively courted the friendships of men like Arnold even before she conceived of a plan to earn the right to be counted among them.

Soon after their move to London in 1879, French-Sheldon and her husband had established a salon in their London home for travelers and others interested in African exploration. Their well-connected compatriot Henry Wellcome engineered the couple's gravitation to the center of an elite circle of world travelers by directing many of his associates to them. Perhaps the most frequent, and certainly the most famous, of visitors to the Sheldon home in the 1880s was the unrivaled Henry Morton Stanley.

Twenty years before French-Sheldon set out on her own trek, Stanley's successful search for the explorer cum missionary, David Livingstone, received unprecedented public attention in the United States and Europe.[9] Stanley, a poor orphan who as an adult tried to hide his ignominious Welsh beginnings behind a veil of American citizenship, handled his sudden rise to fame awkwardly. Under pressure from upper-class British geographers who attempted to cast doubt on the verities of his claims and to disparage his unrefined manner, Stanley took umbrage at the slightest criticism or note of mockery in press reports of his public presentations. He especially resented the uproarious amusement that ensued at his relation of his initial greeting to Livingstone in a remote part of Africa: "Dr. Livingstone I presume?" The obviousness and incongruous formality of this remark would not fail to elicit smirks and laughter for several generations to come. More damaging were criticisms that he exaggerated or fabricated elements of his travels and conquests in Africa. Failure to adopt a dry, scientific tone in his writings, or to succeed at affecting a restrained matter-of-factness more characteristic of British travel writings, put Stanley at odds with British upper-class readers and audiences and made him, paradoxically, a pariah as well as a hero to those belonging to exclusive geographical societies. The criticism he received often dwelled on the self-portraits he painted in his publications of a man who relied on extortion, enslavement, torture, and murder to accomplish his goals. How much violence was essential to the civilizing mission was a heated question in the 1870s and 1880s, as Britain fought to secure and add to its empire across the globe.[10] Even more than his gift for understatement or tendencies towards embellishment, Stanley's rough edges and reputation for brutality as an explorer made him and his daring expeditions a major focal point for British debates over colonial strategies and policies throughout the period.

French-Sheldon, in contrast with London high society, found nothing humorous or contemptible in Stanley's coarseness or untrammeled ambition. Despite her own refined background and impeccable public deportment, she found in Stanley's example a rough-and-ready model of American-style adventurism. Prior to the outbreak of the Spanish-American War in 1898, most Americans were less troubled by the questions raised by colonial expansion that plagued the British, lacking as they did an extraconti-

nental empire and unwilling as they were to recognize their nation as an imperial power facing some of the same issues as Britain. For this reason and as
a consequence of the American celebration of the "rugged individual,"
American audiences and readers in the 1870s and 1880s had less trouble cel-
ebrating Stanley's exploits, rough edges, and braggadocio style. American audiences shared French-Sheldon's hero worship of the man, reveling in his
tales of the "Dark Continent" without too much soul-searching regarding
the ethics of empire. French-Sheldon's unequivocal idolization of Stanley in
the 1880s is revealed in the frontispiece dedication to her translation of
Gustave Flaubert's *Salammbô*, where she praised him as "the great explorer,
who found Dr. Livingstone . . . and created the Congo Free State, which is
destined someday to outrival ancient Phoenicia."[11] She wrote this dedication
in 1886, before conceiving of her own expedition and before events in
Hawaii and the remnants of the Spanish empire had propelled new questions about empire to the front pages of American newspapers. Not too
many years would pass before French-Sheldon would challenge Stanley's
model of aggressive exploration as part of the rise of "anti-imperialist" attitudes in the United States. Although French-Sheldon never ceased to admire
Stanley privately, publicly French-Sheldon utilized Stanley as a foil to throw
(what she claimed to be) her more humane model of colonizer into relief.[12]

Yet the material relations of empire were never far from these imaginary and ideological concerns. French-Sheldon's relationship to Stanley was
grounded on more than a shared interest in the principles of colonization or
the ethics of African exploration devoid from the practical considerations of
the implications of various methods of colonization. In fact, French-Sheldon dedicated her translation of *Salammbô* to Stanley at a time when her
husband and Stanley were conspiring behind the scenes to organize the
building of a railroad line through Central Africa. Stanley had become a
very close friend of Eli Sheldon during the 1880s, even living with him for
weeks on end between trips to Africa. The couple hosted him frequently,
helping him celebrate his accomplishments and decompress from the pressures of public notoriety with intimate, but lively, parties at their London
home. It appears that Stanley hoped to return the favor by folding the Sheldons into his own self-aggrandizing colonial schemes in Africa.

In private letters, sometimes marked "confidential," written to Eli Sheldon in the late 1880s, Stanley promised to offer him an integral role in the
commercial ventures to which he hoped his explorations would give rise.
For instance, Stanley credited Sheldon with the thinking behind the plan
for a railway and expressed his intention to promote him as "Secretary of
the Railway Co. should it come to anything" in one letter to Sheldon written in 1889.[13] Stanley and Sheldon's plan to establish a cross-continental
railway in Africa faltered when King Leopold II of Belgium hesitated to act

Fig. 5. Clowning with H. M. Stanley and Guests
French-Sheldon (center) poses in her London home with her husband, Eli Lemon Sheldon
(upper row, far left) and guests that included Henry M. Stanley (upper row, center)
whose mementos from his recent African travels provided an opportunity for amusement.
Courtesy of Koninklijk Museum voor Midden-Afrika, Tervuren.

to set it in motion immediately following the 1884–1885 Berlin Congress,
as Stanley had expected he would. Nevertheless, privately Leopold continued to encourage Stanley and perhaps inadvertently through Stanley, the
Sheldons, to believe that the realization of the mandate the Congress had
granted Leopold over much of the Congo basin would present unparalleled
commercial opportunities.[14] There was still much reason in 1891 for Stanley and his friends to assume that Leopold would eventually make good on
his promises.

Leopold owed a debt of gratitude to Stanley, who had helped to sway
the American delegation, of which Stanley was a member, and to convince
the other European powers at the Berlin Congress to sanction Leopold's creation of a "free state" in central Africa. The famed explorer helped secure
Leopold's Central African interests in 1887–1889 by rerouting his expedition to rescue Emin Pasha, an embattled German-born commander representing the British/Egyptian government in the Sudan.[15] Stanley took the
very, very long way to the Sudan, disembarking on the Atlantic coast of
Central Africa and traveling up the Congo River through the center of the

continent, both to claim the charting of this heretofore unmapped area for himself and to secure the Belgian king's hold over the region he nominally claimed a "free state." With the help of contacts Stanley made and routes he forged, the vast and rich Congo quickly fell under Leopold's monopolistic control. In the end, however, Stanley's loyalty to the ambitious and manipulative Belgian monarch produced little tangible or financial reward for himself. It garnered even less for Stanley's good friend Eli Sheldon, whose health had started to fail even prior to Stanley's return from the Emin Pasha expedition in the summer of 1890. Perhaps in lieu of further plans with Stanley to promote the career of her ailing husband, French-Sheldon began to look for a way to propel herself into a limelight normally reserved for the men of her race and class.

The relationship Eli Sheldon enjoyed with Stanley was an important stimulus to French-Sheldon's plans. French-Sheldon drew on his inspiring example and took advantage of his fame by requesting from him endorsements for her expedition and letters of introduction. Although privately Stanley exhibited a distinct lack of enthusiasm for French-Sheldon's scheme, his close relationship to her husband made it difficult for him to refuse French-Sheldon's insistent requests for letters of introduction that would legitimate her and direct the officials of the Imperial British East Africa Company (IBEA) to provide her with assistance.[16] In the end Stanley supplied her with several letters. His letters carry a decidedly condescending tone and reveal how unclear he was, and perhaps how cagey French-Sheldon was herself, as to the purposes of the costly but fairly routine trek she had in mind. Stanley described French-Sheldon to IBEA representative George S. Mackenzie and to the director of the Christian mission at Mombasa, as a "litterateur" and "an accomplished writer" who "desires to obtain some local colouring for an African romance." He added, "What she desires to do eventually while in search of it I do not know." In spite of this tepid endorsement, Stanley made it quite clear that French-Sheldon was a "close friend" and firmly informed Mackenzie that it would be "warmly appreciated" if the officials of the company would extend "every consideration" to "gratify her *penchant* for African matters to the full."[17]

Stanley also added a letter of advice to French-Sheldon in which he advised her in no uncertain terms not to venture beyond the mission at Mombasa—"or your own sake"—and not to stay too long, as it would be impossible to avoid getting the fever or triggering some "lurking malady," which would cause her "to certainly lose her good looks." But mostly, he repeatedly warned her to be circumspect in Zanzibar—"a terribly gossipy place"—and to be especially careful and diplomatic around the British Political Agency, those "wide-eyed . . . people of the world." Perhaps Stanley hoped to prevent French-Sheldon from prematurely leaking plans that he and Eli Sheldon yet hoped to implement or, with his eye on a press always hungry for damaging details of his personal life, perhaps he feared she might reveal confidential personal information he had shared in the past with the couple.[18] In any case, though full of vague misgivings and cryptic warnings, Stanley's letters paved French-Sheldon's way to Zanzibar and Mombasa by formally introducing her to the men who would help her arrange the details of her expedition. In addition to Stanley's letters, French-Sheldon also carried with her a letter of introduction from Sir William MacKinnon (founder of the IBEA) addressed to the captain of the *Madura,* and a general letter of introduction and official endorsement signed by U.S. Secretary of State James G. Blaine.[19]

To all of these men, French-Sheldon presented herself as a writer in search of exotic material, the object of her visit one of research for a novel or "historical purposes," as Blaine's letter termed it.[20] She had either purposely obfuscated as to her ethnographic and exploratory intentions or, as she claims later in *Sultan to Sultan,* she only conceived of them once she had embarked upon her journey. Either way, six months from the date of Blaine's letter, the physically-drained "litterateur" in search of "local colouring" stood with the help of a supporting staff to address the largest assembly ever to gather for a lecture at the British Association's Geographical Section E. At this lecture she claimed that her goal had been to write an ethnography that focused on African women, children, domestic arrangements, and the mysterious "inner life" of primitives. Moreover she intended this ethnography to demonstrate the proper method of peaceful interaction with African natives. She claimed her expedition presented a prototype of efficient and effective colonization—one that utilized just, humane, and reasonable methods of uplift without resort to so much as bad manners and, least of all, to bloodshed. French-Sheldon, according to her public lectures and the account she wrote of this trip in *Sultan to Sultan,* was out to upstage her role model Henry Stanley and male explorers of Africa in general with a strategy she imagined no man could have conceived—killing African recalcitrance with womanly kindness.

ON THE MARCH

[I]t is recognized that a caravan going into the interior or
up country in Africa is like a migratory community and
must be provisioned and armed for the entire expedition,
take sufficient goods for barter to insure immunity from
hunger, and be enabled to give tribute to purchase from the
natives a right of way (*hongo*), if required, as well as a variety
of presents for the natives one wishes to negotiate with.

—French-Sheldon, *Sultan to Sultan,* 1892

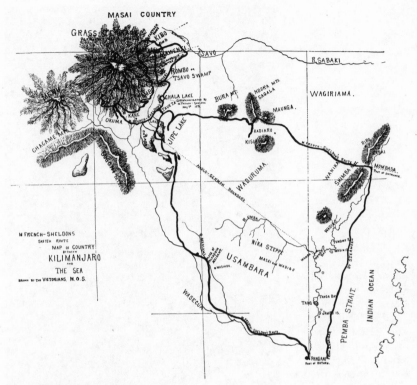

Fig. 6. Map of Route
French-Sheldon's hand-drawn map of her 1891 route through the Kilimanjaro region
of East Africa.

In *Sultan to Sultan* French-Sheldon claimed that between March 1891
when she started out from the mission in Mombasa and June when she
headed home by ship, she distributed many products of industrial civilization, promises of more that would not go unfulfilled, and the gift of her
eminent example wherever she went in East Africa; she strongly advised all
others following her to do the same. Much of her ethnography concerns itself with the many exchanges she initiated between herself and East Africans as well as the exigencies of organizing such a concentrated expedition.

French-Sheldon's journey really began once she arrived in Zanzibar and
entered into negotiations with both British and Zanzibari authorities concerning the procurement of sufficient numbers of porters and *askaris* (armed
guards), food, supplies, and guns to get her through what she estimated
would be a three-month trip. Her expedition took her from the coastal city
of Mombasa on the mainland of what is now Kenya, across territory still in
some doubt as to German or British jurisdiction, not to mention Masai and

Fig. 7. The Sultan of Zanzibar
An audience with Sultan Sayyed Ali bin Said (1854–1893), who governed the island of Zanzibar and parts of the East African coast from 1890–1893, formed a highlight of French-Sheldon's narration of her expedition in her narrative, *Sultan to Sultan.*

Chaga effective control, to the foot of Mount Kilimanjaro. Her return was southerly, through Pangani to the coast of what is now Tanzania.

Despite the letters of introduction from MacKinnon, Stanley, and Blaine, and the influence of Henry S. Wellcome, French-Sheldon had a difficult time obtaining IBEA representative Mackenzie's aid in securing porters. In fact, French-Sheldon began referring to Mackenzie, until he caved in to pressure, as "my obstacle" whenever she made mention of him in her descriptions of her first few weeks in East Africa in *Sultan to Sultan.* The Sultan of Zanzibar, the eminent and powerful Sayyed Ali bin Said, proved to be a far more cooperative and supportive official. Following a memorable meeting with him which formed a highlight of French-Sheldon's later written and verbal accounts of her trip, the Sultan supplied her with a writ of passage granting her official permission to hire porters and soldiers.[21] This writ constituted a guarantee of safety and a modicum of hospitality as

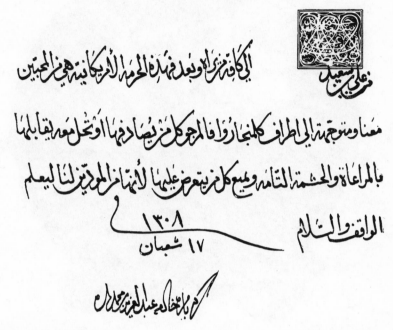

Fig. 8. Sultan's Letter
A letter from the Sultan of Zanzibar was a necessary item legitimating travel through the mainland territory under the Sultan's rule throughout much of the nineteenth century.

long as she stayed within the bounds of the Sultan's influence on the mainland.

Letters of support from the Sultan had been necessary to commission porters and headmen for expeditions into the interior since the 1840s when the German missionaries Johann Ludwig Krapf and Johannes Rebmann had begun the European search for the reputedly enormous lakes that lay to the west. By 1891 porters were in great demand as commerce between mainland Africans, German colonists, and British traders increased. Porters, although referred to often simply as *Zanzibaris,* were drawn from all parts of the region. Regardless of their status as slaves or former slaves, they each received a customary fee of about ten rupees (roughly equivalent to three U.S. dollars at the time or about a week's pay of an average factory worker in the United States) for each month they spent on the trek plus a daily food ration of *posho,* a stiff porridge made from ground cassava (later, from corn).[22]

Fig. 9. The Palanquin
French-Sheldon posing in the litter or "palanquin" in which she rode, wrote, and slept during her expedition.

Some porters would have been accompanied by their own servants or slaves, or by wives who washed and prepared their food and bedding.[23] According to the roll call of porters that French-Sheldon included in *Sultan to Sultan,* she hired five women outright. These women served as porters but also attended French-Sheldon personally when in camp.[24] The loads porters carried averaged between sixty and eighty pounds. In the late 1880s, a tramway, the Central African Railway, had been attempted by the IBEA in the area but proved unworkable. Both British and Germans were hastening to build a viable rail line out to Lake Victoria. In the year French-Sheldon traveled, the IBEA was still in the process of surveying the land for its construction. The lack of any mechanized transport did not deter French-Sheldon, of course. With over 150 porters to carry the goods she needed to sustain her on her expedition, French-Sheldon intended to walk most of the thousand or more miles from the coast to Mount Kilimanjaro and back. The ones she did not walk she intended to float three feet above, nestled comfortably in the silk-covered, down-filled cushions of her palanquin.

French-Sheldon took great pride in her compact yet luxurious palanquin. Although Henry S. Wellcome undoubtedly had a good deal to do with engineering its design and construction, it was French-Sheldon who won an award for it at the Chicago World's Fair of 1893. The palanquin was a round, light (73 pounds) basket made of wicker and fitted with yellow silk curtains and tassels. Built into it were drawers for toiletries, medicines, and documents, also a writing table and seat that unfolded into a bed at night. Four poles extended from each corner for porters to grasp and set on their shoulders. At night the palanquin sat under a tent to afford French-Sheldon some additional privacy and protection from insects.

French-Sheldon set out with a caravan of over a hundred porters, and had to send back word for several dozen more once she was underway. In addition to guns, they carried the many bartering items she estimated she would need for smooth interaction with inhabitants of the interior. Beads, simple toys and mechanical devices, and thin cotton cloth called *merikani* (local slang for American-made calico) were her chief trading goods. Trade routes to the interior had been forged not only by Swahili-speaking Africans in the area but also by the Arabs who had begun using such routes in the 1820s and 1830s to transport ivory, slaves, and other goods. Many of her porters were experienced as veterans of these trading caravans and a few, including her headman, Hamidi, and her translator, Josefe, were familiar with the few *wazungu* (Europeans or whites) who had earlier journeyed in the area. French-Sheldon was wholly unfamiliar with the terrain and entirely inexperienced as a caravan leader, but the porters the Sultan had helped her to retain made her plan a feasible one.

The route French-Sheldon planned to travel presently comprises the two major highways leading through Kenya and Tanzania to the fertile fields and national game parks around Mount Kilimanjaro. The northern route from Moshi to Kilimanjaro was a heavily traversed caravan road in the late nineteenth century, upon which few days in a row would have passed without French-Sheldon's meeting up with other trading companies and even other *wazungu*—primarily British or German colonial officers, soldiers, and perhaps a few missionaries. Once out of the area around Mombasa, however, most of the people that French-Sheldon and her caravan encountered were African. French-Sheldon lists some of them as the Wa-Duruma and Wa-Shenzie, the Wa-Teita and Wa-Taveta.[25] These groups inhabited the environs of the towns, Shenzie, Duruma, Teita, and Taveta; French-Sheldon gives little indication of their group affiliation or identity beyond that. Likely they were ethnically heterogeneous populations of trading towns whose prosperity depended on forging friendly relations with the

Fig. 10. The Caravan Trek
Photo taken by French-Sheldon of members of her caravan while on trek.

caravans that passed through bringing needed supplies in exchange for goods produced locally. French-Sheldon's recounting of the hearty welcome she received from townspeople overlooks the degree to which a vigorous caravan trade represented their economic lifeblood, instead portraying them as overawed with the hyper-racialized presence of a White Queen. In *Sultan to Sultan* French-Sheldon draws a strong moral contrast between such townspeople, whom she largely praises, and the pastoralists who looked upon caravans passing through their territory as political threats as well as a strain upon environmental resources and who could be less friendly as a result. Large caravans depleted the areas they passed through of food stores and often would hunt and let small herds graze along the way to feed their members. Large, militarized pastoral groups such as the Masai and Chaga who dominated the areas between the coast and around the base of Mount Kilimanjaro viewed caravans and other trespassers as sources of supplementary income in the form of tolls as a way to offset the damage caravans caused and as a way to affirm their territorial rights. Several encounters with Chaga and Masai warriors, during which French-Sheldon betrayed no recognition of the legitimacy of their insistence that she pay *hongo,* or tolls, for safe passage through their territory, form the dramatic highpoints of French-Sheldon's text.

Much of the rest of *Sultan to Sultan* consists of French-Sheldon's visits with townspeople who introduce her to their local customs and sometimes

Fig. 11. Python
Illustration accompanying French-Sheldon's recounting of an incident with a python
in *Sultan to Sultan*.

invite her to join in local celebration or rites of passage as an observer. The
text records details regarding native dress and jewelry, local industries, and
housing arrangements. Interactions with children and interpretations of familial relationships are important foci for the sociological analyses the text
offers. Despite the attention to detail French-Sheldon brings to bear in these
descriptive passages, the reader's attention is insistently drawn back to an
appreciation of French-Sheldon's leadership qualities and the physical trials
she was forced to endure through dramatic recounting of such incidents,
such as an eye infection, nearly being swarmed by red ants, and having a
python crawl over her palanquin as she slept one night. The climax of the
text surrounds French-Sheldon's descent to the surface of a crater lake,
Chala, at the base of Mount Kilimanjaro. This feat of exploration, her only,
is rendered in vivid terms as an almost supernatural encounter with the
African landscape.

The less-traveled southern route through what was then German East Africa (currently Tanzania) made French-Sheldon's return to the coast particularly uncomfortable and even a little treacherous. The road was spotty in many places and the various bridges and overpasses not suited to vehicles of any sort. At two points near Pangani, French-Sheldon's porters lost their footing and dropped her and her palanquin into a ravine, injuring her spine and causing the fever she was suffering from at that point to soar. French-Sheldon's description of her return sea voyage from the coast to Zanzibar dramatically depicts her lashed to the main mast and delirious with fever and head injury.

Despite the melodramatic potential of this final image, *Sultan to Sultan* speeds quickly over the last few weeks of French-Sheldon's trip, grueling weeks spent primarily in the German controlled Pangani region at military encampments and a German hospital where she was admitted for "nervous dysentery."[26] French-Sheldon did not intend to leave the reader with the impression that the trip had brought out latent feminine frailties in her; she records only enough of her struggle with illness and injury to avoid any accusation of omission and to acknowledge the kind treatment that the Germans (of whom the otherwise German-hating French-Sheldon had nothing good to say) had shown her. Distributing its weight unevenly, the original text devotes 415 of its 435 pages to portrayals of French-Sheldon organizing her trip and ruminating amid the various groups making their home near the base of Mount Kilimanjaro. French-Sheldon's intentions to market her narrative to British audiences at a time of intense rivalry between Britain and Germany in this region of Africa explains in part this concentration on territory the British claimed control over. But one also gets the feeling that the last half of the journey, time spent recovering from dysentery and fever and hurrying homeward, simply made for less interesting or less self-aggrandizing copy. Like any travel writer, French-Sheldon felt she had to portray her journey as a difficult, danger-strewn one to justify it as an accomplishment while simultaneously avoiding the trap of describing a situation of which she was not in control or betraying herself as somehow less than qualified to meet its challenges. This hazard was multiplied for French-Sheldon as a woman with that much more to prove than a man, as an amateur without training or prior experience, and as a dilettante without apparent purpose to her trip.

For French-Sheldon exploring Africa was as much about discovering a new public sense of self and projecting that self outward in an authoritative way. Rather than viewing her sex as an impediment to that goal, French-Sheldon forged a way through the minefield of late Victorian gender politics that turned the twinned discourses of true womanhood and new womanhood to her advantage and located her opinions on empire centrally amid competing ideas about colonization, civilization, and race in a period when few women spoke publicly on global matters at all. The next four chapters pull in close to French-Sheldon's representations of her experiences, particularly her account of her expedition as it appears in *Sultan to Sultan,* to examine the implications of the strategies of self-representation she pursued following her return from her expedition in June 1891.

TWO

Self-Discovery

One could scarcely believe, as he looked upon a
certain guest at the Wellesley commencement banquet,
last June, that the elegantly arrayed lady was fresh
from the wilds of Africa, but so it was.
—*Critic,* New York City, April 1, 1893

Though her appearance had hardly altered, May French-Sheldon returned from her 1891 African expedition a changed woman. No longer merely a prominent member of affluent circles in England and the United States, French-Sheldon had become a bit of a celebrity on both sides of
the Atlantic. The circumstances of her life also shifted significantly the year
following her return. Eli Sheldon's death in June 1892, while French-Sheldon was in the United States finishing her book, left her widowed at the age
of forty-five. Although Sheldon had experienced success as an enterprising
young investment banker in London, when he died he left his widow with
few assets and significant debt. The extravagance of French-Sheldon's recent expedition would never again lie within her grasp.[1] Indeed, widow-
hood put French-Sheldon in the position of needing to earn a living despite
the near impossibility of that task for women of her class in this time period. Although the machinations of Henry Wellcome prior to her departure for Africa make obvious French-Sheldon's desire for public recognition, perhaps her financial situation following the death of her husband
compelled French-Sheldon to pursue a career as a public speaker and author in earnest.

As she and her good friend and advisor Wellcome had anticipated, the
novelty of her gender and the cultural currency of topics related to Africa
generated the opportunities for remunerative public appearances. With the
aid of J. S. Pond, the New York publicist who had made his reputation arranging American speaking tours for Paul du Chaillu, Henry Stanley, and

other celebrity explorers, French-Sheldon booked dozens of speaking engagements, arranged interviews with reporters, and was reviewed in nearly every major regional and national newspaper in the United States and Canada in the first few years following her expedition.[2] This genteel, polished woman of fashion now commanded the attention of the British and American publics. No longer a mere supporter of the scientific quest for knowledge about primitives, French-Sheldon mounted the podium as an esteemed peer of famed explorers at the express invitation of the most prestigious geographical and anthropological societies of the day. In Britain she was immediately commissioned to speak before the Geographical Section of the British Association, the London Anthropological Society, and the Manchester Anthropological Society. In the United States the following March, her presence before the American Geographical Society next to the famed explorer of Africa Paul Du Chaillu on the stage of Chickering Hall in New York City inaugurated her career in her own country as a minor celebrity and an intellectual authority on Africa and colonization.

One of French-Sheldon's first steps following her return from East Africa was to record her travels in Africa in a form that would attract the attention of the general public as well as enhance her status as an intellectual. In this chapter I examine the conditions under which French-Sheldon wrote and the textual self that *Sultan to Sultan* projects in light of the racial and gendered politics of writing, exploration, and science in this period.

THE WRITTEN RECORD

> The book is handsomely printed on coated paper and is
> bound in a rich African red, silk-finished cloth, stamped in
> gold on the back and side. It is without exception the most
> valuable and most beautiful holiday book of the year.
> It contains besides the most accurate account of the habits,
> customs, and inner life of the natives of East Africa
> that has ever been published in the world. The author
> emphasizes the good rather than the bad qualities of the
> natives, for she went bearing emblems of peace, and
> saw them at their best.
> —Press release from Arena Press[3]

Like May French-Sheldon, *Sultan to Sultan* was praised for its looks as well as its substance. The publisher's physical description of the book, "Handsomely illustrated, printed on coated paper, and richly bound in silk-finished cloth," appeared on the first page of the publisher's press release, just beneath French-Sheldon's photo and her signature, "Bebe Bwana." So jux-

Fig. 12. "Bebe Bwana" in Court Dress
Frontispiece of *Sultan to Sultan* showing French-Sheldon in her "White Queen" costume.

taposed, the description drew a parallel between the author and the book. As travel writing, *Sultan to Sultan* was also necessarily an autobiography and the characteristics the reviewer (quoted above) used to describe its physical form mirror the qualities of the autobiographical self constructed between its pages.

Just as May French-Sheldon's self-presentation traversed numerous Victorian categories of identity, the text of *Sultan to Sultan* belongs to several late-nineteenth-century literary genres at once. *Sultan to Sultan* qualifies as travel writing and social science literature, as adventure story and new-woman didacticism as well. French-Sheldon targeted a wide audience in her marketing of the book by striking a balance between claiming its value as a unique travelogue and presenting it as a particularly innovative ethnography. The Arena Press drew on the exotic attraction that both Africa and new womanhood held for a Victorian readership by foregrounding the issues of gender and race in promotions of the book with its declaration that "other white women have been to Africa, accompanied by, or accompanying white men" but that French-Sheldon's trip "was unique in that she was alone, at the head of a caravan of nearly 200 native men and women, and from the time she left Mombasa, was entirely unassisted or unaccompanied by any white person."[4]

Despite the need to attract attention, French-Sheldon was careful not to allow the dramatic narrative to overshadow the serious content of the work. The suggestiveness of the image the press paints risked cheapening her and contained the potential to undermine the scientific worth of her pronouncements. Self-conscious of her ambiguous status as an untrained ethnographer, French-Sheldon walked a fine line between claiming official scientific authority and dramatizing her story in a way that might render her opinions about Africa and colonization wholly unworthy of consideration. Thus she hedged. She included in a promotional flyer for *Sultan to Sultan* both a denial of any scientific pretensions as well as several quotes from eminent members of scientific societies, such as the London Anthropological Institute and the British Geographical Association, endorsing the book's contribution to a growing body of reliable scientific knowledge of the "inner life" of the "primitive."[5] The defensive tone of these testimonials indicates that French-Sheldon encountered some difficulty establishing the intellectual merit of a narrative that details a relatively brief sojourn along well-traveled caravan routes. The inclusion of such emphatic testimony, complete with Latin flourishes, indicates that the value of the text also lay in its ability to constitute its bourgeois reader as the cosmopolitan possessor of a distinguishing intellect. As the promotionals would have it, the book's physical attributes (note the quote at the beginning of this section) alone provided the owner or giver of *Sultan to Sultan* with evidence of her or his inclusion in the refined circles of the elite.

More to the heart of the matter, a certain social responsibility and moral sensibility clung to the middle-class purchaser of a book whose promotional literature emphasized its author's "just and humane" treatment of the "sometimes savage" African. Despite the fact that the passage most often quoted was the one in which French-Sheldon aggressively quelled a rebellion of her porters by brandishing her whip and guns, critics consistently praised her for being "gentle," "friendly," and "patient" with Africans. The advertising flyer celebrated the "constant outcropping of womanly sentiment" in *Sultan to Sultan*.[6] Readers who accepted French-Sheldon's observations and conclusions were thereby credited with a generous attitude toward women as well as "natives." In terms of race and gender, the publication of *Sultan to*

Sultan made evidence of right-minded thinking on both counts purchasable to the discriminating consumer.

DISCOVERING AN AUTOBIOGRAPHICAL SELF

> Africa reveals to everyone who sojourns there any
> length of time, himself.
> —M. French-Sheldon, draft of speech[7]

> If travelers, she said, would only act in a manly
> and straightforward way.
> —*Spectator,* 1891

> Finally among themselves they talked in a subdued tone,
> casting inquisitive glances at me, evidently studying my
> attire, and christened me "Bebe Bwana" (woman master).
> —French-Sheldon, *Sultan to Sultan,* 1892

Travel narratives, autobiographical texts that often frame themselves as stories of exploration and discovery, tend by their nature to aggrandize their authors. As such they lend themselves to a significant degree of self-consciousness. *Sultan to Sultan* represents a particularly ungainly example of autobiographical writing, as the projection of a subjectified self in Victorian women's literature was no mean, or "straight-forward," feat.[8] Indeed, autobiography, strictly defined, was not a genre engaged in by women in the nineteenth century. Like biography, autobiography took as its subject the public, even historic, activities of great men. The private transformations of self that middle-class women underwent in the Victorian era were more likely to be recorded in a personal diary, the histories of their lives embedded within a family memoir, and the news of their daily existence serialized in the voluminous correspondence in which they engaged one another. Though the new-woman novel provided a publishable form in which Victorian bourgeois women might posit semi-autobiographical protagonists, for the most part the only non-fictional genres open to nineteenth-century female authors who wished to publish as well as tell stories of themselves were the few slave narratives that emerged during the middle of the nineteenth century and the travelogues that proliferated near its end.[9] *Sultan to Sultan,* as a travel story, represents one of the few non-fictional forms open to French-Sheldon in her endeavor to re-invent herself as a public person. Indeed, the act of writing a narrative of exploration and ethnography rather than simply a traveler's memoir propelled its Victorian narrator past the boundary of private/public and into the company of historical actors. Given the severe emphasis in the Victorian period on sexual difference, and on that difference as corresponding to a split between a masculine, public world of great deeds and historical change and a feminine, unchanging world of private emotions, it is difficult to imagine how any Victorian woman could have envisioned herself and convinced others to envision her as important enough, individual enough, public enough to warrant a narrative all her own. Travel among peoples even farther removed from the status of Subject than they themselves represents one of the few scenarios capable of imbuing Victorian women with sufficient subjectivity to authorize them as the protagonists of their own stories.[10]

French-Sheldon shrewdly harnessed to her narrations the colossal Anglo-American fascination for a barbarized Africa to lend her struggle for self-invention subjectifying meaning. Offering herself as guide, she led her readers on a journey into the "heart" of Africa, painting for them pictures of Africans' "inner lives." In *Sultan to Sultan* and other accounts, however, French-Sheldon goes beyond the role of *guide* to the primitive. She lays claim to a peculiarly American version of the civilizing mission to position herself as a *steward* of the colonized. Debates over the nature of the civilizing mission took on particular relevance in the United States—a country rent by race conflict—in this period. In the 1890s middle-class black Americans publicly struggled to replace race markers with class markers as the defining characteristic of civilized culture.[11] Turning the discourse of the civilizing mission to their own purposes, middle-class black Americans tended to see their duties towards less-privileged members of their own race in terms of "racial uplift." Both the civilized mission and uplift were ideas that relied on similar notions of progress, evolution, and civilized deportment. But uplift, when wielded by black Americans toward other black Americans, failed to contain the distinctions of race as a determinant of culture. Black male and female reformers employed the term to refer to their responsibility toward lower-class blacks in an effort to protect their own standing as members of the same race. Black and white middle-class women may have meant very different things by it, but uplift was a compelling rallying cry for both, incorporating as it did elements of class paternalism, Christian millenarianism, and social Darwinism.[12] Both white and black female reformers in the Progressive Era relied on a discourse of uplift to insist on public careers as missionaries, social workers, and educators. Turning the black American discourse to her own purposes, French-Sheldon's frequent use of the term to describe her intentions with regard to Africans collapsed the distinction between colonialist objectives and the class goals that middle-class black women strove to establish in this period.[13]

French-Sheldon's successful positioning of herself within the rhetorics of civilization as they existed at the end of the nineteenth century depended implicitly upon her ability to project a womanliness that conformed to class-specific expectations. In the racist imaginary of the time, only white middle-class women were imagined as harboring the required attributes permitting them to shoulder the civilizing mission or to contribute to a white supremacist definition of racial uplift. Violating the central tenet of true womanhood, that is, confinement to domestic pursuits and the avoidance of the public sphere, made the self that French-Sheldon presented in her travel writings and presentations vulnerable to the charge of *un*womanliness—a charge that risked her class standing rather than just her gender identity and thus threatened the whole purpose and thrust of her self-presentation as an uplifter of Others.[14] Typically, in the attempt to remain within the boundaries staked out by the doctrine of true womanhood, women explorers of the period met the challenges of this paradox by loudly eschewing stances associated with new women such as the espousal of dress reform or support for woman suffrage. They tended to insist upon their loyalty to conventional notions of femininity despite their obvious violations of those conventions.[15] French-Sheldon went further than most, exaggerating her femininity even while she refused to be confined to the private sphere on the basis of it. French-Sheldon relied on a tangential but potent attribute of true womanliness to establish her subscription to the norm. Along with the characteristics identified by historian Barbara Welter (including purity, piety, morality, and domesticity), an important expectation of a true woman was that she had an attractive appearance and feminine demeanor. From the society pages of papers published in London the year French-Sheldon traveled to Africa, one can see that French-Sheldon mastered this requirement superbly.

> Dearest Amy,—We were at Whiteley's on Saturday morning, and chanced to see the adventurous lady who is off and away on a journey through Africa. I fancied her a tall and masculine woman, with a hard voice, resolute face, and that sort of conscious superiority that often places people who are doing unusual things quite outside the line of our sympathy. But Mrs. French Sheldon has a slight and pretty figure, a bright, animated face, a low and pleasant voice, and the kindliest grey eyes I ever looked into. . . . Maud and I felt attracted to her at once.[16]

At age forty-three, French-Sheldon was attractive. But, I would argue, her allure stemmed less from a possession of indisputably beautiful features than from the magnetic exhibition of hyper-masculinity she brilliantly framed within an ultra-feminine molding. Her genteel and ladylike demeanor relieved middle-class observers like the one above and reassured audiences on both sides of the Atlantic that her ambitions presented no threat to the notion of gender as Difference incarnate. However, the undeniably masculine stance French-Sheldon struck in her writing and public lectures discloses that more was at stake for French-Sheldon personally, and for her audiences collectively, than just a reaffirmation of Woman's beauty and mild, "pleasant" nature. French-Sheldon, as her African title *Bebe Bwana* announced to the world, was a "Woman Man," even a "Woman Master" as she often translated the phrase. Her rendition of her powers of command over black men deemed at least half savage ensured that her audiences would not overlook her capacity for public authority.[17] The following incident from *Sultan to Sultan,* by far the most quoted by reviewers, commentators, and biographers after her death, pointedly captures her ability to be masterful. Her "men became surly," she recounts, "evincing symptoms of insubordination" and, throwing their packs to the ground, claimed *"Bebe* (woman) did not know the road."

> Then or never I realized I must demonstrate to these mutinous, half-savage men that I would be obeyed, and that discipline should be enforced at any cost. Only for one instant in perplexity I paused, a vulture flew overhead, I drew my pistols and sent a bullet whizzing after it, and brought it surely down at my feet, to the astonishment of the revolting men.
>
> With both pistols cocked, suddenly I became eloquent in the smattering of the Swahali which I knew, without interpreter, inspired with fearlessness and strength I started through the centre of the rebellious throng, pointing first one, then the other pistol in quick succession at the heads of the men, threatening, and fully prepared, determined, and justified to shoot the first dissenter.
>
> As with unflinching, angry eyes fixed upon them, I exclaimed, "Get up! take your load! One! two! th—!" . . . "Every man who is not on his feet with his load on his head, when I have counted three, I will shoot!" They knew I would. (*SS:* 132–133)

This self-portrait of French-Sheldon, in light of the "slight and pretty" figure that observers reported French-Sheldon cut during personal appearances in London, evinces a sharply contradictory combination of stereotypical manliness and womanliness. Her slides between masculine and feminine ideals are perhaps the most dramatic example of a double-voiced narrator in all of Victorian women's travel writing. French-Sheldon straddled the Victorian gender divide brilliantly; she neither yielded her claims to masculine authority nor relinquished her middle-class feminine charms. French-Sheldon's self-portrait in *Sultan to Sultan* is double-edged in its intent both to exploit the strangeness of a woman speaking in a male voice and to render that strangeness less strange, even natural, for a true woman to adopt. Race and white privilege in particular were the keys to French-Sheldon's successful resolving of the two aspects of the persona she urged her readers and audiences to embrace.

The hybridized persona that resulted was realized in the title that French-Sheldon claimed Africans had bestowed upon her in recognition of her ability to project both masculine and feminine qualities, *Bebe Bwana*.[18] French-Sheldon translated this phrase for her readers and audiences variously as "Woman-Man," "Woman-Master," or "Lady Boss." In her primary text and many oral presentations, French-Sheldon used the terms *Bebe Bwana* and *white queen* interchangeably, suggesting with both that her racial status had a strong effect on her gender identity from the viewpoint of Africans. She often attributed her successful neutralizing of African hostility to the power that the combination of her race and gender produced. This tendency is most pronounced in passages of *Sultan to Sultan* depicting her ability to assert authority over males. "Simama! Simama! Bebe! (stop! stop! lady!) suddenly yelled my askari, Masai! Masai!" one memorable episode begins. According to French-Sheldon, "[T]his was certainly a trying moment," but merely at the sight of her, the Masai "squatted abjectly upon the ground, their long bows and arrows planted straight up and down in front of them, their startled countenances, with eyes opened wide in amazement, speechless to see such as strange apparition of a *mzunga* (white man) as I presented" (*SS:* 113).

French-Sheldon, an elaborately dressed "lady" flanked only by other Africans and advancing confidently toward a group of Masai warriors, may have been as strange an apparition to her Anglo-American readership as it was to the Masai. French-Sheldon claimed her gender as an advantage, sufficient to render warriors, with their long pointy weapons passively planted in the ground, "speechless" before her and suggested a way of making sense out of this by pointing out the unique role that white womanhood accrued to her in Africa.

Like the other white women traveling without white male escorts at the edges of the British empire in the late nineteenth century, May French-Sheldon experienced the thrill of masculine authority, purchased by virtue of her race, class, and national affiliation. She experienced her gender as a malleable thing, not biologically determined but contextually situated. She understood this experience to indicate that some women, even if only a handful like her, harbored the capacity for autonomy and even leadership. Surely she believed this, in part, to be true before she set out, but the experience itself gave her the confidence, the evidence, and the language with which to assert its verity to male audiences and to share it with female readers who were invited to participate vicariously in the experience. Africans very well may not have considered her a "Woman Man," called her "Bebe Bwana," or at the very least meant what French-Sheldon believed was meant by the term, but French-Sheldon's ideas about what Africans thought of her affected her self-image and the image of herself that she promoted publicly. Successfully asserting herself to have been virtually worshiped by Africans as a white queen both elevated French-Sheldon to a rank eligible for Subject status and accelerated the racialization of the politics of women's emancipation in Britain and the United States. In this ideological way, among others, the periphery helped to shape the metropolis.[19]

A HYPHENATED HEROINE

An American heroine has appeared before the public, who possesses not only the perseverance and positive pluck necessary for such an adventurous undertaking, but with it the refinement and culture of a true woman. She shines equally well as hostess at an intellectual social function in her own drawing room, or as sole leader and commander of a caravan of black men in the wilds of Africa.
—*Chautauquan*, 1893

Mrs. Sheldon has French enthusiasm, American pluck and English determination, and the courage of all three nationalities.
—*Toledo Commercial*, 1892

As the hyphen between her maiden and married names and the space that stretched between the two halves of her title "Bebe Bwana" both symbolize, the self that French-Sheldon presented to readers and audiences was a doubled one. But the gender divide between Victorian ideals of masculinity and femininity described above was not the only border she straddled. Although new-woman literature was better developed in Britain and female British role models were at least as available to French-Sheldon as American ones, her U.S. nationality was not lost on British or American audiences. French-Sheldon's ability to parlay her expedition into evidence of her emancipation from "old world" attitudes adhered to her projection of an idealized American womanhood. Still, the endorsement of British geographical institutions and authorities was crucial to French-Sheldon's ability to assert the verity and worth of her experiences to both Anglo and American audiences. Thus, in addition to the radical oscillations between masculine and feminine ideals, French-Sheldon's presentation of self also alternated between American and British models of the explorer as hero.

French-Sheldon carefully tailored the heroic features of the self she presented in her writings and her person to satisfy two related but nationally distinct views on geographic exploration. Though the British press tended to extol adventurousness and risk-taking for its own sake, performance, achievement, and demonstrable success mattered most to pragmatic American audiences. By the turn of the century, Lisa Bloom argues, Americans were more likely to celebrate the leader of an expedition who had demonstrated the traits of a technologically proficient "scientific manager," while British audiences admired personal sacrifice to an abstract ideal such as "science" or "progress" or stoicism in the pursuit of the unattainable.[20] The British public looked less to empirical measures of success than to the nobility of the undertaking and the manner in which the hero had comported himself, imagined as intimately bound up with the manner to which he was born. By contrast, in a gesture reminiscent of the popular celebrations of the "self-made" man, American audiences measured the worth of their heroes by the concrete gains they could substantiate. (Had they really reached the North Pole or not? Could the source of the Nile be identified with certainty? What was the precise height of the highest mountain peak?) To satisfy the American half of her audience, French-Sheldon promoted herself in the 1890s as the self-made woman with her heroism figuring very much a consequence of her accomplishments. At such moments in the text, her literary voice took on the tone of the objective, technically proficient scientist as much as her untrained, womanly sensibilities would allow. Her grandest triumph, the "discovery" of Lake Chala, took on definitive scientific worth in her retelling of it.

> The gradual ascent from Taveta to the rim of the crater lake on the western side is only a little above the level of the plain, and on the southwestern end there are abrupt peaks two hundred to four hundred feet high; the level of the water, as shown by our aneroid, attained a level of one hundred and ninety-five feet below the encampment, and about four hundred and forty-seven feet above Taveta. And the temperature of the water near the surface was only one and one half degrees lower than the atmosphere registration. The lake, is near the western side of the stream Mfuro, or, in the Masai language, Naromosha, but according to some travellers misnamed the Lumi. *We* find Lake Chala north of Taveta on the northeastern side of Kilimanjaro, about 3° 22' south latitude, 37° 17' east longitude, over three thousand feet above the sea level. (*SS:* 172; emphasis added.)

Suddenly, from nowhere it seems, there is a *we* in French-Sheldon's text. Merely the page before there had only been a defensive and emphatic *I.* "It will be well to state," she claimed, that "absolutely in no instance was my rule and order of command relinquished to any temporary guest or friendly escort during my entire expedition, nor in any way have I to acknowledge the successful carrying forward or completion of my expedition to the auspices or patronage of any European resident in East Africa, however grateful I may be for certain courtesies" (*SS:* 171). The sudden switch into the present tense and a clipped dry tone indicates that the *we* in the former passage is not a slip revealing her partnership with the English officer Anstruther, who had joined her for this part of her expedition. Instead, her use of the plural is an attempt to distance her subjective personal self from the narrative and lend an air of appropriate scientific detachment to her description of the lake.

Measurement did not comprise merely an aside in French-Sheldon's account, it was the usual goal of exploration in this period and formed the basis for her one semi-legitimate claim to actual discovery. According to French-Sheldon, she had measured and circumnavigated what no previous man had ever measured or charted or graphed before. In truth she knew the missionary Joseph New had already spied the little crater lake years before. French-Sheldon's claim to "discovering" Lake Chala was based on the fact that she had taken measurement of it—a modest accomplishment that impressed absolutely no one but the untutored general public, especially the American one. An American hero's ability to master the natural world through the language of science mattered to a middle-class public that imagined its own glory reflected in every demonstration of empirical proficiency and technological prowess by Americans abroad as much or more than at home.

Wandering back and forth between two national zones of idealized masculinity, French-Sheldon attempted to satisfy British expectations for heroism with a romanticized projection of self that forsook the scientific persona her measurement of Lake Chala evinced in favor of a stoic and determined one. The juxtaposition of the two sensibilities exemplifies the intensely heteroglossic character of her self-representation in *Sultan to Sultan*. Her descent to the lake's surface, following closely upon her empirical discussion of the lake's measurements, begins with the voice of a physical scientist but shifts into romantic reverie of excessive proportions. "There was a weird attractiveness overhanging this place that overawed even the natives," she reports, though their "vague accounts" of the dangers merely made her all the more eager to "taste of the forbidden fruit" herself. At this point the narrative takes a decidedly supernatural and erotic turn as French-Sheldon found herself, "attempting to penetrate through a girdle of primeval forest trees, tossed as it were, by some volcanic action against the rock base, and seemingly as impenetrable as any stockade. . . . [E]very moment's tarriance seemed to imperil my equilibrium; and as I dared to venture on other uncertain surfaces which presented a footing, it required cat-like agility to crawl or slide down, sometimes landing in a bed of leaves, which must have been the accumulations of centuries." An *unheimlich* sense of disturbing the natural order of things pervades French-Sheldon's writing at this point—but only in ways that reify her stature as a virtual force of na-

Fig. 13. Lake Chala
The circumnavigation of Lake Chala, a small crater lake at the foot of Mount Kilimanjaro, supported French-Sheldon's only claim to African "discovery."

ture herself: "[A]fter great effort and considerable peril, [I] succeeded in laboriously attaining some other foothold, step by step advancing, again and again to be opposed by gigantic trunks of trees, which, lightning-smitten, had fallen as a barricade, or through some potent eruptive force had been uprooted and turned themselves top down in solemn humiliation. . . . The danger attending every movement and the spectral weirdness of the place inspired me and even affected my men with awe. . . . All this filled me with an excitement and imparted fresh courage, and re-enforced my determination to overcome the difficulties of the uncanny spot, cost what it might, so long as I should be able to climb, or crawl, or slide, or step, or simply let myself go with utter blindness" (*SS:* 173–174).

A literary movement in voice from that of the in-control American scientific manager to that of the dauntless and romantic British adventurer-hero ends with French-Sheldon depicted as a goddess of the natural world. "Through gaps in the massed trees, through which the sun could scarcely filter, the arboreal darkness was pierced by a radiant gleam of light, and the flashing lake greeted my expectant eyes. There arose a general shout from the men, 'Chala!' 'Chala!' and behold! I found myself rewarded by being upon a rugged, rough tangle of prostrate trees and wild tumble of white and gray rocks, whilst the limpid, restless waters were laughing and dashing themselves into a jubilant foam at my feet," she writes. The rhetoric of British stoicism and self-sacrifice merges in this account with the language of command detailed earlier in this chapter. Her self-discipline and determination impresses her "awe-stricken" African porters, in whose eyes, presumably, she gains respect not normally due a woman. Such respect spills over onto the natural world, a world that spontaneously and ecstatically humbles itself at her feet (recall the trees that "turned themselves top down in solemn humiliation"). The magnitude and complexity of the egoism exhibited in this passage is staggering. French-Sheldon's gender strategies combined with her split national identity to produce in her travel narrative a complex interweave; British pomp and stoicism merge with a characteristically American goal orientation, all of which enhances her as a commander of nature and of black men. French-Sheldon weaves the languages of sentiment and science into a close-knit mantle and wraps herself in it to appear before audiences and readers as a modern-day hero, all the more glorious for the gentle and genteel character of her heroism.

The seemingly opposing voices of science and sentiment in French-Sheldon's published work is unusually pronounced, but not unique to travel narratives of this period. Mary Louise Pratt has argued, "[I]n travel literature, . . . science and sentiment code the imperial frontier in the two eternally clashing and complementary languages of bourgeois subjectivity."[21] In narrations of what she calls the "anti-conquest," Pratt explains that "the two discourses could not be more different . . . because they are so much defined in terms of each other; they are complementary and in their complementarity they stake out the parameters of emergent bourgeois hegemony."[22] As Pratt's work brilliantly elucidates, both languages share crucial characteristics paramount of which is the innocence they attach to the subject who speaks them.[23] In this way did French-Sheldon's gender strategy cohere to those deployed in travel narratives generally. French-Sheldon's utilization of the languages of science and of sentiment built on the rhetorics of true womanhood, racial uplift, and the civilized mission. As such they helped cover the tracks of French-Sheldon's colonialist ambitions and put a humanitarian face on her relations with Africans.

GLOBAL HOUSEKEEPING

> Mrs. Sheldon set out upon no crusade of conquest;
> projected no new disturbance of the creeds of science;
> paraded no promise to add other sheaves to the never
> fully gleaned harvest of geographical knowledge.

> She had a purpose not less determined, not less
> thoughtful, not less adventurous than any of these.
> In her burned the woman's will to know, the woman's
> generous desire to communicate, the woman's
> indomitable bravery to master, the home laws and
> habits of the aboriginal Africans, at the thresholds
> of whose dwelling-places every previous explorer
> had been turned away uninformed.
> —Clayton McMichael, editor of the *North American*[24]

Sultan to Sultan, like other examples of new-woman literature in the 1880s and 1890s, took as its mission social reform and pronounced the particular talents of women essential to that mission. Borrowing from arguments for "social housekeeping" that assigned responsibility for "cleaning up" the corruption, immoralism, or inefficiency of the public sphere, French-Sheldon applied Progressive ideologies of gender to a larger arena. Visiting African villages instead of city slums, and dispensing technological wonders and "modern" scientific wisdom within the *boma* instead of the tenement building, French-Sheldon transfigured the charitable social obligations of a society woman into those of an ethnographer and progressive social reformer without seeming to violate any class-bound rules of feminine propriety. Even if she had difficulty impressing academics and specialists—especially in Britain—with such arguments, the popular press adored her for it. By wisely restricting her investigation to an inspection of "the habits and customs and the family life and relationships of the natives," French-Sheldon enlarged American popular ideas of the Victorian sphere of new womanhood to include within it the fields of ethnography and colonial policy making in Africa.

French-Sheldon's exploration entailed less a discovery of territory than it did a survey of domestic economies, civil services, and social structures, especially in terms of the ethnic variability of East Africans. The purpose of such observations and categorizations of Africans was to gather impressions and information on their "inner life," presumably to determine the appropriate conditions of the white stewardship that she and many of her contemporaries deemed inevitable. Much of *Sultan to Sultan* resembles Jacob Riis's classic text of urban types wherein prosperity is causally related to physical appearance and assumed states of morality.[25] According to the French-Sheldon, the Wa-Nyika are "unseemly," "grovelling, intimidated, unclean creatures," as are the Wa-Teita generally and the Wa-Sagalia especially. The Wa-Sagalia "are grovellers, devoid of self-respect, and evince a shameless state of beggary. . . . [T]heir indolence and the prevailing demoralization of the women too often reduce this tribe to a sad state of penury. The flagrancy of the women is most disgusting. . . . Neither the men nor women are comely of feature or fine in figure." Conversely, the "pure-blood" Wa-Taveta are "untrammelled, so natural," "thrifty," "their teeth beautifully white and polished;" "the damsels are very fine in figure." Accordingly the "plantations" of the Wa-Taveta are splendid; their ways gentle, pastoral, peaceful, and orderly; and their valley prosperous and clean. The content summary of the chapter French-Sheldon devotes to an ethnographic description of the people of "arcadian Taveta" lists character traits alternately with employments:

> Attributes of Character. Farm Products. Rotten Egg. Tanning Leather. Clannish Selection of Ornament Sumptuous Display of Native Jewelry. Marriage Customs. Mixed Family Relations. Native Medical Clinic. Childhood's Limits. Education by Ob-servation. Circumscribed Language. Fire-Sticks Shooting Fish Universal Kindness to Children. Harmless Freedom in the Intermingling of the Sexes. (*SS:* 63)

Although French-Sheldon often depicts character traits and cultural mores as innate aspects (or even constitutive) of ethnic differences, paradoxically in other points in the narrative she tends to link the traits she discerned in different African groups to structural conditions. As any Progressive Era reformer might have, French-Sheldon follows up her observations by proposing specific reform measures to remedy the conditions she had documented. In her view, the "depraved Wa-Teita" suffered from the ivory traffic across Africa that forced many of them into slavery as porters. Such exploitation, in French-Sheldon's opinion, constituted a silent "plea for proper and human transportation, to which obviously Christians, humanitarians, commercial promoters, colonizers, should lend unanimous voice" (*SS:* 146). Silent on the subject of her own employment of porters as tantamount to slavery, she argues, "[T]here remains no relief to the poor Zanzibar porters, nor immunity for the natives from slavery until a railroad is constructed" (*SS:* 146).[26] The building of a railroad, presumably commissioned and administered by white colonials, involved all of the interests she identifies in the previous sentence in the "development" of Africa.

French-Sheldon, as a Progressive and a neo-Darwinian, asserted her faith in the inherent potential for improvement of even those Africans most degraded in her view. Some, like her favorites the Wa-Taveta whom she praises for their "simplicity," seemed more readily disposed than others to improvement. French-Sheldon argues with those who would dismiss Africans as hopelessly savage that the key to successful colonial penetration lies in the methods one employs. "If at the outset," she insists, "these particular, amiable, and amenable tribes of East Africa have sagacious, peaceful, fair treatment, and their natures are enlarged and they are led at a gradual pace to accept the ways of civilization, there is much to hope for in their intellectual enfoldment" (*SS:* 168). A strong supporter of capitalism, French-Sheldon promotes a doctrine of self-help and finds a commercial use for every trait she encountered, whether admirable or not. She finds that even though "extortion seems a latent trait with all African tribes . . . properly directed in connection with their trading propensities may in good time result in converting them to thrifty commercial peoples, and in uplifting them beyond dependence upon philanthropic indulgence and helpless subserviency" (*SS:* 126).

As part of her secular civilizing mission, French-Sheldon performed inspections of Africans' living conditions, affective relationships, employments, technologies and available facilities, their habits, and their predilections. Like a social worker on an international field assignment, she concerned herself with the condition of roads, children, livestock, waterworks and sanitation. She vaccinated every woman and man in her one-hundred-plus caravan and attributed the success of this endeavor to "the excellency and purity of the vaccine and certain hygienic laws I unremittingly persisted in having the men observe" (*SS:* 134). She took pride in the hygienic and scientific example she felt she was setting for Africans who, she believed, scrutinized her "[e]very move, every gesture, every word" for clues as to "civilized" deportment (*SS:* 168). She made recommendations for the uplift of Africans in the direction of industrial capitalism based on specific, detailed observation of African life and on personal trial and error. Each anecdote provided her with the opportunity to demonstrate to her reader "the importance of striving to understand the peculiar characteristics of different tribes, in order to know what impression they are likely to receive when experimented upon" (*SS:* 181).

French-Sheldon's text amounted to a teaching manual for future colonizers. The goal was to more efficiently and successfully guide African evolution in the direction of Western civilization to the mutual benefit of both Westerners and Africans. Whatever her original intentions might have been, upon her return French-Sheldon asserted that the primary value of her expedition lay in showing the way to other explorers, settlers, missionaries, traders, and colonial administrators. By her example French-Sheldon hoped to "contribute something substantial towards the betterment and enlightenment of the natives, as well as to be instrumental in convincing their future rulers and teachers that more humanity and practical commonsense will be more fruitful" (*SS:* 251). French-Sheldon saw her mission as directly antithetical to the clumsy, callous, and destructive assaults on Africa launched by previous (and here she meant male) explorers. Nor did she endorse the impractical and misguided (in her view) efforts of religious missionaries who, with their emphasis on intellectual and spiritual training, both overestimated African capacities and underestimated their material needs. According to promotions of *Sultan to Sultan,* she "strongly advocates the methods of civilizing the African people not wholly by missionaries and tracts. She would solve the problem by industrial training." French-Sheldon elaborated on this theme in her personal appearances. The *New York Times,* in an article reporting on her first official lecture in the United States to the American Geographical Society, credited her for such enlightened views. "Mrs. Sheldon," the paper reported, "has at heart the freedom of the slaves but not by emancipation, which is only an encouragement to idleness." Perhaps with the recent and current arguments about black Americans' role in the economy of the American South uppermost in mind, the paper went on to explain that French-Sheldon "desires that these East African slaves should be freed through their own exertions, by which means, while engaged in the task of emancipating themselves, they may at the same time be learning some useful craft or calling, which will enable them to live honestly and independently after their freedom has been accomplished."[27] Noting that French-Sheldon was "besieged with requests for tools, such as saws, hammers, and the like," the *New York Times* asserted a kind of colonialist agenda in line with domestic racial policies that undergirded the development of Jim Crow segregation in the United States.

French-Sheldon, Tuskegee-like, recommended the introduction of "simple, useful industries such as Zanzibar mat braiding" that she thought contained commercial possibilities.[28] She praised the work of Drs. Stewart and Moffat (the latter a nephew of David Livingstone), who had established an industrial mission "on the most practical lines," one that "aims to teach the natives some craft or avocation, according to the trend of their minds and physical capabilities, which will fit them to fill the existing demands, or those which may be created, of the country and not such as will have no outlet" (*SS:* 90). By way of contrast, her encounter with a girls' school run by a ladies' mission in Mombasa provided her with the opportunity to warn against the "utter impracticality" of a curriculum centered around literacy that, without any remunerative expectation or eventual employment plan for its students, "must necessarily undermine their self-reliances [*sic*] and leave the imprint of irresponsibility upon the native pupils." French-Sheldon expressed relief that "[t]he woman missionary workers happily are not so much swayed by supercilious sentiments, and with an amount of practical common-sense seem to realize that all natives rescued from slavery by the mission have not by nature the aptitude which makes them eligible for teachers" (*SS:* 90). The future of Africans from this "sensible" viewpoint was a bright but limited one.

French-Sheldon, like an earlier brand of "*sociale exploratrices,*" strove to bring the colonized within the orbit of middle-class reform.[29] She justified her own quest for knowledge, adventure, and fame by wrapping that quest in a double layer of industrial capitalism and maternalistic uplift. Borrowing from the argument for social housekeeping posed by reform-minded women in the Progressive Era, French-Sheldon's justification of her penetration of the exclusively male preserve of exploration and social science depended upon a conventional view of true women as better suited to the role of civilizer than men.[30] In the foreword to *Sultan to Sultan,* she identifies the proving of this principle as the supreme objective of her expedition and her publicizing of it. "I have completed the work," she claims, "while endeavoring fortitude to do my best to make my readers better acquainted with the possibilities of the natural primitives whom I am proud to call my friends and be called friend by, and to demonstrate that if a woman could journey a thousand and more miles in East Africa, among some hostile tribes, unattended by other than Zanzibaris [*sic*] mercenaries, without bloodshed, the extreme measures employed by some would-be colonizers is unnecessary, atrocious, and without the pale of humanity" (*SS:* 59).

Men, unarmed with feminine empathy and patience and bereft of the benefit of female company, she strongly implies, were apt to judge rather than empathize. They were thereby likely to antagonize rather than befriend and, in the face of such antagonism, to lose sight of the humane goals with which they began. Women, on the other hand, with their greater sensitivity and mild manner were more attuned to "native" ways and so could easily recognize African attempts at reciprocity, however pathetic they might be. French-Sheldon, by contrast, is able to evaluate cultures on their own terms, in her telling of it, as a direct consequence of her feminine insight into human nature. French-Sheldon doubts white men's abilities to maintain civilized standards even for themselves, if left alone too long without the benefit of true women's company. Men, she claims, who had been "thrown promiscuously together and too much upon their own resources" were wont to drink and wallow in loneliness (*SS:* 92–93, 104). But more to the point, they were unlikely, even under the best of conditions, to exhibit the same tact and delicacy that cross-cultural encounters demanded, and so, French-Sheldon asserts, many episodes went to show "how much superior in some ways is the position of a woman going among this tribe over that of any man, however crafty and savant he might be [in the conducting of ethnographic research into] the habits and customs and the family life and relationships of the natives" (*SS:* 208).

If there were at least some ways in which men had an advantage over women as emissaries of the West in Africa, French-Sheldon's text remains quiet on them. Indeed, French-Sheldon protested, "Every time a white man chanced to be with us, my porters were discontented and at times positively sullen; they seemed somewhat apprehensive lest the white men might be installed in my place as leader." French-Sheldon attributes their apprehension about white males to the suspicion that men were more likely to "make some demands upon them, or might be desirous of subjugating them, or fighting with them." Africans' reaction to her, on the other hand, was one of childlike trustfulness, "Like children they would flock about me to express their delight," she writes. "So it was proved disadvantageous," she asserts, "for me to entertain or to be joined, when on the march, by white men, no matter who they might be (*SS:* 171–172). Despite the often contradictory nature of her text, French-Sheldon's argument for women's contribution to the very public and political task of bringing Africa under Western control remained determinedly focused on the ability she claimed she harbored as a woman to win the hearts and minds of Africans.

French-Sheldon cleverly, perhaps even brilliantly, solved the dilemmas posed by her gender in a way that gave her currency in Europe and the United States. She portrayed herself, in the end, as a kind of self-appointed ambassador for the industrializing West on a fact-finding and networking mission, her peace offerings of *merikani,* mechanical gadgets, and tools doubling as salesman's samples for an eventual business relationship between Western industrial entrepreneurs (such as Wellcome) and Africans. She meant to show how neo-colonial relations with Africa could be accomplished cheaply, efficiently, and without compromising the humanitarian principles that served to characterize the West in the minds of her readers and audiences. With the American flag flying above her tent and serving as the mascot for her expedition, French-Sheldon turned what could have been seen as a mere lark into a humanitarian mission as well as a national service. Her writings do not permit readers to overlook the moral and commercial purposes behind her expedition, as she had intertwined them. As I detail in the next chapter, nearly every page of French-Sheldon's text makes explicit the links between the rhetorics of ethnography, racial uplift, and new womanhood and the economics of New Empire at a key moment in the development of Anglo and American colonial imaginations.

THREE

Forging a Feminine Colonial Method

The ground was not wholly unfamiliar, for travellers
and their books had taken away much of the novelty.
Nevertheless, a woman's eyes see much of interest
that a man is apt to slur over, and Mrs. Sheldon is
a wide-awake observer and a bright story-teller.
Full of the joy of physical life and keenly studious of
human nature in "our primitives," she saw much
besides ebony skins and shovel spears.

—*Critic,* 1893

Mrs. French-Sheldon . . . was very anxious to disclaim
any scientific purposes for her journey, geographical, or
otherwise, in that she made no profession of possessing
the necessary scientific attributes. Her plan, she says
"was simply to study the native habits and customs free
from the influence of civilisation and in their primitive
condition. . . . Her curiosity on the matter of native
habits and customs, if it had no scientific end, and was
merely feminine curiosity, seems hardly a very useful
or a very laudable one."

—*Spectator,* 1891

Since May French-Sheldon was not a trained ethnographer, her challenge
lay in how to add an official patina to her self-presentation without exposing the scientific quality of her observations to the scrutiny of professional social scientists. French-Sheldon met that challenge through obfus-
cation. She consistently referred to *Sultan to Sultan* as an ethnography
rather than a travelogue but tempered such hubris by modestly if also paradoxically disclaiming any "scientific purposes" to her work. Equivocating
on the subject of her contribution to the scientific study of primitives, she

drew a shaky line rather than a firm one between her and professional specialists in the field of ethnographic analysis. This tactic succeeded more with popular audiences than with reviewers from prestigious journals. The reviewer from the *Critic* (quoted in epigram above) for instance, conceded the high-mindedness of French-Sheldon's endeavor without granting her account any scientific authority. Acknowledging that the extent to which the "object of the journey was not a mere haphazard quest of adventure," the reviewer granted that *Sultan to Sultan* was "an intelligent desire to know Africa, for the betterment and enlightenment of the natives, and the 'convincing of their future rulers and teachers that more humanity and commonsense will be more fruitful.'" In the fashion of a backward compliment, the reviewer praised the volume for not amounting to a "pretentious addition to science or literature," labeling it instead a "most fascinating travel-story from London to London by way of the interior of Africa.[1] Even while this reviewer took pains to differentiate French-Sheldon's narrative from the more "haphazard" works in the genre, he declined to label her "travel-story" scientific in any way.

Other reviewers were even less generous. The reviewer from the *Spectator* (see second epigraph quoted above) counterposed "feminine curiosity" to scientific inquiry in an effort to undermine the significance of French-Sheldon's endeavors. Even more damning was a vicious letter written to the *London Times,* following French-Sheldon's and the induction of over a dozen other women into the Royal Geographical Society in 1892. In his letter the writer deplored the recent upsurge in women's exploratory research, contesting "*in toto* the general capability of women to contribute to scientific geographical knowledge." Seemingly aiming at French-Sheldon in particular, he explained that women's "sex and training render them equally unfitted for exploration, and the genus of professional globe-trotters with which America has lately familiarized us is one of the horrors of the latter end of the 19th century."[2]

Published responses to French-Sheldon's account of her expedition ranged from misogynist invective such as this to the more modulated comments in American periodicals such as the *Critic* and the *Nation* and glowing reviews from reporters at the *New York Times.*[3] Apart from those discussed above, nearly all commentators, especially those writing for popular newspapers in small cities in the United States and Canada, accepted without question the quotes included in *Sultan to Sultan's* promotional flyer that identified French-Sheldon as a "recognized scientific authority" on Africa, primitives generally, and the process of colonization especially. Even harder to support factually, these newspapers confidently announced variations on the theme that her "geographical researches . . . have been recognized by learned bodies of men as authentic and wonderful discoveries."[4] As this chapter will demonstrate, the difference of opinion about French-Sheldon's ethnographic expertise expounded in mass-circulation dailies and review journals was as much about competing standards of social science and women's relationship to scientific authority as it was about French-Sheldon's personal scientific acumen.

WOMEN, SCIENCE, AND ETHNOGRAPHIC EXPERTISE

French-Sheldon's public lectures and written work drew on a model of ethnographic literature from the mid-nineteenth century that had relied exclusively on the reports of travelers. By the end of the century, this model was under attack; anthropology was attempting to particularize its practices and gain exclusive right to confer judgment on the scientificity of epistemological pronouncements about "the primitive." By defining the untrained traveler as outside the parameters of the anthropological project, professional anthropologists hoped to monopolize the authority such pronouncements carried with them. Though French-Sheldon managed to give her ethnographic observations purpose and definition by utilizing the rhetorics of racial uplift, her untrained and deeply gender-coded "commonsense" flew in the face of the increasingly professional orientation of anthropological study.

Still, amateurism and professionalism overlapped a great deal in ethno/ anthropological research in 1891 and French-Sheldon exploited the fluctuations and ambiguities that characterized social science inquiry in this decade. Debates on monogenesis versus polygenesis (the rift that had sparked, in part, the initial separation between ethnological and anthropological societies in 1863) had been a topic of hot debate for decades among academics and laypeople alike, in seminars and lectures that were open to the public and exceedingly well attended. The immediate political repercussion of questions, such as whether humans were related as divergent members of a family (monogenesis) or members of entirely separate lineages (polygenesis), as well as the fascination of traveler's testimony typically presented as evidence in these discussions, made talks given at the Geographical Section of the British Association, the Anthropological Society of London, the Manchester Geographical Society, and those of the Chautauquan Society and the American Geographical Society in New York, enormously popular with mixed-class audiences well into the late nineteenth century. Following her return from Africa in the summer of 1891, French-Sheldon appeared on the stages of all those organizations and many more. Her reputed stage presence and speaking ability, her charm, and the exoticism of her topic filled these halls and galleries with enthusiastic audiences. Even May French-

Sheldon's foremost detractor, the *Spectator* reporter quoted at the outset of this section, though disbelieving many of French-Sheldon's claims, had to concede the unusually enthusiastic audience she had attracted to the British Association and that it was "the largest audience that the Association has yet been able to assemble."[5]

Just as she would in her written text, French-Sheldon made the most of her gender in lectures, claiming to have out-performed some of the greatest African travelers and observers without the benefit of previous experience or academic training, equipped only with such feminine "skills" as patience, kindliness, concern, and attention to detail. The key to whether French-Sheldon received a rousing endorsement or a condescending or even scathing review lay, not unsurprisingly, with the particular reviewer's reception of her claim to a gender advantage over men of science. The *Spectator's* critic scoffed at this idea along with the notion of French-Sheldon's delicate sensibilities. He at once cast doubt on her womanliness and impugned the veracity of her account on the basis of it.

> What she particularly insisted on in her lecture was the fact that, though quite prepared to accept things as they were, "she went into Africa with all delicacy and womanliness";—also, we suppose, with a hundred and thirty Zanzibari coolies and a raw-hide whip,—or perhaps those items are included among the things that she had to accept.[6]

This writer mocked French-Sheldon's plan to study Africans "in their native condition," by pointing out the "obvious" inconsistencies that existed between the ethnological project and middle-class female propriety (i.e., encountering African nudity). He jeered, "When the primitive condition, however, happened to be also an unclothed one, her plan seems to have broken down, though even in this matter she assured her audience that the wild savages hastened to meet her half-way."[7] Chivalric gloves off, he snidely queried, "Who applied the rawhide whip? . . . Evidently the spirit to whip was there; but, indeed, we should think that, however willing the spirit was, the flesh must have proved too weak." While he viciously attacked the veracity of French-Sheldon's account, he especially ridiculed her assertion that gentle manners and good form were all that a colonialist needed to arm herself or himself with. Disparaging the very qualities French-Sheldon asserted made all the difference in interactions with Africans, the writer for the *Spectator* pointed to the presence of an escort of well over a hundred men to explain French-Sheldon's successful completion of her expedition. The "special consideration on account of her sex" that this columnist accused French-Sheldon of requesting, rendered her, in his opinion, a "sham Lady-Errant" rather than a "real 'Woman-Master.'"[8] However misogynist, the author of this mean-spirited piece was perceptive; he discerned in the simplicity and modesty of French-Sheldon's claims to scientific acumen a resistance to male monopolization of the ethnographic enterprise. He perceived a "feminine spirit of unrest, and the uneasy jealousy that is for ever driving the fair sex into proving itself the equal of the other." And he warned the British Association against encouraging it.

Most commentators were not so harsh nor so skeptical of the gendered slant French-Sheldon lent to her ethnographic expertise. In general the argument that women had particular gifts stemming from either their functional roles in the home or their biological natures held great persuasive appeal with readers and audiences used to thinking about middle-class women as the "angels in the house."[9] The *New York Times,* in both its report of French-Sheldon's lecture to the American Geographical Society and in its book review of *Sultan to Sultan,* endorsed this point of view and French-Sheldon in her role as social scientist on the basis of it. The *New York Times* reporter who was assigned to her lecture especially delighted in French-Sheldon's feminine "shrewdness," attributing much of her "easily-won success" to the "gorgeousness of her apparel." "Throughout her journey," the journalist chortled,

> Mrs. Sheldon made a point of impressing the chiefs with the gorgeousness of her apparel, appearing before them at all formal palavers in a magnificent white silk ball gown, trained, and trimmed with silver. The chiefs evidently appreciated this formality and reciprocated by appearing in all their own finery. One of the chiefs remarked that she was very different from the white men, who appeared before them in rags and were no better than themselves.[10]

Nine months later, in its review of *Sultan to Sultan,* another writer for the *New York Times* elaborated on French-Sheldon's ability to make manifest the cleverness of Woman as well as the peculiar audacity of American womanhood in this regard. Claiming that the Parisian fashion house of Worth "made this dress for the express purpose of furnishing the wearer with an irresistible means of conquest," he queried, "who but an American woman would have conceived the idea of making a Worth gown help her win her way into the interior of Africa? But that gown was a part of a well-devised plan, based upon the penchant of savage and semi-barbarous persons for finery in dress and ornaments."[11] Although French-Sheldon was given her due in this review, it is important to note that her success was attributed to a certain wiliness in Woman's character. Moreover, in an unexpected twist of this logic, her ability to relate to the "savage and semi-barbarous" figured as the result of a perceived similarity between women and "savages" that lay in their mutual "penchant" for finery.

French-Sheldon's argument from gender difference, like the suffragist and social housekeeping argument that women's intervention was required in the public sphere because of their superior moral training in the private, suffered from a circularity that threatened to undermine her efforts to lend scientific worth to her exploits.[12] For instance, the *Nation,* like the *New York Times,* was far kinder in its review of *Sultan to Sultan* than the British *Spectator* had been to French-Sheldon a year before, and went so far as granting that in her work "many little details, such as would have escaped the notice of a man, or been deemed by him too trivial to record, are given, and enable the reader to form a very vivid idea of these interesting savages." But though the reviewer facetiously declined to comment on the literary character of the book out of a chivalric respect for the "affliction" she was under during its writing (French-Sheldon was in mourning for her husband), he made it abundantly clear that the "little details" that might have escaped a man were indeed "too trivial" to constitute a contribution to the official literature. In a patronizing tone, he declared, "She does not appear to have had any sufficient reason for her adventurous undertaking, and she adds little or nothing to our knowledge of the regions through which she passed or their inhabitants, but she does give many lively pictures."[13] The biggest danger inherent to French-Sheldon's gender-conscious strategy was that critics would accept her womanly virtues as advantages in conducting ethnographic research but would disregard her conclusions as scientifically inconsequential for the same set of reasons.

Despite the scantiness of the evidence supporting French-Sheldon's claim to a scientific contribution, she managed to become one of the first women accepted as a member of the most honored and prestigious of organizations when she became a Fellow of the London Royal Geographical Society in 1892.[14] Her timing may have been just right for inclusion in that quasi-professional and semi-academic institution; but it was off in terms of expecting a short safari more accurately labeled "from IBEA post to IBEA post" than from "sultan to sultan" to render her a veritable scientist, at least as far as specialists were concerned. Although as late as the mid-nineteenth century explorers legitimately saw themselves as "auxiliary scientists"[15]—collectors of raw data and novel, undiluted information— the "aneroid-carrying and calipers-brandishing traveler actually [became] a figure of fun" by the 1890s, and travelers like French-Sheldon, "who hungered for recognition as authorities on the places they explored and the peoples they studied, settled instead for the role of the 'theorizing' traveler, one who observes and evaluates evidence, because he can no longer collect it."[16] French-Sheldon was not the only explorer at the turn of the century who found herself a late comer to the European game of "being-the-first." As would increasingly become the habit of travelers to

Africa in the ensuing decades, she resolutely proclaimed that her contribution to the ethnographic project lay in the unique perspective she brought to the field.

Undoubtedly, part of French-Sheldon's ambivalent stance vis-à-vis science stemmed from her awareness of her individual inability to lay claim to an original "first," but it also may have stemmed from her accurate perception that the field of ethnographic study was changing in the direction of an emphasis on quality of observation and method of field research and away from a fixation on the "undiscovered." French-Sheldon was not a student of Franz Boas, who had yet to establish his reputation at Columbia University; but her presumptions about her work—her emphasis on the participatory methods of her field experience, her attention to the varieties and diversity present in each locale, her assertion of inductive purity, and her belief in her freedom from prior prejudice or culturally specific standards—prefigured the historical particularism and cultural relativism that Boas would make central to twentieth-century anthropological inquiry.[17]

These changes in anthropological methodology, which were only embryonic in 1891 when French-Sheldon published her "ethnography," would prove far more conducive to female contributions to the study of colonized peoples in the twentieth century than had the tendencies of nineteenth-century ethnology with its emphasis on entirely novel penetrations of uncharted regions. "Participant" observation in the intimate domestic life of those subject to anthropological inspection could be seen as utilizing what were thought of as uniquely feminine skills, thereby putting the supposed domestic orientation of Victorian women to their advantage as anthropological researchers.[18] At least French-Sheldon tried to make this case. In *Sultan to Sultan* and in her anthropological article "Customs among the Natives of East Africa, from Teita to Kilimegalia, with Special Reference to their Wom-en and Children," French-Sheldon highlighted the participatory nature of her expedition, with tantalizing images of secret blood brotherhood rituals, rites of passage, and sultan's "harems" to which only she, as a woman, had special access. She claims her way was smoothed in Taveta, for instance, by an influential African woman who was "so eager that I should be a witness of all her tribe's strange customs and habits that she gave me the open sesame to them all, and even at midnight, when the moon dances were taking place, she would steal to my tent and take me off through the forest to witness them, unseen and without their knowledge. I was thus enabled to become very familiar with the customs forbidden to be witnessed by the white man."[19]

Since "savages" were beyond the reach of industrialization and were thought to inhabit stateless societies, their world, much like that of middle-class white women, was believed to consist of the ahistorical, unchanging,

Fig. 14. Woman of Taveta
French-Sheldon claimed that this Tavetan woman imparted to her domestic
information and secrets of tribal initiation ceremonies hidden from other
explorers and travelers in the region.

and inherently "private" tasks and relations which lay outside of "civil" society. Anthropologists' primary concerns were with kinship, domestic economy, marriage relations, and (even more private) the native's "inner life" or
"nature." Who but a white middle-class woman could penetrate such a
world and come to understand it on its own terms? By subtitling her anthropological article "with Special Reference to their Women and Children," French-Sheldon intimated that anthropology's primary concerns
were well within the purview of a true woman. Professional or academic social scientists may have been slow to accept such logic, but the *New York
Times* promoted and popularized it without hesitation and accepted, with-

out question, French-Sheldon's ability in particular to demonstrate its effects. "Mrs. Sheldon undertook her journey with the purpose of winning and holding the confidence of the natives, especially of the women," the paper explained, "by mingling if possible in their family life as a male traveler could not hope to, and she was highly successful. In this way she was able to make many curious and original observations, and to secure objects which have never been seen out of Africa before." The paper credited French-Sheldon with utilizing her privileged relationship to what Westerners viewed as the private sphere of home and familial relationships, claiming that "with the private household life of the natives Mrs. Sheldon was very familiar, having been to all intents and purposes an inmate of several native families," and that these "rare favors" permitted French-Sheldon to contribute to the anthropological record "many hitherto unknown details concerning the treatment of children and about the ways and the feelings of African womankind."[20] French-Sheldon's emphasis on the nature of her field experience rather than on the unfamiliarity of the peoples she encountered evaded the issue of "being-the-first" and shielded her somewhat from the fall from relevance and prestige that travelers and explorers were suffering.

Women, even when they did chart new regions and encounter wholly unfamiliar peoples, labored under the burden of proof—never a far-off danger to the integrity of travel texts in any case. Female travelers suffered in particular from attacks on the veracity of their accounts, and French-Sheldon was not invulnerable to the misogynist belief in women's inability to resist hyperbole and embellishment. French-Sheldon escaped the brunt of these attacks on women's competence and character by exaggerating, not refuting, her femininity and her possession of the traits assumed to be innate to Woman's nature. Her reliance on and redeployment of conservative beliefs about women side-tracked most would-be sexist denunciations and side-stepped the fact that she lacked any official training in social science research. Taking as her project a humanization of the civilizing mission, French-Sheldon avoided being held to a masculine standard of objectivity or the formalities of scholarly qualifications that were possessed almost exclusively by men in the 1890s. She gained moral legitimacy and scientific credibility with general audiences instead by claiming the skills peculiar to the true woman. Such deft negotiation of extremely complex and potentially hazardous cultural terrain resulted in her essentially feminine, and therefore, inherently anti-scientific, perceptions about Africans taking on definite scientific worth and lent to her person the unmistakable aura of scientific authority at least in the minds of general audiences especially in the United States.

THE MYTH OF RECIPROCITY

> My method of procedure was to harmonize and
> attract towards me rather than to bully and
> subdue them by any rough methods.
> —May French-Sheldon

> I confess that in all history that I have ever read,
> no other explorer, to my knowledge, has ever
> invaded East Africa as she did.
> —Mary Livermore

Despite the need for French-Sheldon to proclaim her capacity for masculine authority in *Sultan to Sultan,* she spent most of the narrative stressing her womanly sensibilities. Her womanliness provided her with an "anti-conquest" device with which she cloaked the aggression underpinning her colonial attitudes toward Africans.[21] As part of her self-presentation as both a refined woman and an enlightened civilizer, French-Sheldon could hardly afford not to present herself or even view herself otherwise. Observers, even the few less-sympathetic ones, universally lauded her sensitivity, her magnanimity, and her manners. The imagery and language that French-Sheldon inspired and promulgated produced a dramatic and overblown picture of a genteel lady. For instance, the promotional flyer for *Sultan to Sultan* proudly announced that present in the hall was another explorer who has returned from Africa, a "woman, whose deeds have been unlike those of any other explorer."

> She visited kings, and so she went in her best clothes. She went as an elegant woman should go, superbly dressed, and simply with the words, "Good will to men." She came back to tell us what Stanley never did tell us,—of the home life of the natives, of their loves, their marriages, their daily habits and their thoughts of God and duty. She had no trouble whatever with the natives; she went to win their love and such a method has succeeded always and always will.[22]

This paean employs the idioms of the Victorian fashionable set and therewith portrayed French-Sheldon as, above all else, the perfect bourgeois guest, neglecting to note that she was not an invited one. French-Sheldon explored Africa "as an elegant woman should, superbly dressed" and with the best of intentions in mind. Her reward for such gracefully presented altruism was African recognition and affirmation of her superior status. Denying the possibility that French-Sheldon had compromised her dignity

as a respectable woman, the pundit just quoted ended his admiring assessment of her manner in Africa by noting, "not once in all her journeying did
she receive one insult; never did she see one indecent act." The elegant explorer claimed to have withered African resistance to her free-wheeling access to their land and their "inner lives," with nothing more than the fact of
her racial superiority, manifested by her costume, confirmed by her exhibition of impeccable bourgeois manners, and declared by the iron-clad logic
her race and class hubris put at her disposal. Arrogantly announcing, "I did
not pay *hongo* (tolls) to any tribe during my safari," she claimed that she
merely had to put the matter clearly and firmly to the young, male warriors
who approached her with their demands for tribute, explaining to them, "'I
am your guest; I am as a white queen coming to you. Would you ask *hongo*
of the sultan of such and such a tribe should he visit you?' and it successfully
relieved me from further parley or exaction" (*SS:* 169).

French-Sheldon claimed to have made a significant contribution to the
civilizing of Africans merely by being the perfect lady in front of them. A
reporter for the widely read *Chautauquan* commended her efforts by noting
the "tribes" she had encountered, "had been in the habit of mincing their
food all together, making it into balls, and crowding it down their throats
with force, in a horribly gluttonous fashion. Sometimes a thousand at a time
would come down from the mountains to see the white woman eat," and
now, this reporter averred, "where she has passed through, they eat with
knives and forks."[23]

Lest we ignore the links that Victorians drew between personal demeanor and morality, it is important to notice the connections the *Chautauquan* reporter and others drew between discussions of French-Sheldon's
toilette and manners and the more serious issues of empire-building. More
than displaying the effects of exemplary manners on the uncivilized or the
calming effect that French-Sheldon's gentility seemed to have on the savage
character, *Sultan to Sultan* was "commended by the fact that it records an effort to separate exploration from murder." Another commentator labeled it
"a lesson in that supremely womanly virtue: mercy." This reviewer went on
to mysteriously speculate, "[T]he book may well act as an instrument to
erase the blood marks from other recent tablets of history" (by which he
likely meant African slavery).[24] French-Sheldon's scientific pursuit of
knowledge and sentimental quest for cross-racial engagement was viewed as
not only non-aggressive but positively uplifting and, as such, harbored the
potential to redeem the project of colonization from the depths of ig-
nominy where European-sponsored slave traders and explorers such as
Henry Stanley had left it mired. In her telling and in the impression her self-
presentation made on her white middle-class audiences, her exertions, at

great sacrifice to herself, amounted to a noble effort of humanitarianism on "behalf of the primitives."

French-Sheldon painted colonialist relations between Europeans and Africans as mutually beneficial. Key to every encounter between herself and Africans was what Mary Louise Pratt calls the "mystique of reciprocity."[25] French-Sheldon carefully recorded all the many gifts she brought with her and listed them frequently in *Sultan to Sultan* for the reader. Beads, as the item of barter in East Africa, were of obvious importance to the success of her expedition and she bought a significant quantity on the coast to take with her. But of more importance to her presentation of herself in the text as an ambassador for European and American commercial interests were the many industrially produced items she thought to pack, including

> metal wires, the cloths, the silks and velvets, gold-lace, and other presents which one takes for chiefs, of all kinds and sizes, the most valued among which will be British soldier coats, flaunting red, with gaudy gold-lace and plenty of brass buttons; European hats, and red umbrellas, tooting horns, music boxes, clocks, matches, razors, knives, bells, rings, bracelets, metal belts and jewelled weapons, needles, sewing thread, pins, fishhooks, tops, kites, dolls, picture books, clay pipes, tobacco, snuff, tea, sugar, silverware, china, cups, knives, spoons and forks, paint boxes, mirrors, sewing machines, tools. (*SS:* 106)

French-Sheldon characterizes her exchanges as benefiting Africans far more than herself, even as she crows over the inestimable worth that would accrue to her from the African items she procured in exchange and would later represent as rare anthropological "finds." Effacing the immediate commercial value of objects in favor of the professional status and exotic appeal they could confer upon their bearer, the products of African labor appear in her accounts to be both of inferior quality to the industrial trinkets and toys she tendered and perfectly available to whites, virtually there for the taking. "They were so pleased to have the 'white queen' with them," she claims, "there was nothing among their possessions which I really craved in the end they did not give me. "Of course," she hastens to add, "it is well understood that these gifts were always reciprocated by me, if not in kind, certainly in excess of value, but that does not in any way detract from the fact that they were willing gifts and presented with a free, open hand, without expectation of return, as a tribute to the 'white queen'" (*SS:* 157–58).

French-Sheldon believed she had found a way to pacify a "half-savage" continent without engendering any resentment or even encountering any resistance. Even the most reputedly menacing of East African peoples, the Masai, were hardly a threat to French-Sheldon; their "quaint way of forbid-

Fig. 15. Angry Bebes
French-Sheldon admitted to frequently inciting the ire of Africans with her aggressive bartering for their personal items.

ding passage through their territory," by the placing of a bullet crossed with two twigs in a path, she carelessly "kicked aside," and their aggravation with her she "soon appeased with a few lumps of bluestone" (*SS:* 200). Likewise, after she "concluded to go and see for myself," the Rombos, long "deemed a ferocious people, tricky in their dealings with other natives, and the marauders of passing caravans," were as it turns out, "the delighted people most civil, and eager to do Bebe Bwana homage. They were neither uncouth nor unkind nor ungenerous, and certainly far from being hostile. They loaded me with gifts of beautiful furs and such other of their worldly possessions that I chanced to admire" (*SS:* 179).

Simply by virtue of her race and gender, apparently, Africans rushed to bestow valuables upon her and enter into exchanges that French-Sheldon represented as freely entered into and wholly reciprocal in nature. Even in light of their enthusiastic participation, however, Africans had to be guided with patience and forbearance at times, for, according to French-Sheldon, as "primitives" they had only the most rudimentary understanding of the ethics of exchange versus those of gift-giving. French-Sheldon tells of "one sprightly bronzed beauty—a beauty according to the accepted rule of that country" who offered French-Sheldon her own delicately beaded necklace as a present. French-Sheldon denies misunderstanding the young woman's intentions and instead characterizes the young woman as having changed her mind about the meaning of the act later once the caravan had left the area. French-Sheldon records the awkwardness of the moment when the woman, after having traveled for miles, finally caught up to the caravan and, repenting "of her free gift," demanded it paid for or returned. The callous ending to this episode, "she was pacified with the glitter of a few pieces and a name ring," that French-Sheldon records reveals her contempt for the very ethics of exchange that she meant readers to credit her with.

The crack that this ending introduces in French-Sheldon's deployment of a peculiarly white and feminine commitment to reciprocity widens later in the text of *Sultan to Sultan.* Desiring a beaded cloth symbolic of a married woman's identity and faithfulness, French-Sheldon badgered the African woman who owned it until she finally relinquished it. "They have never been known to sell, give or barter one of these cloths after having worn it, until I procured the one in my possession," French-Sheldon boasts and gives as the reason, "the idea that if they should give to any *mzunga* such a cloth, or he should obtain it in any way, the woman would be under some sexual subjection to this man; that he could take her from her husband and tribe to the ends of the earth." French-Sheldon's cultural sensitivity ("the reason for this is very rational from their standpoint") was entirely over-ridden by her condescension ("considering the people from whom it emanates"), and did nothing to hinder her from exerting an enormous amount of pressure on her African "sister" to relinquish such a precious item. "When I argued with the women that I was a woman, a *bebe* like themselves," French-Sheldon begins,

> that I could not possibly work such magic over them, and that it would be a graceful thing for one woman to give to another woman such an evidence of her friendship, they argued and protested at first, always refusing to comply with my request; then as I made firmer friendship with them, bestowing gifts and kindnesses upon them, possibly administering to them medically if they chanced to be overtaken with illness, the heart of one woman softened towards me and she professed that she was willing to give me her cloth if her husband would only consent, for which favor I avowed my willingness to give her sufficient material and beads to make two others. (*SS:* 207–208)

French-Sheldon assures the reader that this exchange, however aggressively negotiated, was a reciprocal one with her pointed last phrase ("sufficient . . . to make two others") and the one following: "Yet she kept settling back in wonderment over the peculiarity of my request, and that I, a woman, and the master of a great caravan, could possess her cloth and yet not care to possess her" (*SS:* 208). In the end French-Sheldon, despite "all manner of blandishments on my part," insists that the exchange was not a result of bullying or even tough bargaining practices but instead reflected the reciprocity inherent to the non-competitive relations innately existing between women, a relation self-evident even to "savages" apparently. "After a lapse of many days," she recounts, the woman who had followed her safari for over fifty miles, "finally came and tossed it into my tent, exclaiming, "Bebe Bwana, take it, take it: you are my sister, take it!" (SS: 208). French-Sheldon's only embellishment on this ending is to announce that "this episode goes far to evidence how much superior in some ways is the position of woman going among this tribe over that of any man" (SS: 208).

The explorer passes over the raw brutality she exhibited on several occasions with the blithest of references to cultural sensitivity and her earnest desire for "harmony" between herself and the Africans in her employ. "A Masai woman's corpse was nosed out of the bush," she unapologetically reports, "with all her armor of iron wire leglets and armlets upon her stark stiff body untouched, however much coveted, through superstition. Personally I nerved myself to the removal of her leglets," French-Sheldon continues dispassionately, "which had become so imbedded into the flesh and muscles of her legs, amputation was necessary." She explains that she could have insisted that the porters "attend to this matter," but their "nameless superstitions" would have made such a command obnoxious and "put a damper on their exalted estimations of me for so outraging their sentiments." And so she performed the amputations personally and without apology.

French-Sheldon's commitment to "maintain a policy of harmony" with Africans "when consistent" obviously was whenever French-Sheldon deigned her desires consistent with her ability to maintain control, and when she really wanted something neither cultural sensitivity nor stereotypical "womanly sentiment" stood in her way of getting it. Corpses were not the only African bodies French-Sheldon violated. French-Sheldon proudly recounts in *Sultan to Sultan* the method by which she acquired some precious "jaw-shaped" armlets worn by men that had been "placed upon the arm in youth before the muscles are developed, and become imbedded in the expanded flesh to such an extent that removal is almost like amputation, so painful and difficult is the operation." "Upon the three arms from which I took the armlets I have in my possession," she boasts, "the scars were so pronounced and disfiguring that the owners of the surrendered ornaments insisted that they should have a substitute of sufficient metal armlets to entirely cover the scars" (SS: 159).

Heightening the castrating connotations of the pictures she draws for readers of disfigured and scarred arms and her severing of them from their disgruntled owners is the sexual meaning she attaches to these particular ornaments. She maintains that she "was told by a very intelligent elder that the figures graven on the reverse side of these armlets represented the male and female organs of generation" (*SS:* 159). Whereas French-Sheldon sexualizes the African woman ("a sprightly bronze beauty") who demanded further payment from her, she symbolically castrates African males and reduces them in the passage to their body parts (in this case, arms). Africans in general were dehumanized by language that typically separates them from their body parts and by a skewed interpretation of "reciprocity" that served to separate many of them from their valuables.

Throughout *Sultan to Sultan* French-Sheldon effaces the inequalities of these "trades" by foregrounding her insistence on upholding the ethics of exchange and respect for private property. She clarifies for readers that she neither cheated Africans nor was bullied by them. Maintaining such a claim, in light of incidents such as the one recounted below, was not a simple or straightforward matter. French-Sheldon's report of her confrontation with a Masai warrior concludes on a note of pure violence. "A warrior, hideously bedecked in his war paint and war toggery, having heard that I refused to pay hongo to the Masai who tried to exact it from me whilst in Kimangelia, and not in Masai land, came rushing up to me brandishing his spear violently, then uplifting it as though he aimed to cleave me in two, planted it into the ground before me, yelled in a deafening tone as he bounded high in the air 'Wow! wow! wow!'" she excitedly recounts. "Quick as a flash," she continues, "I reached behind me and seized my gun, rushed forward with it, pointing the muzzle towards him, and in turn yelled, 'Wow! wow! wow!' discharging it in the air." French-Sheldon does not hesitate to follow her depiction of this confrontation filled with bravado with a smug expression of victory over the male warrior: "Suffice it to confess, I own that spear," she crows (*SS:* 204).

As the last statement in this passage makes abundantly clear, French-Sheldon was determined to enforce the rules of civil exchange as she defined them. Her refusal to pay tolls, or *hongo,* for passage through Masai territory (territory that was not covered by the writs of passage she had acquired from the Sultan of Zanzibar) stemmed from her presumptions of racial entitlement. Further, she justifies her confrontational style by referring to attempts to intimidate her into paying *hongo* as blackmail. Yet French-Sheldon was not entirely comfortable with ownership by such acquisition, even if she viewed it as arising from an attempt at extortion, inasmuch as it did not satisfy the terms of reciprocity she herself had laid bare for readers. She makes her discomfort explicit in the next two sentences in the passage about the expropriated spear. "It was never called for. It cannot be denominated as either a gift, or a find, or a capture." She immediately follows up her report of this incident with an anecdote designed to soften her image a bit and lighten the moment. She recounts turning suddenly "from a lurking place where I sought to evade observation, for more than all other tribes the Masai have a dread of a camera," to capture "a large body of warriors, all accounted" with her lens as they passed in full view (*SS:* 204). In a textual turnaround, and couched in a self-deprecating tone more typical of her fellow African explorer Mary Kingsley, French-Sheldon admits that what she thought was her camera was actually her water bottle.[26] Instead of capturing the Masai's image, she found herself deluged with liquid from the upturned bottle. "So much for blind zeal!" she exclaims self-mockingly.

French-Sheldon meant to pass lightly over the incident with the spear-carrying Masai by inserting this light anecdote, an additional intent of which was to apologize for the disrespect with which she treated Africans who did not wish to be photographed. But the awkwardness she displays in the truncated passage reveals her discomfort with the exchanges, even photographic ones, that she has to admit were forced.

The moral of the water-bottle incident, immediately following as it does on the heels of her boasting about how she deprived a Masai warrior of his own spear, reasserts the primary message she hoped to demonstrate throughout the text. Although French-Sheldon likes to present herself as someone whom Africans could not best, "blind zeal" was not something French-Sheldon meant to encourage in those white explorers and travelers who might follow her. Despite what I have been depicting as exacting demands on African hospitality, French-Sheldon meant to advocate responsible governing, meaning rule by law, respect for property, and honoring of contracts. *Sultan to Sultan* is a cautionary tale aimed at "fine, energetic men who are fired with ambition" and Africa-bound, to convince them that "[a]bility, steadfast work, patience, abnegation, and time are the only stepping stones" to the successful conquest of the continent (*SS:* 102).

Almost every page of her over four-hundred-page narrative extols the values of the self-made man, of respect for property, and of capitalist development. In light of debates rife in the late nineteenth century regarding the slave trade and the complicity of explorers in that trade, French-Sheldon was conscious of her role as an employer and presents herself as supremely fair-minded, responsible, and reliable. She pushes this image even to the point of attributing to herself a self-sacrificing tendency she links, once again, to her gender. French-Sheldon describes her efforts to fulfill commitments made on her journey in just such terms. "Despite my serious illness, so exhausted I could not articulate an audible sound, suffering excruciating agony," she records near the end of *Sultan to Sultan,* "I feel a glow of pardonable pride, in which my friends and my sex must join me, in the fact that I personally discharged all of my men, and saw them disband, and that I made full settlement of every payable obligation connected with my caravan, as completely as though in the possession of my normal health"

(*SS:* 250). The enjoinder aimed at her female readership demonstrates the added pressure French-Sheldon was feeling, as a woman, to convince her readers that she understood the logic underpinning capitalist market relations. French-Sheldon's emphasis on the payment of debts and the reciprocity of her dealings with Africans invests her with a sense of honor usually applicable only to men in Victorian society.

The ability to recognize the rights of property, the necessity of reciprocity, and the sanctity of contracts were not only central to French-Sheldon's conception of honor, they also were necessary to the implementation of her capitalist vision. In the space of three pages in the original text, French-Sheldon demonstrates the mutual benefit that could accrue to Europeans and Africans alike if the set of values she demonstrated were inculcated in Africans. The "Sultans" Mireali and Miriami were her most illustrious example of the untapped potential of Africans to participate in a world organized by capital and private property. "Mireali has not been free from the crime of raiding lesser tribes," she explains, "but he aims to improve himself, and seeks to imitate the more enlightened ways of the mzungu." She continues to describe this headman as someone who "represents all that is superior and intelligent among these tribes." She is equally impressed with another headman, Miriami, who had rendered her several services and received many presents from her in appreciation but who was not satisfied with the sorts of trinkets she normally distributed. When pressed, Miriami admitted to wanting a hammer and saw with which "to build an English house and live like a white man." In response to French-Sheldon's assurances that she would send the items upon her return to London, Miriami doubtfully exclaimed, "Ah, yes, white men all promise, but they all forget; the mzungu always lies." This impertinence produced a verbal cuffing from French-Sheldon, "Stop, Miriami, you must not speak to Bebe Bwana in that way. I never lie. I will send you the saw." French-Sheldon claims in *Sultan to Sultan* that even while her delirium from an illness she contracted near the end of her trek raged, "this thing haunted me with other promises I had made these poor trusting natives, and I never rested, day or night, until every one had met a fulfillment, through the consideration of the scrupulous guardian of my honor, and Miriami has his saw" (*SS:* 220–21).

Her interchanges with Mireali and Miriami reveal the degree to which French-Sheldon viewed every exchange as a means of bringing civilization to Africa. A saw and hammer were no more crucial to Mireali's and Miriami's attempts to leave behind a life of crime and "imitate the more enlightened ways of the mzungu" than were the bourgeois ideals French-Sheldon meant to inculcate through explanation and example. A vision of Mireali and Miriami getting jobs, cultivating a respect for property, and becoming trustworthy home owners testified to the mutually beneficial possibilities colonialism presented to Africans and Euro-Americans alike. Such possibilities, of course, could only be realized if Africans, who resembled nothing so much as wayward teenagers, were managed properly by incoming whites. "So it is," she argues,

> I think, if people when visiting the country of natives, instead of taking useless, showy trumpery, would give them implements useful and simple to understand, and take a little trouble to teach them the uses thereof, they would be found ready and appreciative people, evincing gratitude and no mean amount of aptitude.
>
> The natives' sufferings from the cold in these districts, where the bleak wind rises at four in the afternoon, and the thermometer falls down to fifty-four degrees and even lower, is very pitiful; and although they have quantities of furs, they are constantly asking for cloths and blankets to keep them warm. Various fibres, papyrus, bamboo, m'whala, and others, and grasses which abound throughout East Africa, are susceptible of being converted into fabrics, exactly as such have been utilized by the people of Madagascar and Peru; therefore, if simple looms, without any mechanical intricacies, were introduced, the natives could very soon supply their own requirements, as well as produce a commercial commodity. (SS: 221)

These two paragraphs appear to form a non sequitur. But the underlying message of the former (that Africans are eager to learn industrial ways) only has meaning in view of the latter (with the appropriate imports, East Africans could be a source of inexpensive labor and light industrial products). There were commercial advantages to be had, French-Sheldon maintained, and African needs could be American or European opportunities. It was a national flag that French-Sheldon flew from the center-pole of her tent, not a mission's, and it was capitalism she intended to encourage, not merely philanthropy. Supporters of the commercial penetration of Africa agreed and relied on French-Sheldon's reports to make the case for economic and cultural imperialism as opposed to formal colonization.[27] And since the "white man's burden" French-Sheldon advocated was a secular "mission," not an ecclesiastical one, a way had to be found for it to pay for itself. "If the slaves who are now in Africa had some means of self-liberation, by which they could pay for themselves by their own work instead of becoming the paupers of a zealous philanthropy, and if they were treated as the children they are in all matters appertaining to Christianity and legal codes, the future of these people would be assured."[28]

The colonial relationship between Africa and her readership that French-Sheldon envisioned and did her best to facilitate, was one firmly centered around Euro-American appropriation of resources, management of populations and services, and administrative control of economies, rather than settlement or territorial acquisition through warfare. Yet as the several incidents in which French-Sheldon unilaterally claims a right to trespass through African lands and expropriate African labor, goods, and body parts make clear, a militant attitude of entitlement and racial mastery was never absent from this "anti-imperial" vision. Indeed, French-Sheldon's explicit exegeses of suitable methods of forging and sustaining an imperial relationship to Africa were characteristic of American contributions to debates over colonialism in the 1890s, and her ethnographic research was geared to the production of useful, pragmatic suggestions for the "New Empires" under construction in this period.

FOUR

Sex and the Sultans

May French-Sheldon's account of her first trip to Africa appealed to readers for other reasons besides its classy exterior, intellectual merits, and seemingly enlightened attitudes toward women and supposedly inferior races. The narrative draws on a popular taste for orientalist imagery by foregrounding elements of East African society that would have reminded Victorian readers of such popular classics as *A Thousand and One Arabian Nights*. A major portion of the narrative focuses on French-Sheldon's sea voyage through the Mediterranean and the Suez Canal, along the coasts of Egypt, Sudan, and Somalia, and on her stay on the island of Zanzibar. Perforce, the first portion of the text concerns itself primarily with Arab culture and Islamic customs. In her narrative French-Sheldon took the opportunity to state her views on "Eastern" ways and to develop theories about the relative stages of civilization and moral development of East African peoples. In French-Sheldon's telling, Africa becomes an extension of Arabia, albeit an even more primitivized one. Although *sultan* was used widely in this part of East Africa to refer to headmen, for French-Sheldon's English-speaking readers the term carried connotations of Eastern despotism and cruelty and gave rise to fantasies of licentious living and barbaric sensualism. In light of this predisposition, her orientalist depictions of East African leaders along with her sexualized descriptions of her interactions with them lent her tale an erotic and exotic air. The idea of a charming and attractive white woman traveling "alone" with a 150 armed black men through the "dark continent" to meet with "sultans" could not have failed to tantalize French-Sheldon's readership with its suggestive possibilities.[2]

ONE FRANK AMERICAN WOMAN

> A plucky woman . . . a womanly woman, as feminine in her
> instincts and dress as the stay-at-home who has never gone
> to New York alone. In wonder the child-like, easily
> impressed savages looked upon this Bebe Bwana
> as a being from another world.
> —Advertisement printed in the
> *Philadelphia Times*[3]

French-Sheldon encouraged Africans to view her as a White Queen by dressing up in an elaborate costume complete with platinum blonde wig (see introduction for a detailed description) to convey and exaggerate her status as a white woman. Although Africans may not have, in fact, drawn a connection between French-Sheldon's jewel-studded tiara, blonde wig, and shiny gown and a European queen's rank, American reviewers and critics especially were impressed and intrigued by her elaborate costume and the gender-, race-, and rank-specific issues it raised. Reporters rarely failed to comment on what they perceived as a clever tactic to gain the respect and admiration of unsophisticated natives. The effect of French-Sheldon's ultra-feminine and racially exaggerated appearance on Africans became a central theme of most discussions of French-Sheldon as an explorer in the first few years of her public-speaking tours.

Steeped in their assumptions about white superiority, white beauty, and black sexual rapaciousness, French-Sheldon's white audiences and readers might have concluded, even without her explicitly claiming it to be the case, that African men were attracted, perhaps uncontrollably, to her as a white woman. Rather than dismissing or attempting to downplay at least the racialized sexual tension such assumptions lent to her enterprise (as other female travel writers in this period tended to do), French-Sheldon sought every opportunity to amplify the eroticism.[4] In *Sultan to Sultan* she refers repeatedly to Africans' expressions of desire for her and admiration for her Caucasian features. Yet somehow her portrayal of herself as desirable to blacks did not result in her textual objectification; in fact she accomplishes just the reverse. French-Sheldon contains the potential degradation that tends to threaten the dignity and self-possession of female protagonists in travel writing by dismissing black desire as fatuous but, at the same time, not entirely without consequence. In a deft reworking of the familiar trope of white woman as coveted sexual commodity, she achieves a position of control, even of mastery, in her narrative. Each sexually charged incident in French-Sheldon's account demonstrates her inviolability to readers and establishes her personal triumph over sexual degradation while simultaneously reducing the threat of black male sexual prowess.

The first incident in *Sultan to Sultan* is a trivial episode but one fraught with sexual tension and veiled thinly in metaphor. As soon as French-Sheldon's husband exits the narrative, her "reputation" as a "brave lady" was established with the help of a rat aboard ship. "The impudent rodent explored my legs and tested my nerves!" she reports. Yet for some "unknown reason," she "was not in the least excited only surprised and anxious to know how to rout the enemy." French-Sheldon admits to not a shred of feminine hysteria and claims that no panic on her part repelled the rodent, who finally ran off when French-Sheldon inadvertently emitted a sneeze. Completely undaunted by the classic terror of stereotyped womanhood, French-Sheldon proceeds to describe her befriending of this pest with suggestive language: "Throughout the voyage this rat was a constant visitor to me. . . . He never molested me only to manifest his presence by passing his rough, coarse, hairy paw over my face." French-Sheldon exhibits no distaste for such "nightly" attentions, not even permitting a trap to be set for the rodent (*SS:* 70–71).

No sooner was French-Sheldon out of port and beyond the reach of her husband and other white male protectors than she confirms her ability to protect herself by neutralizing unwanted advances. The suggestive anecdote reveals her need to address the issue of her sexual vulnerability, even if only obliquely. Victorians, distinctly unaccustomed to scenes in which respectable women discuss their legs and something "exploring" them, would have sensed the sexual threat that the rodent symbolized. The passage establishes not only French-Sheldon's "bravery" but also her position as a respectable "lady" by demonstrating her unflappable dignity and resourcefulness in "rout[ing]" an "enemy." French-Sheldon's lack of concern and even bemusement at her own composure ("For some unknown reason, I was not in the least excited") is vindicated when a simple, unlooked for, sneeze takes care of the problem. The implication of this solution is that French-Sheldon's natural instincts were capable of neutralizing sexual danger. In other words, she did not have to do anything but be her controlled self and the threat would be exposed for what it really was—an innocuous episode bereft of any power to humiliate her or bring out the latent vulnerabilities of Woman. Her repositioning of herself as a kind, maternal figure in the passage ("I would not consent to have a trap set to capture him") further diminishes the horror of her "nightly visitor" by establishing her protective authority over "him." French-Sheldon was in no way defeated or sexually defiled by this experience, nor by any of her other encounters on her journey. She intended to elicit from her reader a respect for her staunchness on this point with her calm reiteration of the rat's potentially menacing sexual advances, the "rough, coarse, hairy paw" which passed over her face each night of the ship's journey. If this incident with the ship's rat was a foreshadowing "test" of her nerve and her ability to defuse future sexually tense situations, French-Sheldon assures her readership she was up to the task that lay before her.

Though the rat incident aboard ship is clearly a gratuitous one included merely for the purposes of conveying the quality of French-Sheldon's nerve, the invocation of women's sexual vulnerability followed swiftly by a reaffirmation of self-possession and dignity repeats itself throughout *Sultan to Sultan* and in doing so reveals a fundamental tension in the narrative regarding sexual vulnerability, middle-class respectability, and public authority. The pattern appears at key moments in the text, such as the occasion of French-Sheldon's first meeting with an African authority, the Sultan of Zanzibar.

The Sultan of Zanzibar, whose palace was located on the island itself, claimed control over a vast area of the mainland coast for hundreds of miles to the west, north, and south of the island. French-Sheldon required the cooperation of the Sultan to secure porters for her expedition and had to meet with him personally to obtain a writ of passage that mainland peoples would honor. In the passages describing this meeting, French-Sheldon reveals her nervousness at going alone to meet the Sultan, whom she imagines as being used to receiving women for the purpose of engaging in sexual liaison. She recalls being "sandwiched between" two of the Sultan's "dragomen" as they guided her through the "narrow, dirty apologies for streets" in Zanzibar town with "all the black people gazing." In the late Victorian period, "the street" was a precarious venue for respectable middle-class women, whose reputations were vulnerable to the charge that they had allowed themselves to be put on public display. The fear was that they might be mistaken for common prostitutes or subjected to the ogling that degraded even legitimate working-class women who could not avoid appearing in the street unchaperoned. French-Sheldon addresses the danger of defilement that hovered above the images of the self she had conjured for her readers and, within the very same sentence, dismisses it as powerless to affect her. "The thought came flashing into my brain," she writes, "that even these wretched blacks, in their debasement, imagined the very worst thing possible about the white woman, and I felt choked with self-indignation that a freeborn American woman should have sought the opportunity to conspicuously place herself in such a questionable position; then the absolutism of my one determination asserted itself, and the humiliation was from thence a mere detail, albeit keen and uncomfortable" (*SS:* 96–97).

In her account French-Sheldon "sandwiched between two marked drag-omen, with all the black people gazing," comes close to being demeaned by the gaze of the "wretched blacks" who, she assumes, imagined her no more in control of her sexuality than she and her white readers would have presumed that black women were in control of theirs. At first she blames herself for being vulnerable to public insult, that is, for making herself "conspicuous"—few crimes against true womanhood were not summed up by such a notion. Yet before even ending this sentence she has recovered her sense of self-possession, her composure, and an ability to assert her right to the public space of the street. Importantly, as we saw with the incident of the rat aboard ship, no alteration of the circumstances are required. Her resolution to the problem is merely to assert her will within an emphatically racialized context to reinterpret the meaning of the relations of power being enacted. In doing so she denies her black oglers the power to humiliate her. She encourages the reader to understand their insulting view of her as a reflection of their own debasement and racial status, rather than her decision to violate the strictures of true womanhood that would have her remain at home. The embarrassment is all on the Sultan's side as he hastens to apologize to French-Sheldon as a woman worthy of the respect he denies women of his own race and class. "Subsequent to these delicate civilities," French-Sheldon recounts that the Sultan explained "with evident embarrassment, that it was not his custom to ceremoniously receive ladies, nevertheless he was quite desirous to be of service to me in every possible way" (*SS:* 97–98). French-Sheldon's recollection of the way that the Sultan put himself at her service as "he wrapped his splendid gold-embroidered *joho* about him with a certain majesty and said imperiously, 'Command us and it shall be done,'" reverses the ignominious situation threatening French-Sheldon out in the street and establishes her ontological difference from the women of his society.

In the next scene, French-Sheldon takes her readers on a titillating tour of the women's quarters, the Sultan's "harem." Even the most privileged of Zanzibari women, members of the royal family, are only to be pitied in French-Sheldon's narrative. She describes the Sultan's daughter as draped with symbols of her commodification and confinement.

> The heavy gold anklets worn by this little child, but five years of age, impeded her moving with any freedom. Her crown, studded with jewels, must have pained her tender brow; and the gorgeous as well as curious necklaces suspended one upon another to the number of a dozen, and numerous bracelets and finger rings, certainly must have been burdensome. (*SS:* 99)

The Sultan's daughter seems more than merely physically burdened by the jewels she wears. From French-Sheldon's viewpoint, they represent a lack of the very mobility that figuratively and literally comprises French-Sheldon's status as a "freeborn American woman," a subject uncompromised by gender. The irony of French-Sheldon's own donning of an excess of jewels and elaborate costume to put such "freedom" into effect apparently escaped French-Sheldon's notice and, presumably, would have escaped the notice of her readers in the 1890s as well.

The climax of the harem scene comes when French-Sheldon is ceremoniously introduced to the Sultan's numerous wives. French-Sheldon's portrayal of these tragic and demoralized women is meant to ironize any presumed shared sisterhood between them and "freeborn American" women. French-Sheldon's dramatic skills are in great evidence in this passage as she strives to describe how the head wife or Sultana, "a haughty woman, gorgeously attired," and "possessed with all the imperious disdain of an empress," greeted her with outraged expression. "Poor woman," French-Sheldon writes, "did she presume I was another usurper of her legitimate place?" Graciously setting aside her repugnance at the thought that her gender grouped her with the Sultan's wives, French-Sheldon remembers rising and extending her hand "to greet the first, who was a fine, frank-looking creature" only to be waved down by the Sultan who discouraged her from troubling herself, explaining that "there are too many, all alike, and not worth it." Yet time constraints notwithstanding, French-Sheldon reports that, at the command of the Sultan, each of "these poor degraded concubines," some "sad-eyed and full of sorrow, others . . . defiant and triumphant, and yet others . . . envious . . . bathed my right foot in rose-water, and in recognition of my superiority and evidence of their humility, each gave me one of her jewelled rings. The sum total was one-hundred and forty-two" (*SS:* 99–100).

In this scene French-Sheldon wonders incredulously whether the Sultana could possibly draw the absurd conclusion that French-Sheldon might covet her position. The rhetorical question is aimed directly at the reader, who is expected to concur that the life of a (middle-class white) American woman is vastly preferable, given the humiliation even a Sultana is forced to endure at the hands of an Eastern man. However much sympathy for them French-Sheldon exhibits, she betrays not a trace of empathy for women with whom, ultimately, she feels she has nothing in common. Referring to her closest counterpart, the Sultana, as a "fine, frank-looking creature," French-Sheldon establishes her own subject position as a human, not a sexualized, "creature," and as an individual, not one of "too many, all alike, and not worth" even greeting.

French-Sheldon's rendering of this scene corresponds to the growing body of stories featuring resilient, liberated white women adored by African or Asian men who exhibit only disgust for the slavish women of their own societies. The stereotype of the plucky Western feminist developed in such stories as French-Sheldon's seem to exempt Western women from the degradation innate to women everywhere else. French-Sheldon's privileged location of herself in relation to her nationality as well as her race comprises a key strategy French-Sheldon utilizes repeatedly in *Sultan to Sultan.* In response to the Sultan's request for her opinion of his household, French-Sheldon reminds readers of the inherent contrast between American women and Zanzibari women. "With true American frankness, I declared it [the Sultan's polygamy] atrocious. He said he would gladly renounce his harem," if it could be done without harming his political position (*SS:* 100). Apparently even the Sultan could see that one "frank" American woman was worth more than 142 slavish ones.

French-Sheldon's visit to the Sultan's harem was one of the most recurrent stories she told to live audiences and the press over the next forty years. Setting up a striking polarity between herself and the degraded Sultana, French-Sheldon positions herself and the male potentate on equal planes, both physically and ontologically. As with her description of the Sultan's daughter, she exoticizes and objectifies the Sultana with references to her clothing, jewels and accessories, and body parts. She attaches such childish qualities as sullenness and quaint ritualism to the Sultana to emphasize her own rationality and maturity. The Sultana takes on the degraded characteristics of enslavement, revealing her position of prestige to be a sad artifice. In fact, the Sultana, in French-Sheldon's telling, is reduced to a sham empress, while the White Queen is revealed to exhibit the marks of true sovereignty—dignity, self-possession, and mastery of others. French-Sheldon sets up her story of her encounter with the Zanzibari Sultana in such a way as to counter the earlier image she gives of herself in the street, thereby displacing sexual objectification and defilement away from women of the West and onto African women.

THE SEDUCTIONS OF THE MARCH

The harem scene afforded French-Sheldon an unparalleled opportunity to draw readers' attention to a contrast between her own subjectified experience and African women's desubjectified one. Yet throughout the text of *Sultan to Sultan,* French-Sheldon finds even more occasions to position African men as objectified, sexualized, and emasculated by comparison with her. French-Sheldon admits to the sexual tension that days and nights spent alone with a 140 or so porters prompted. This situation posed no threat to her because of her ability to convert what she represents as African men's lust for her into a childish desire to please her. The best example of this appears early on in her relation of the expedition when French-Sheldon coaxed a particularly strong porter to volunteer to carry a double load. Her physical description of Kara, "the strong man," both sexualizes and lampoons him for the amusement and titillation of her white readers. "There was a decided rustle," she fondly recalls,

> then a jostling and parting at the back of the throng of porters, and forcing his way through there came forward a tall, stalwart fellow, with a beaming face, his smiling open mouth revealing his glittering teeth. He stood out conspicuously apart from the others, and announced proudly, "Bebe, I am that strong man." Then whirling himself like a spinning top round on his heels to display his muscular superiority, he stretched out both his arms, clinched his fists and forcibly drew them tightly up to show off his pronounced biceps, saying, "Bebe, command me." (*SS:* 117)

The character of Kara resembles a trusted and faithful, strong but stupid, fictional slave-hand from nostalgic accounts of the Old South. Kara, whom French-Sheldon refers to as "my Samson," is dependable and gallant, even bringing French-Sheldon "beautiful flowers and grasses" and making the brightest of fires for her. Yet French-Sheldon is clearly more impressed with his physicality than his personality. Declaring that "this same porter had as tremendous a voice as he had a body, and was always talking garrulously," French-Sheldon shows Kara to be no more sophisticated than a child who was in the habit of babbling nonsense. "Frequently I thought he would drive me distracted," she complains. Whether it was his body or his voice that distracted her is not entirely made clear in a passage that switches back and forth between admiring the porter's physique and complaining about his intellect. French-Sheldon expresses her ambivalence by concluding, "[W]hereas I did not wish to diminish his strength, I did care to silence his lusty voice" (*SS:* 118). Apparently Kara was never so pleased as when he, with great difficulty, managed to obey his mistress's command to be silent on the march and thereby prevented himself from being sent to walk at the rear of the caravan. "At night," French-Sheldon reports that she called him at the end of the day to compliment him on his effort to keep quiet drawing forth from the porter a "burst of enthusiasm" with which he exclaimed, "Ah, Bebe Bwana, I am so happy! because I have sweat prickles from my marrow all day trying to be quiet" (*SS:* 119). French-Sheldon pities and patronizes the porter, calling his remark "quaint" and congratulating him on the aptness of his use of "simili" (in reference to his "marrow").

Fig. 16. Strong Man, Kara
French-Sheldon included in *Sultan to Sultan* this postcard and labeled it, "Kara, Strong Man," to represent a favored porter in her employ. Such postcards, depicting African or Oriental "types," were a frequent device in travel literature in the nineteenth century.

Fig. 17. Porters at Leisure
French-Sheldon's amateur photography successfully captured the individuality of her porters that her narrative often effaced.

French-Sheldon's attraction to her porters is both revealed and veiled in these passages. Though she acknowledges Kara's "tremendous" body, his "pronounced" muscles, and "lusty voice" which nearly drives her to "distraction," her descriptions infantilize him and thereby diminish the possibility of any sexual desire to develop on her part. Kara's excessive gratefulness paired with French-Sheldon's teacherly comments regarding his speech confirms the distance between mistress and porter, white woman and black man, and demonstrates French-Sheldon's mastery of the men in her employ.

Despite French-Sheldon's depiction of Kara as an exceptional porter who stands out from the others for his extraordinary strength and character, she does not present him as an individual but as a type through which she can communicate her control over her porters to the reader. Although *Sultan to Sultan* includes many photos French-Sheldon personally shot of her porters (figure 17), Kara's image (figure 16) is represented not by an actual photo but by a postcard featuring a large black man with a fierce expression on his face, dressed in a contrived costume meant to identify him as vaguely North African. Despite the obvious studio quality of the photo, French-Sheldon pretends that it is of Kara himself by subtitling it simply, "Kara, Strong Man." The point she communicates is that it might as well be Kara, since he is of a similar type. French-Sheldon's purpose here is not to fool her readers that they are viewing an actual photo of Kara so much as it is to convince readers that the African men she surrounded herself with were classifiable, knowable, and thus, manageable. Kara is not just strong and obedient and loyal, he knows his place. He only violated French-Sheldon's supreme injunction, "Touch Me Not" once in the text, and then only out of fear for her safety, begging her forgiveness for his indiscretion nonetheless. As French-Sheldon was just about to step on an ant's nest, "like a whirlwind," she recalls fondly, "something suddenly grasped me about the waist, lifting me up from the ground." When she looked around, Kara, or "my strong man," as French-Sheldon refers to him, had "prostrated himself, his face pressed close on the ground in the dust, pleading pathetically, "Bebe Bwana: siafu! siafu!" (ants, ants!) in a desperate act to appease her for violating the rule against touching her (*SS:* 120). French-Sheldon credits Kara, a "half-civilized" porter, with "chivalry" not only for his actions to protect her from biting insects but also for his expressions of his distress at violating her person. Even as such scenes evoke the fantasy of inter-racial sex, they demonstrate the harmlessness and placidity of even the largest, manliest of African men French-Sheldon encountered.

All the black men French-Sheldon meets in Africa, however imposing they may seem when considered in the abstract or upon first viewing, are shown by French-Sheldon to be pliant, servile, and entirely non-threatening. The sultans she meets along her trek are no less docile than her porters and seem all the more ridiculous for their assumption of parity with French-Sheldon. In the following scene from *Sultan to Sultan,* French-Sheldon spies an African leader named Mireali who, from a distance, cuts an impressive figure, silhouetted against the sky on a crest of a hill. French-Sheldon's interest in him is piqued by the deferential crowd around him, but as she quickly discovers upon approaching the headman, Mireali's intimidating reputation is ill-deserved. "As we approached Marungu, Sultan Mireali's province, had crossed the last ravine, and were ascending the last hill to his boma, a very stony, difficult pull for my weary porters, there could be heard the buzz and hum of distant voices. . . . [O]n searching for a solution of the hubbub," she discovered that the "pivot of attraction consisted in personage standing upon a huge boulder,"

> a native, tall and distinguished, who appeared a perfect guy, tricked out in a pair of German military trousers, with side stripes, a white knitted shirt with a brilliant pin on the bosom, a celluloid high collar, a cravat of the most flaming color, a striped woolen Scotch shooting-coat, a flamboyant pocket-handkerchief, and a pair of Russia-leather shoes, exposing blue silk clocked socks. His fine head was disfigured by wearing a black silk pot hat, which was canted backwards, bonnet fashion, by the long porcupine quill ear ornaments thrust through the rims of his ears. He carried an English walking stick with a huge silver knob, and held in his hands a pair of kid gloves. This clown then was Mireali, conceded to be the handsomest native man in East Africa, the most noble and most majestic sultan if not the most powerful. This chivalrous sultan, notified by his couriers at last, after his weeks of expectancy, I was coming, had summoned all of his subjects—several thousand—to bid me welcome, and add lustre to the honor he desired to pay Bebe Bwana, and to italicize the function had ridiculously bedecked himself in this cast-off finery of various persons of different nationality, who had but recently left his province. (*SS:* 216)

French-Sheldon's description trivializes and mocks Mireali's attempt to take on the pomp of a European military commander. While ignoring the degree to which her White Queen costume inaccurately represented her own bourgeois social rank, she emphasizes Mireali's inability to live up to the aristocratic status his clothing implied by recounting his difficulty executing the proper European greeting.

> Remembering that he had been told to uncover in the presence of a guest, Mireali found himself in a sad dilemma as to how to do it; however, one of his many subjects stepped up behind him and tilted the hat over backwards, and scraped it off from the embarrassed potentate's head. It is a shame a man like Mireali should be so imposed upon by those who should have known better. (*SS:* 216)

"Those who should have known better," the reader is meant to understand, are the Europeans who thoughtlessly donated the items of Western clothing to Mireali, succeeding only in cruelly mocking his inadequacies by doing so in the eyes of French-Sheldon. As if to show how vulnerable and imitative African men are, French-Sheldon infantilizes Mireali by taking away responsibility for his choice of self-presentation. "Mireali, why do you wear these clothes?" she reprimands, "they make you look like a goat. I want to see you in your own native cloth, and see you as Mireali, the great African sultan that you are" (*SS:* 217). The African leader, according to French-Sheldon, merely hung his head in response to her chiding, and returned the next day dressed in more usual attire.

More than mere condescension, French-Sheldon accomplishes the symbolic castration of Mireali on several levels with this account. First Mireali is coded as an effeminate dandy by virtue of his "cast-off finery": a cravat of the most flaming color; flamboyant pocket-handkerchief; hat canted backwards, bonnet fashion; and kid gloves. Then he is exposed as an imposter even as an effeminate white man, when his subordinate has to assist him in performing the gestures of a gentlemen dandy, removing his hat by knocking it unceremoniously to the ground, or "scrap[ing] it off from the embarrassed potentate's head." The transfer of the phallic power from Mireali to French-Sheldon is finally accomplished when Mireali, "in a spasm of desire which overcame him," offered to trade "his own personal spear, his sceptre as it were" for French-Sheldon's music box, typically referred to in the text simply as her "box." French-Sheldon, "happy to possess the spear," gave up her coveted "box" readily. As if these suggestive references are not enough to communicate French-Sheldon's phallic one-upmanship of Mireali, she renders his emasculinization complete with repeated references to the drumming Mireali had received recently at the hands of a rival sultan named Mandara (*SS:* 218).

In *Sultan to Sultan* French-Sheldon donates an entire chapter to Mandara, the last sultan she recounts meeting in East Africa. She begins this chapter with a long and impressive build-up that spans several pages, beginning with the declaration: "It would be impossible to narrate half of the rumors current as to the extremely crafty and atrocious deeds of the ambitious, brutish, and abominable Sultan Mandara; but without doubt he is much feared for his cleverness and duplicity. He is a keen, intelligent observer and a deep student in his way, despite his marked deficiency in uprightness, justice, mercy, or morality" (*SS:* 233).

With such an introduction French-Sheldon establishes for the reader that this sultan, unlike others she described, warranted caution and perhaps even grudging respect for his military prowess and his rule. She reminds her readers of the sexual risk she, as a white woman, ran in daring to visit a man reputed to harbor such hypermasculine appetites by reporting that "Mandara had been exceedingly curious to see a white woman," to the extent that he had issued an offer of "forty, eighty, and even one hundred cows if some Arab caravan would fetch him a white wife" (*SS: 235*). Heightening the suspense for her readers, French-Sheldon admits to vowing to be "more guarded" than ever when approaching Mandara's territory, even going so far as to break with her habit of traveling unaccompanied by white men. She allowed the nearby German commander at Moshi to send along a dozen soldiers to protect her.[5] Still, she thought to herself as she picked her way down the hillside to Mandara's compound, "perhaps it was rash." However, one sentence later, the reader follows as she is escorted inside Mandara's gateway "with considerable pomp and many salaams, to Mandara, who was prostrate by paralysis, unable to move his body below the waist." Once again French-Sheldon finds that the rapaciousness and masculine vigor attributed to African men was hardly warranted. "In his helplessness and emaciation, one could scarcely believe this man possessed the power to terrorize all the lesser chiefs of the Kilimanjaro district, and from recent accounts cause the Germans a large expenditure of gunpowder" (*SS: 236*). With this final anticlimactic meeting, French-Sheldon demonstrates that African male sexuality poses no danger to white women, rendering white women's dependence on white men for protection from black men entirely superfluous.

Though French-Sheldon depicts Mandara as harboring an intense desire for French-Sheldon as a white woman, his impotence, both physical and sexual, rendered such desire unthreatening and even pathetic. French-Sheldon writes, "He was fairly jubilant on seeing me, extended his hand, but in a piteous voice said, 'Ah, now I have lived to see a white woman, and here I am so helpless'" (*SS: 237*). French-Sheldon describes Mandara begging to feel her hair, running it through his hands, and harshly comparing it to that of his wives. "He stroked it in a strange, caressing way," she remembers, "called out to summon his wives to come and look at the white woman's tresses. When I gathered them loosely up and replaced the pins, he indulged in an undertone conversation with these women, who, overcome by curiosity, ventured to ask why I did not shave off my hair, as they did theirs; and Mandara sneeringly retorted, 'It is too *mzuria sana* (it is too beautiful); why should she cut it off?' And then he continued in an incisive tone, 'She is a white queen, and you are all slaves and black'" (*SS: 237*).

In this scene French-Sheldon seems to revel in the dual concept of her racialized attractiveness and Mandara's helplessness. Mandara appears disgraced by his inability to act on his desire for her. The presence of his wives, whom Mandara impatiently reminds French-Sheldon are valueless compared to white women, only increases his frustration. As in the case of the Sultan of Zanzibar, Mandara's expression of contempt for his wives serves to link slavishness in these women to their racial identity and their African-ness. Instead of making this assertion herself in her narrative, French-Sheldon leaves such pronouncements to African men of authority, such as Mandara and the Sultan of Zanzibar. In this way French-Sheldon further naturalizes the connection between blackness and feminine degradation, as if it is an unavoidable conclusion rather than an expression of race hatred. Mandara's reported treatment of African women debases them. According to French-Sheldon, he "drive[s] them into his harem like cattle" and when tired of them, hands them over to his "favorites" (*SS:* 238). Mandara's supposed desire for French-Sheldon, however, has no power to demean or objectify her. As if to confirm this, French-Sheldon refused to allow Mandara to add a photo of her to his commercial collection of photos and postcards of white women in spite of his earnest request, unless Mandara allowed her to take a photo of him first. Mandara protested against the idea, explaining his shame at his own (sexualized) feebleness "in a tone of injured vanity." "But see, Bebe Bwana," Mandara pleaded, "I cannot stand, I cannot hold my spear, I cannot aim my *bunduki* (gun)" (*SS:* 238). If the subtext of his words are not enough, French-Sheldon's recollection of Mandara's subsequent exposure of his emaciated lower limbs to her view makes plain his impotence to her readers. French-Sheldon's position as holder of the gaze not only symbolically castrates Mandara, but it also signals her successful appropriation of the phallus that might have otherwise accrued to him as a result of her earlier endorsement of his masculine prowess. This appropriation is made even more explicit in the narrative when French-Sheldon reports growing literally erect and flushed in angry reaction to Mandara's strange way of displaying his respect for her: he spit onto her hands. "The blood flushed to my cheek," she admits, "and in a moment of anger I rose to my feet and took my pistol from my belt" (*SS:* 237). The German officers accompanying French-Sheldon for her protection have receded into the background at this point in the narrative as there is no need for a more masculine or symbolically phallic response than that of French-Sheldon—turgid with outrage and armed with the loaded pistol she tellingly kept hidden beneath her belt.

French-Sheldon's phallicism, absolutely dependent as it was on her racial status, flattered white readers and may have served to calm their fears of black male sexual potency and African military might. French-Sheldon's portrayals rob Africans of authority, dignity, and subjectivity, in part to assure her Victorian audiences that her reputation remained unsullied in spite of her questionable position as a "conspicuous" woman but also to assure them that their hierarchical relationship to Africans, and all black people by extension, was best protected by the kind of empowered woman that French-Sheldon modeled. In *Sultan to Sultan* Africans are submissive, not resistant; they are open to suggestion and, as I have noted in previous chapters, to capitalist penetration if all "would-be colonizers," as French-Sheldon terms them, would follow her gendered lead. Yet *Sultan to Sultan* is not completely consistent even on this point. The concluding chapter of this part of *White Queen* will reveal the tensions between the many sexual, economic, and political discourses French-Sheldon sought to bring under her control and the ambiguity and anxiety that lay just below the surface of French-Sheldon's otherwise triumphal story of colonial conquest.

FIVE

Confessions of a White Queen

I was not enabled to find that any of my porters had
heard of any one descending to the surface of the lake,
or to meet any native who had gone to the water's
edge or who could be induced to descend thereto;
and instead of being the subject of curiosity, which I
had apprehended and was desirous to avoid, when the
natives knew I intended to descend, and witnessed my
preparations, they flew back, terror stricken, into their
mountain villages, and not one intrusive eye would
gaze upon the white woman on the Devil's water.

French-Sheldon, *Sultan to Sultan,* 1892

Despite *Sultan to Sultan*'s successful dissembling, French-Sheldon's account was not entirely free of the consciousness that her presence in
Africa was that of an outsider who might stir up trouble. Perhaps this is
most evident at the moment of French-Sheldon's only viable claim to scientific "discovery." When describing her descent to the surface of Lake Chala,
she edges her recollection of the "weird, weird beauty" of Chala with
touches of malevolence. She notes with trepidation the great flocks of birds
that "cawed and screamed and whirled about," diving into water that
swirled with the commotion of countless crocodiles" (*SS:* 175). She recalls
that a "strange suction" tugged at her paddle and threatened her control of
the pontoon (*SS:* 176). Still, none of this proved to reveal a truly inhos-
pitable environment, just one dangerous enough to dub French-Sheldon a
genuine conqueror of nature, and her pleasure at the thought that she had
finally proved her mettle as a discoverer was immense. She muses in *Sultan
to Sultan* on "the hours spent upon this lake at different times [that] held me
in a thralldom of wonder." She recollected at such times that "there was little said, very much thought, and [that] imagination thrilled my brain with

Fig. 18. Circumnavigating Lake Chala
French-Sheldon included an illustration of her circumnavigation of Lake Chala by pontoon in which she was accompanied by an IBEA representative named Anstruther.

Fig. 19. A Mystical Mood
A mystical mood often pervades French-Sheldon's written and photographic descriptions of her experience of Africa.

the ineffable pleasure which I had craved and sought for years, of being the first to visit a place undefiled by the presence of man before" (*SS:* 176).

This orgasmic moment utilizes a sexual metaphor that places French-Sheldon in the oddly cross-dressed position of "defiler" of virgin territory, rendering her sail upon Chala a maiden voyage of truly carnivale proportions. She is overwhelmed almost by the surreal nature of her experience of this position, dwelling for some time in the narrative upon the "weirdness" of the place and the fact of her presence in it. "All contributed," she recalls, "to make it seem as though I was in some phantom land. Everything was most eldritch and immense" (*SS:* 176). Although French-Sheldon appears to be far more awe-struck than frightened, the threat that her actions might have some unpleasant reverberations is not wholly absent from her mind even amidst her joy. "At the firing of a gun the reverberations came back like a thunder-clap—sharp, crashing," she recalls. The jarring sound of her own gun gives her a creeping feeling of being watched, of the colonial gaze being reversed. "I should not have been surprised to have seen the whole lake covered with some uncanny creatures, or to have seen the apparition of some mammoth forest king issue forth and assert himself as monarch of all we surveyed, and crush us out of existence as invaders," she admits (*SS:* 176). Curiously, French-Sheldon seems to abandon the position of "monarch of all I survey" just when she is most authorized by the circumstances to claim it.[1] Moreover, she concedes the position to a phantom African male authority, to whom she acquiesces in both fear and acknowledgement of the invasive nature of her presence.

There are other moments in the narrative that reveal the same "weird, weird" mixture of awe and dread, moments that hint at French-Sheldon's awareness that she was an "invader" as she suspects, rather than an honored White Queen or some innocuous, well-mannered guest, as most of the text asserts. Much earlier in *Sultan to Sultan,* in a passage that invokes the birth of self that her expedition and her writings were meant to facilitate, French-Sheldon describes the "weird splendor" that electric lights lent to a night transit through ninety-nine miles of the hazardously congested and narrow Suez Canal separating a European world from an African one. According to French-Sheldon, the introduction of the canal was "a boon to the commercial world almost without parallel; reducing the distance from London to India from 11,397 miles to 7,628, thereby shortening the voyage by the Cape thirty-six days." Although conceived of by the Pharaoh Necho, 600 B.C., she tells us, it was made possible and navigation through it made efficient and safe by the introduction of Western technology (that is, electric lighting) and, as she explains further, the European imposition of "absolute law . . . impartially applied to all" in its regulation of ingress and egress from the canal (*SS:* 71–73).

Seemingly, this passage presents the reader with cold facts concerning the Suez Canal. However, the description of the moment when French-Sheldon passed from metropolis to periphery prepares the reader for four hundred pages of text asserting and naturalizing a set of class, race, and national hierarchies in support of the colonial appropriation of East African labor, goods, property, and sovereignty. This moment is not lacking in ambiguity or ambivalence. French-Sheldon's description of her passage through the Suez is bounded by two statements that reveal the central contradiction at the heart of turn-of-the-century philosophies supporting the civilizing mission in Africa. French-Sheldon precedes the passage with a gratuitous racist affirmation that in Port Said Jetty, "Egyptian and native laborers make the line of distinction between master and servants unmistakable," and she closes the passage on a philosophical note that presumes a history of human progress and the relative democracy of the present inasmuch as it mawkishly celebrates "the wondrous changes that time has wrought" (SS: 72). Her philosophical reverie was prompted by a glimpse of the Empress Eugenie's chalet on the banks of the Red Sea, built for the Suez Canal's inaugural celebration, the sight of which, according to French-Sheldon, "provokes the thought of the downfall of an Empire" (SS: 72–73). With such an introduction to her text, the reader of *Sultan to Sultan* is assured early on that the rule that French-Sheldon came to establish in Africa represented a break with the empires of the past. The days of illegitimate and tyrannical empire-building belonged to a long-gone era, and modern colonial relationships, though based on unequal racial relationships, would not be of the same despotic ilk. Her efforts, she assures her readers, would help usher in a new day characterized by a regulation of the movement of goods, services, and people governed by the principles of efficiency and commitment to "absolute law . . . impartially applied to all" (SS: 72).

Despite such assertions, French-Sheldon's portrayal of nights on the canal in this first chapter of *Sultan to Sultan* betrays some of her unease about her position as the bearer of a new and enlightened rule. However well lit, the channel at night in her description is not without a certain haunting quality that hangs like a pall over the "weird splendour" of it all. The electric light enables her vision less than it magnifies a treacherous landscape. "The nearness to the white sand banks at times painfully glaring," she bemoans, "and the far-away mountains cut across the sky in ragged peaks, limiting the lateral horizon" (SS: 72). By the time the steamer came to drop anchor for the night in the Gulf of Aden, described by French-Sheldon as "Hell's Harbor," a place of "burning sands and treacherous coasts," she found herself surrounded by "spectacular wrecks of vessels [that] loom up out of the water, suggestive of a fierce struggle with the elements, and as a phantom warning to those who course that way, against the high winds and insetting sea which prevail" (*SS:* 74). In setting up the reader for her dramatic and triumphant overcoming of fear and natural adversities, French-Sheldon allows some of the nagging ends of her colonial conscience to fray with references to the fierceness of past struggles, phantom warnings, and the "downfall of Empire, and later the downfall of a man who, at one time, was on the pinnacle of fame." Her self-representation as an "anti-conquest" heroine, of empathetic predilection and sweet disposition, strains a bit under the stress produced by the murky half-vision of the electric lights and her invocation of Napoleon Bonaparte's defeat. From the deck of the *Madura,* French-Sheldon spied and then attempted to photograph a woman onshore who glared at her and indicated with gestures her anger at being targeted and ogled by French-Sheldon. French-Sheldon's recorded response was utter disdain for the woman's sense of privacy and dignity, noting that she could not understand the woman's imprecations and railings which were in Arabic. Imprecations "about what?" French-Sheldon rhetorically asks the readers of *Sultan to Sultan,* and then dismisses any need to ponder the answer to the question with a pitiless "ah! ask the Arabs who heard" (*SS:* 73).

The "defiant glance" flung at French-Sheldon by an unveiled Arab woman on the banks of the Red Sea was the first, and one of the only, hints of African animosity and rejection that French-Sheldon allows to mar her account of an otherwise universal and spontaneous welcome in Africa. The attitudes she exhibits in this encounter stand out markedly from the perceptive, sensitive, and courteous attitudes she generally credits herself with and strives to give examples of in her narrative. Yet in this episode she reveals an unapologetic disgust for the Arab members of a caravan she sees from the ship whom she describes in the next sentence as "villainous landsharks. . . . Unclean, utterly miserable, degraded beings, knowing only a migratory life, in common with their camels and their vermin, devoid of principle, eking out a questionable existence by cunning, extortion, and mendicancy" (*SS:* 73). French-Sheldon does not stop in her excoriation of such "barbarians" to entertain any cultural relativism, unlike later moments in *Sultan to Sultan* when she allows an idealization of Africans to cast doubt on her assumptions about Western superiority.

Indeed, in strong contrast to Arabs French-Sheldon often refers to subSaharan Africans as her "long-sought ideal primitives." Though often orientalized by French-Sheldon's references to sultans and harems and often disclosing the same "Eastern" perfidy, despotism, and avariciousness, she also views them as possessing "noble savage" hearts and, as I have shown, an untapped if childlike "brilliant potential" for commercial development. Even this tack is not without its own hazard however. At her most laudatory, French-Sheldon exaggerates African noble savagery to a degree that almost pushes her to question the legitimacy of the civilizing mission. "In talking with them as to the English occupancy in their country and the benefits to accrue therefrom," she confesses that Africans "sometimes answered rather dubiously . . . and I fain discovered a tinge of regret, and in their hearts I believe they would be content to go on in their happy, pastoral way, without bothering their brains about education, government, and all the confusing principles of civilization." French-Sheldon defends this attitude by adding that these Africans "live to enjoy, and enjoy to live, and are as idyllic in their native ways as any people I ever encountered" (*SS:* 170). The rhetorical logic of "noble savagery" almost, but never quite, forces the imperative of uplift into the form of a question. French-Sheldon's condescension becomes more vehement as she struggles to justify white incursion without sacrificing her image as a sympathetic ally of the native. French-Sheldon's special contribution to the civilizing mission was to make the transition to stewardship a gentle, smooth, and guilt-free one. Whatever ambivalence she may have experienced on her trek in Africa, in French-Sheldon's narrative, Africa waits hungrily for white civilization to arrive.

CONCLUSION TO PART I:
AN AMERICAN QUEEN IN AFRICA

> Many hundreds of years ago Ethiopia was invaded by an
> Assyrian queen. In these modern days the invasion was by
> an American queen, and the honors showered by the
> kings of Ethiopia upon Semiramis were renewed in
> those which were given to Bebe Bwana.
> —Press release by the Arena Press[2]

In the Africa French-Sheldon found once she was through the straits of Aden, whites did not have to be aggressors; after all the very trees "turned themselves down in solemn humiliation" at her approach and the waters laughingly "dashed themselves into a jubilant foam at her feet" just to celebrate her arrival (*SS:* 173–174). Africans themselves were no different, drenching her with warmth and praise, and scrambling to be the first to "bid me welcome, to bring me tributes of all kinds, to say to the white queen, as they persisted in calling me, that, they had looked for me for two moons, and almost despaired that I would ever arrive" (*SS:* 149).

Overall the text of *Sultan to Sultan* rings with the sound of Africans hailing French-Sheldon and the civilizing mission. The few negative notes that filter through the chorus of praise would have attracted little of the Victorian reader's attention, even if they do upon reflection manifest the strategies French-Sheldon used to redefine Victorian imperial ideologies and negotiate a subject-position for herself within them. If nights spent on the Red Sea encroached with ominous portent at times, "the days were glorious. . . . A hot sun, but sprightly fanning breezes, a steady awning ship, were winsome enough to make the Red Sea delightful" (*SS:* 73). And in pondering her situation as she prepared for what lay ahead of her in Africa, French-Sheldon found in herself the wherewithal to go forward, and a joy in the sheer amazement of intellectually "probing every topic to the heart and thrashing out the subjects thoroughly." Onboard the *Madura,* and on her way to what she hoped would be glory, she composed her thoughts and her plans, prepared herself mentally for the emergencies she anticipated encountering, and generally "fortified" her health and strength for the adventure that awaited her. "It was," she reports, "like gathering one's self up to enter an arena as a combatant." She expresses surprise at her ability to rise to the occasion despite the lack of guidance available to her: "In making classifications for my future work, writing out leading questions, jotting down points for anthropological and ethnological observation in order to lose no opportunity, when once in the field, of probing every topic to the heart and thrashing out the subjects thoroughly, gradually I discovered in myself a latent gift for organization." The result of all this intense concentration was "self-amazement" and confidence that as a "thoughtful, earnest person in quest of knowledge in new fields where there is no precedent to follow" she would succeed beyond all expectation (*SS:* 73–74).

With thoughts of the self-aggrandizing responsibilities her ethnological work might place before her (the "good work" her ideas would hopefully "put into effect") and "self-amazement" at evidence of her own intellectual rigor, French-Sheldon "gathered her self up" to confront Africans as a thoughtful, earnest scientist, a concerned and conscientious global social worker, a non-aggressive yet tireless "combatant." The sea willingly echoed her happy thoughts, "gradually assuming the color of a lovely turquoise green, with thousands of gleaming, glittering whitecaps." And "the far-reaching horizon at the rim of the peerless, spotless blue-gray dome" rose up to greet the arrival in Africa of a great White Queen as She[3] (*SS:* 74).

Part II

AGENT FOR EMPIRE:
INTERVENTIONS
IN CENTRAL AND
WEST AFRICA,
1903–1908

SIX

An Imperial Spy in the Congo

Botofi bo le iwa (Rubber is death).
—Congolese proverb[1]

By 1895, after a few exciting years of life as a minor celebrity and public pundit, interest in May French-Sheldon's 1891 expedition and analyses regarding colonization and "the Primitive" had waned. The nature of geographic discovery and ethnographic research dictated this inevitability, dependent as the value of both were upon currency and novelty. The death of French-Sheldon's husband, Eli, had left her without the financial means to add to her experience on the colonial frontier and placed her in the socially awkward position of an unmarried woman lacking independent income sufficient to maintain her upper-middle-class associations. Even her ability to exploit the distinctiveness of being a woman explorer became eclipsed in the final years of the century. With other female explorers such as Isabella Bird Bishop and especially Mary Kingsley returning home from their travels in Asia and Africa with new information and fresh evidence of Woman's insight regarding colonial methods and relationships, French-Sheldon was forced to retire from the limelight.

Despite her near disappearance from the lecture circuit and popular press by 1900, in the first few years of the next century French-Sheldon re-emerged as an important, and highly controversial, observer of the colonial process unfolding in Africa. September 1903 found French-Sheldon applying for a new passport from the U.S. embassy in London in order to make another journey to the continent of Africa. Her mission would take her to an area controlled not by the British or the Germans but by the Belgian king, Leopold II. A desire for glory once again fueled her intentions to travel in Africa, but this expedition would not be merely one of her own planning and purposes. This time around French-Sheldon's personal ambition was augmented by a small salary and her travel plans coordinated by a few men in the vanguard of an emerging international reform movement. French-Sheldon left in October 1903 as the undercover detective for a group that would, within a few short months, unveil itself as the Congo Reform Association (CRA). Unlike her first expedition, which she publicized extensively before embarking upon, this trip was shrouded in secrecy initially. And unlike the welcome French-Sheldon's opinions received following her first trip, the reports French-Sheldon made to the public following her second expedition to Africa placed her distinctly at odds with other British voices on Africa and embroiled her in the most explosive international controversy of the day. In this chapter, I examine the role French-Sheldon played in the political crisis that put Africa at the forefront of twentieth-century debates over the economic, political, and moral consequences of empire.

RED RUBBER:
THE POLITICS OF INTERNATIONAL REFORM

> [R]emember also my warning that the man who goes
> out to the Congo with the intention of investigating
> the evil deeds of the Congo State, and going out
> unattached to the missionary's societies, State,
> or Co's. takes his life in his hands.
> —Private correspondence from E. D. Morel
> to W. T. Stead regarding French-Sheldon

As early as March 1903, the much-respected British editor of the *Review of Reviews* and former editor of the *Pall Mall Gazette,* W. T. Stead, began enlisting the support of May French-Sheldon in the campaign against King Leopold II's administration of the Congo Free State. Recently, rumors of Belgian "atrocities" in the Congo had mushroomed into an international scandal, and Liberal reformers such as Stead were intent on documenting the accusations leveled at Leopold that his administration was both inhibiting free trade in the region and making a mockery of the civilizing mission.[2] Although the British-led Congo reform movement eventually would come to hinge on the latter point, the economic issues at stake were formidable. British commercial interests cast envious and resentful eyes at the lucrative concessionaire system that Leopold had set up. His system undermined competition and maximized profits by relegating the details of administration to private companies to whom he granted exclusive permission (or "concessions") to operate in a given area in exchange for a large percentage of the profits. British, French, and even American business groups complained to their governments that Leopold's concessionaire system violated free trade agreements. But the case for free trade, though loudly proclaimed in the Anglo and American press of the day, evoked little emotive response from the British and American publics. Colonial atrocities carried more sensational weight and commanded more newspaper copy. In 1903 Stead decided to send a scout surreptitiously to the Congo to buttress the growing case reformers were building against Leopold's concessionaire system by returning with juicy tales and images damaging to Leopold's public reputation. That scout was May French-Sheldon.

All through the spring of 1903, by telegram and letter, Stead flattered French-Sheldon with invitations to speak at small gatherings of friends and like-minded colleagues in England. At these talks he encouraged her to remind her audiences of her unique contribution to the colonization of Africa. Once again French-Sheldon's gender along with this framing of her colonial persona positioned her in ways most relevant to the historical moment and made her an ideal choice for Stead's purposes. In her book *Sultan to Sultan,* her other published writings, and in the countless public appearances she had made a decade earlier, French-Sheldon explained her value as an explorer in terms of her womanly sentiment and genteel manner. For those who held up French-Sheldon's experiences for admiration, the meaning of her expedition lay in its worth as an exemplary model of exploration. Such a reputation harmonized perfectly with the impression the CRA strived to attain as a politically neutral as well as beneficent watchdog over colonial activities in Africa. Bringing a humane sensibility to colonial efforts in Africa, or the civilizing of the "civilizing mission," was both French-Sheldon's unique gift and the CRA's raison d'être. Stead, the internationally well-known crusading Liberal journalist and one of the architects of the still-embryonic CRA, hoped to exploit French-Sheldon's prominence to put her substantial appeal to work in the service of international reform.

French-Sheldon responded positively to Stead's private overtures asking her to consider the issues raised by Leopold II's policies in the Congo Free State. She attended the frequent debates he and other Liberals arranged on topics such as the "alleged superiority of the white races" or "the whole question of the treatment of African natives in connection with the Congo" that were held in the spring of 1903.[3] Within a few short months of his initial entreaties, she had agreed by secret contract to travel to Africa as the undercover agent of Stead and his even more determined colleague E. D. Morel. Morel, Leopold's foremost critic in England and founder and editor of the recently established reform paper the *African Mail,* hoped French-Sheldon would supply reliable eyewitness accounts of the abuses he believed were proliferating under Leopold's system. The terms of the contract between Stead and French-Sheldon dated September 22, 1903, bound her to produce by January 1, 1904,"a series of bright and lively letters suitable for publication in a daily paper, of say 2,000 words length, describing the

Congo as it is after twenty years' Belgian rule, foreign trade, and Christian Missions, it being understood that you write for no other, publisher, editor, or person, during your stay in the Congo."[4] At stake for Morel and Stead was their ability to capture the attention of an international audience and to appear sufficiently politically neutral enough to lend an aura of credibility to accusations that could be viewed as serving British interests in the region. Their hope was that French-Sheldon's shining reputation as an insightful and neutral observer of colonization in Africa would make hers a powerful voice in aid of their cause. The impression that French-Sheldon had long given as a sympathetic ally of Africans and opponent of violence gave them confidence that she would view the situation in the Congo with extreme disfavor. The evidence does not permit us to speculate as to the degree to which French-Sheldon shared their baleful view of Leopold II's actions in the Congo prior to embarking on her undercover mission. Whatever preconceived leanings French-Sheldon may have harbored, what is clear is that the trip to Central Africa Stead and Morel proposed represented an opportunity to reignite her career as a public authority on Africa and colonial policymaking that she was unlikely to resist.

For his part of the bargain, Stead would pay French-Sheldon five hundred pounds up front and provide maps and contacts to facilitate her movements. In what may have been slightly galling to French-Sheldon (in light of the way she viewed Mary Kingsley as a competitor for the spotlight on women explorers of Africa), Stead made sure French-Sheldon was acquainted with the issues and the terrain she would be covering by sending along with the maps "both Miss Kingsley's books," thereby giving her "plenty to read" while en route to the Congo.[5] He also laid out the matter at hand in an explanatory addendum to the contract by listing the accusations he expected her to confirm. There were five primary issues. The first, and perhaps the driving force behind Britain's concern in the matter, was the issue of free trade. When Leopold was granted personal possession and control of an area of Central Africa thirty times the size of Belgium at the 1884–1885 Berlin Conference, he firmly committed himself to a policy of free trade. Despite his affirmation of free trade in principal, in fact Leopold's system of private concessionaires gave him a tenacious grip on all commerce conducted in the "Free State." The confiscation in 1900 of a British merchant's trade goods by the French, who were beginning to emulate Leopold's concessionaire system in their own part of the Congo Basin, had touched off a strident outcry in England against the concessionaire system in general and against the greedy Belgian monarch in particular.[6] French-Sheldon was to decide whether "the Congo [was] open to the trade of the world, or what would be the chance of an English or American trader who wished to do business in that region."[7]

Second, Stead instructed French-Sheldon to determine the extent to which Congolese were being compelled to collect rubber in the *Domaine Privé,* Leopold's personal fiefdom, under threat of murder, torture, or other force, and to determine whether the forced labor Leopold would admit to amounted to the same thing as enslavement. Leopold had couched his initial interest in the region as motivated to some extent by the desire to rid the continent of the practice of slavery and the effects of the slave and liquor trades. Partially as a result of this strategy, he had won to his side the English public and the American delegation (which had included Henry Stanley) at the Berlin Congress. In 1885 English Liberals such as Stead and Sir Harry S. Johnston (an early explorer of the region and someone who had supplied *Sultan to Sultan* with public endorsements) had thrown their editorial and personal influence behind the Berlin Conference's arrangement with Leopold in the belief that they were "doing a good thing for humanity, for Free Trade, for civilisation, and for the welfare of the natives" by supporting Leopold's personal command of the area.[8] Stead expressed to French-Sheldon his deep feelings of responsibility and was echoed by Johnston a few years later in the latter's introduction to E. D. Morel's 1906 exposé *Red Rubber.*[9] Men like Johnston were angry that their exploratory efforts were serving Belgian interests rather than British ones and were horrified by the taint that now stained their efforts as a result of Leopold's excessive regime. They looked upon the growing influence of Belgian Catholic missions in Africa with only slightly more concern than they did Protestant missions from Britain. They wondered how their attempts to "uplift" Africa could have gone so awry. The turning over of the civilizing mission to interests incompatible with their own propelled them to act. They sought to recruit someone without ties to religious organizations, someone from their own ranks yet shorn of any links to British government offices or colonial administrations who might appear to compromise objectivity. Anti-Catholic and anti-missionary, and laboring under the assumption that the reported atrocities in the Congo were an anomaly in colonial Africa, Stead and Johnston charged French-Sheldon with corroborating their suspicions that abuses of colonial power were being institutionalized there.

In particular Stead's letter called upon French-Sheldon to ascertain whether the "human instruments" of the Belgian administration, its European officers and "cannibal armies," were "a curse or a blessing."[10] Approximately fourteen thousand Africans were enrolled under the white officers who served the Belgian monarch and another ten thousand Africans were employed in 1903 as riflemen for the rubber concessionaire companies Leopold ran as a private businessman. These soldiers were the direct agents of the violence that had attracted attention of late, though it was the collection policies of government officials and commercial agents guaranteeing that rubber would be squeezed out of plants and labor out of Congolese by any means necessary that precipitated the violence. In fact, Leopold's policy of declaring any land "vacant" that was not "effectively cultivated" by its owners and the blind eye he turned to the methods used by his armies to force Congolese to work paralleled the widespread uses of torture, impressment, and murder in places such as the new British South Africa and Portuguese-controlled Mozambique—indeed throughout colonial Africa at this time. The Belgian methods of resource extraction differed little in effect from British, French, Dutch, or Portuguese. Yet Belgian officials were quickly gaining a reputation for excessive violence even given the high tolerance for abuse that colonial culture in general promoted. International rivalry as well as repressive colonial policies bearing the Belgian monarch's personal stamp encouraged such impressions to spread. Leopold instituted a system of quotas and bonuses for district commissioners and imposed "taxes" on Congolese, who could only pay them by harvesting the sticky resin or handing over some hotly prized ivory. Leopold's salary incentives and his "secret decree" of September 21, 1891, stating that the "one paramount duty of officials was the taking of urgent and necessary measures to secure for the State the nominal fruits, notably ivory and rubber—and the forbidding of natives to sell ivory and rubber, buy it, or even to leave their village without special permit" made violence the most efficient method for the achievement of state and commercial goals.[11] Though in 1903, before French-Sheldon arrived on the scene, that decree was publicly condemned and Leopold had committed publicly to reform the bonus system, in fact he instituted no permanent changes. Bonuses for every male adult and male child recruited for tax-collecting purposes were immediately reinstituted before the end of that year and the "camps of military instruction," in which they were held, were fortified.[12] To beef up the conscripted armies already in place, company officials were directed to redouble their efforts to procure men and children through raids on villages or purchases from slave traders. Considering the British public's anti-slavery sentiments, in combination with the abject fear that whites had of arming black Africans for any purpose, confirmation of such accusations as these were sure to inflame popular sentiments in Britain and the United States against the Belgian king, should French-Sheldon provide the evidence.

In his contract with French-Sheldon, Stead connected the use of torture and enslavement with travelers' and former rubber industry employees' perceptions that the African population in the Congo Basin had sharply decreased. Missionaries in the Congo were claiming that the drop in certain regions was drastic. They cited statistics that showed there had been an elimination of 80–100% of the population in specific high-rubber extraction areas. At their most extreme, these reports claimed there had been an elimination of tens of millions of people or nearly two-thirds the population of the Congo overall in the thirty years of European intervention.[13] Stead requested that French-Sheldon investigate the charge that massive depopulation was the result of nearly a decade of systematic violence, starvation, and deforestation. The idea that genocide was occurring was capable of wholly undercutting any claims by the Belgians that theirs was truly a civilizing mission.

Third and fourth, Stead had two other matters he wanted French-Sheldon to address in his reports. One was the nature of missionary work in the Congo. As might be expected, British Protestant groups and Belgian Catholic missions issued various and conflicting reports on the subject of atrocities. American (mainly Protestant) missionaries, with fewer ties to monied interests in Europe, produced the most condemning charges. However, missions were not perceived by the public as reliable, inasmuch as they were seen as rivals engaged in battles with each other and with colonial authorities for control and influence. Not only did the secular Stead and Morel bear little affinity for evangelical Christians, but all the direct evidence of atrocities had thus far come from individuals such as Protestant missionaries whose charges against Catholic Belgians were too self-serving to be persuasive. Stead asked French-Sheldon to see whether she could differentiate between the methods and effectiveness of the Catholics and the Protestants, implying that neither could be counted on to remain independent enough of the colonial administration to be reliable witnesses or uninvested enough in the exploitative colonial practices that often brought desperate and dislocated Africans under missionary control to be entirely forthcoming. Furthermore, Stead questioned the very goal of religious conversion. He asked her to "ascertain whether the missionaries are making any progress, whether the natives are the better for being Christianized."

The last thing Stead requested of May French-Sheldon in the letter he attached to her contract was "to keep [her] eyes open specially to the position of women in those regions; whether it has been improved or made worse by the creation of the Congo State." If "barbaric" treatment of women could be established, Belgian rule could be shown to have violated a supposedly central tenet of Western civilization. As the previous chapter demonstrates, this could be considered the most damaging of accusations, at least in terms of public sentiment. Rape, torture, miscegenation, prostitution, and sexual slavery played important roles in the colonial imagination. Stead, perhaps as interested in selling papers as in launching an international reform campaign, needed rich, emotionally laden stories in addition to sober statistics to gain public attention. He hoped that French-Sheldon's "special interest in women" might be put to good use toward that end.[14] Recognizing the potential explosiveness and immediacy that images carry, he urged her especially to return with as many damaging photographs as possible. Stead hoped that such "scientific" evidence would incite the British public to put pressure on their government to re-open the entire question of Leopold's right to the rich heartland of Central Africa. If the same coalition that had come together to create and sanction Leopold's hold over the Free State could break that hold, it would be accomplished through a re-deployment of the language of philanthropy and the interventions of persons like French-Sheldon who had already gained the public's trust and respect in colonial matters.

Stead and Morel banked on the fact that French-Sheldon's reports, unlike those of missionaries and disgruntled ex-employees from the region, would be viewed as impartial and independent of any special interests or national agenda. Probably for this reason, he demanded that French-Sheldon keep secret her connection to Morel and himself. In a letter dated September 28, 1903, he explained that he was sending a copy of a letter regarding French-Sheldon from E. D. Morel rather than the original "because I do not think it is desirable that you should have anything in your possession which would imply that you were in communication with Mr. Morel or myself." Communication while she was abroad posed a particular problem. Stead insisted that they communicate only in code and paraphrased "the A. B. C. code" for her, but demanded that she, under no circumstances, telegraph him.[15] A fragment of a letter from Stead dated October 2, 1903, giving some last minute instructions reads: "I do not expect to hear from you for good or for ill until the end of the year. I am quite willing to trust you to do the best you can without reference to me. . . . If you have an opportunity of writing . . . without betraying anything or anybody you had better . . . "; the fragment ends there.[16] Undoubtedly, Stead was highly aware of the delicacy with which one orchestrates an attack upon a man as powerfully connected as King Leopold II. All available evidence indicates that French-Sheldon kept her contract with Stead a complete secret. Even after returning and refuting the CRA's charges against Leopold, French-Sheldon never revealed to the public or to close personal friends the real impetus for her trip to the Congo Free State in 1903–1904. But *was* Stead's assignment the real impetus for her trip?

French-Sheldon may never have intended to fulfill her contract with Stead to provide him with damning reports of atrocities committed by Leopold's officers and soldiers. The evidence supporting the view that she was in fact secretly working for Leopold the entire time is considerable. In the first place, covertly employing French-Sheldon as a counter-agent would not have been outside the usual modus operandi of the Belgian sovereign. Leopold, as was well known among the journalists and government officials at the time, went to extreme lengths to prevent documented testimony concerning conditions in the Congo Free State from emerging. He informally and often surreptitiously employed a large number of speakers, writers, and journalists to promote his image as a great humanitarian and to counter bad publicity. According to historian Stanley Shaloff, who quotes from a 1907 "character sketch" of the king, Leopold was said to have a "wide network of paid agents, some professional and some amateur, [who] pictured the reform campaign as 'an attempt of England to bully Belgium' or alternatively as an 'overt attack of the Protestant missionaries on a Catholic government.'"[17] Furthermore, Leopold's system of concessions which made him half owner of scores of Dutch, French, German, U.S., and British Congo companies gave him a broad base of support for his policies. Leopold used this influence to bury stories and close pulpits to those who opposed him or his policies.[18] Leopold was not averse to exerting his influence in person as when, in the 1890s, he called at the London offices of the *Times* in an attempt to prevent them from publishing a damaging expose of the Congo.[19] Leopold was a master manipulator of people and succeeded for many years by relying on his talent for getting people invested in schemes that in the main benefited him. Even as early as 1903, Leopold was aware of Morel's establishment of the CRA and sought to undermine it through espionage and infiltration. There is no conclusive evidence identifying French-Sheldon as Leopold's plant in the CRA prior to her departure in October 1903. Yet as enthralled as French-Sheldon was with the trappings of majesty, as admiring of Henry Stanley's "founding" of the Free State, and in light of the indirect links French-Sheldon and her husband had attempted to forge with Leopold through Henry Stanley a decade earlier, it is as likely that she would have been predisposed towards Leopold as it is that she was personally swayed by the CRA's arguments against him.

Conclusive evidence exists that French-Sheldon was at least in contact with Leopold before departing on her mission. Leopold provided French-Sheldon soon after her arrival in the Congo Free State with a telegraphed command, "stating that she was the freest and most independent person in the Free State, and was to have perfect liberty to see and hear everything without hindrance or equivocation, wherever and whenever she elected."[20] Obviously, French-Sheldon had informed Leopold of her intention to conduct an investigation, even if she had not disclosed to him that it was the CRA who was paying her to do so. Furthermore, French-Sheldon continued to keep in touch with Leopold during her travels through the Free State. He responded to her via a minister who once telegrammed French-Sheldon that "His Belgian Majesty [was] sorry, but no steamer could be released" from its duties of re-supplying stations for her personal use.[21] Clearly, French-Sheldon expected quite a bit from the monarch she was ostensibly out to topple.

The suspicion that French-Sheldon was firmly in league with the Belgian monarch throughout this period is supported by her actions in the years and decades following her defense of him in 1905–1906. Finding ways to express publicly her lasting loyalty to King Leopold came to occupy much of her time and attention. Indeed, from the many correspondences French-Sheldon sent to Leopold as well as to the nephew who succeeded him on the throne and from the effusiveness of her expressions of admiration for the monarchy of Belgium in public interviews, it is no exaggeration to say that Stead's one-time employee devoted a good deal of the last thirty years of her life to an abject worship of the Belgian monarchy.[22] Of course, the most suspicious fact indicating French-Sheldon's possible predisposition toward King Leopold is that, after fourteen months traveling through the interior of the Congo Free State at the height of Leopold II's abuse-ridden system of expropriation and torture, this eagle-eyed overseer of the colonial condition found no atrocities to report and only a praiseworthy system of colonial overlordship in place.

CONGO: "WITHOUT FEAR OR FAVOUR"

> I went out to the Congo with a thoroughly
> unbiased mind. I saw everything.
> —French-Sheldon[23]

First thing upon her arrival in Africa in November 1903, French-Sheldon arranged to meet with British Consul Roger Casement—the man who was poised to strike the greatest single blow against Leopold in the matter of the Congo.[24] Among French-Sheldon's papers exist photos depicting French-Sheldon and Consul Roger Casement at the residential Telegraphic Post in St. Thôme. Another taken on the same day features a beaming French-Sheldon, her face upturned to absorb some observation being offered by the gesturing consul. The caption beneath the title, most likely recorded decades later by French-Sheldon's long-time companion and executor Nellie Butler, reads: "British Consul Casement recounting the atrocities of the Congo to Mrs. French Sheldon." French-Sheldon's polite and receptive expression belies the affiliation she may have already forged with Leopold and the plans she had in mind for her own rubber concession in the region. The diametrically opposed positions Casement and French-Sheldon were to adopt publicly in the controversy concerning atrocities in the Congo lend an ironic twist to the camaraderie these photos evince.

Three years before French-Sheldon set sail a second time for Africa, Casement arrived in the Congo region as British consul. Assigned to Boma, the small capital city that Leopold had designated his administrative center,

Casement had little opportunity to address the charges of abuses being leveled at Belgian colonial administrators and militia until June 1903, when the Foreign Office instructed him to travel to the interior to gather "authentic information."[25] In May a debate orchestrated by E. D. Morel in the House of Commons concerning Leopold's monopolization of trade, disregard for British merchants and missionaries, and public outrage against the decimation of the Congolese as well had prompted these instructions. Throughout the summer of 1903, Casement made a thorough investigation into a situation he had long suspected personally and, when French-Sheldon arrived in November, was himself preparing to leave for England to deliver his report to a waiting legislature.

Casement's report of extensive abuses—both in terms of violation of the principle of free trade and regarding of atrocities committed against the African populations—was the turning point in the international effort to deprive Leopold of his Congo holdings.[26] The sixty-page report, complete with precise details and names, painted a devastatingly negative picture, so convincing that not even the most pro-Leopold member of the British legislature continued to defend Leopold following its publication. Neither could members of Parliament decide to suppress the document, as Leopold had requested they do. Leopold deeply feared the public consequences of this report. He sent Sir Alfred Jones, the consul for the Congo State in Liverpool (as well as the director of one of Leopold's concessionaire companies, the Compagnie Belge Maritime du Congo), twice to the Foreign Office to threaten the British that if they forced Leopold's hand he might respond by "hand[ing] everything over . . . to Germany."[27] Though the British were not convinced by this show of desperation, at the urging of Lord Percy (the parliamentary under-secretary) they did edit the report severely, eliminating all specific references and names. Furthermore they proposed appointing an international commission to verify its claims.

Not surprisingly, Casement was livid at the suggestion that a corroborating commission was called for. During the early months of 1904 while Parliament mulled over his report, he met several times with Morel and Stead.[28] Soon after Casement's report was submitted to Parliament, Morel officially announced the birth of the CRA to help channel the public outrage against Leopold into an effective protest.[29] Despite this development Consul Casement spent the rest of 1904 frustrated with the Foreign Office's delay, with Parliament's intention to set up a commission to check out his accusations, and with a general lull in the controversy that existed in spite of all Morel's and the CRA's efforts to keep the issue before the public. Casement's role in the controversy was essentially over. The lull, however, was not a sign of the end of the matter. A special international commission was quickly assembled, albeit handpicked by Leopold himself. Overlapping with French-Sheldon's sojourn in the area, the commission arrived in the Congo Free State in October 1904 and returned in February 1905 with a report that utterly dismayed the Belgian monarch: the international commission confirmed nearly every detail of Casement's charges and announced to the world that Belgian atrocities in the Congo were a reality.[30]

With the submission of the negative report to Parliament, French-Sheldon's investigation to the contrary became all the more important to Leopold. She too had traveled extensively in the region, especially in the *Domaine Privé*, the area most deeply implicated by other travelers and missionaries. "Nothing escapes me," French-Sheldon confidently wrote on the back of a postcard addressed to her companion Nellie Butler in February 1904.[31] Indeed, French-Sheldon had been thorough, covering large amounts of territory and visiting with scores of rubber plantation officials and business interests. She made a point to visit the installations of the Abir company, a concession under particular scrutiny for its extremely violent methods. On a boat called *Deliverance,* she sailed up the Lafari and Marangi branches of the Congo River apparently in the determination not to leave without examining the interior as well as the larger settlements and plantations. But in December 1904, she returned fired with the conviction that Leopold should be no less than commended for his administration of the Congo. "I went out to the Congo with a thoroughly unbiased mind," she insisted,

> I saw everything, and when I found anything wrong I exposed it. The white population is only about 3000, and I had the fullest opportunity of questioning a large number of them. The evidence is absolutely conclusive that the labours of the Congo Free State have added to the material prosperity, the happiness, and the development of the natives, whilst the opening up of the country and the introduction of order and system in place of chaos for ever redound to the credit of King Leopold and those with whom he is associated.[32]

In response to the specific accusations leveled against the Belgian king and his administration, French-Sheldon responded by dismissing the issue of free trade as, firstly, not an "atrocity," and secondly, not unique to the Belgians and not likely to improve under the French or any other stewardship.[33] As reason for the "slowness" of justice for abuses of power by soldiers or colonists she cited the poor transportation and communication systems and the terrain and weather constraints, and she declared point-blank that "the law protecting the blacks as against the whites is largely in favour of the blacks. The most insignificant black can gain the ear of the Administration; the laws are most humane for women and children."[34] "As one who knows Africa," she went further to state that she considered the protection given already to the blacks as against the whites is something phenomenal. If a black man makes a complaint against a white man the case is always strictly investigated, and if the charge is proved, very severe punishment follows. Flogging a raw native who is not classed as a workman (*un travailleur*) is strictly prohibited, and as for a white man flogging a black woman, it is unheard of.[35]

As to the ghoulish tales of mutilation and amputation of limbs of those whose rubber harvests fell short of quota, French-Sheldon (not someone who recoiled at the thought or even the practice of dismemberment as my discussion in previous chapters makes clear) implicated African culture and rejected the notion that desire for profit produced such heinous offenses. She explained in one article how "this question of atrocities is very closely wrapped up with the deep-rooted and almost ineradicable practice of fetishism on the part of the natives. The cutting off of hands and what is known as the ordeal of poison, as well as other barbarous customs, are still in vogue, and it will take a long time to make such people accept civilised laws."[36]

In a letter to the *Times* she explained that although flogging was routinely used to enforce the compliance of African soldiers, the experience of "military training is a most thorough and perfect system for the material, moral, and hygienic uplifting of the black."[37] Despite French-Sheldon's explicit rejection of violent methods in the scores of interviews and speeches she had given over the years, she calmly defended the violence perpetrated in the Congo. Her reasoning in support of "discipline" was clearly self-serving, even circular: "discipline is fine in forcing blacks to recognize the necessity of obedience." French-Sheldon contradicted her former repeated assertions of Africans' "common humanity" by suggesting that physical punishment did not pain Africans as it would whites. She claimed that flogging "is a means of chastising which hurts the spirit more than the body, for any people who submit to the extraordinary and exaggerated tattooing must have a remarkably thick and insensible epidermis."[38]

French-Sheldon dismissed the abuse that Congo critics were most in agreement on: the systematic overwork of Africans who, reportedly, were compelled to toil for as many hours a day and days in a row that it took to bring in the desired amount of rubber in any given month. Upon her return, French-Sheldon recalled that "natives" seemed under-employed most of the time and had only themselves to blame if at the end of a work period they were hard-pressed to produce the quota assigned them. She denied the veracity of the outcries "against rubber and the hardships and vicissitudes it entails to the native collectors." "After having visited hundreds of native villages and penetrated into the forests, in order to see the natives gather rubber," she asserted that, "there is a great exaggeration." Her investigation revealed no coercion whatsoever and instead discovered only African laziness and recalcitrance that formed the true cause for consternation and frenetic work patterns at the end of each month. "The natives in their rubber en-campments," she observed, were often "singing and dawdling about until the time arrived when it was necessary to furnish their imposition to the State of 4 kilo per month, when they would run about wildly and, in consequence, would feel the work to be hard."[39]

Evident depopulation, according to French-Sheldon, was the result of a combination of factors. The physical hardships Africans experienced were, in her view, principally due to a lack of motorized transport or good roads, the natural scarcity of food in arid regions, and "their brutish natures [that] have collectively nearly destroyed them."[40] In general French-Sheldon put down the many problems in the Congo to the "general character of the country" and the state of human development in the Congo. "It must be borne in mind," she cautioned, "that the Congo is the very last country of any great area which it has been attempted to civilise. People now predicate their ideas of civilisation upon the most improved, progressive, and oldest savage countries, and they want the Congo to start with the same degree of perfection that has taken centuries to bring about in other places?"[41] In her letter to the *Times,* she continued in this vein, castigating those who spoke as if ignorant of the suffering which, according to her, inevitably accompanied the enforced "uplift" of natives.

Consistent with opinions she expressed in *Sultan to Sultan* and other publications, French-Sheldon exhibited disdain for sentimentalists who failed to recognize the limits of philanthropy and the benefits of commercial development.

> It were useless to deny everything in the development of the country hinges upon commercial possibilities. There never has been and never will be a colony or State organized and maintained by philanthropy unsustained by the large contributions coming from that country's self. There is no precedent or parallel in the annals of the world by which to compare the giant strides and the prodigious progress that have been made in the Congo Free State in face of the almost overwhelming difficulties.[42]

French-Sheldon portrayed Leopold II as shouldering a "white man's burden" that few others were willing or would have been able to adequately bear. "To those unacquainted with the formidable obstacles with which the Congo is beset," she impatiently explained, "it is almost impossible to pass a fair judgment upon certain events, which have evolved out of the primary efforts to arouse in the natives an interest in a civilization which is forced on them, as it has been forced upon people of every country which has been invaded by the white."[43]

French-Sheldon countered critics' images of cruel white officers pushed to emotional extremes by the sudden thrill of unchecked power and by jungle conditions that brought out the "heart of darkness" within them, with images of missionaries victimized by an overexposure to sun and fever. She quipped that though missionaries "have said that the officials are occasionally affected by the climate. . . . I can only infer that the same fever must sometimes attack the missionaries themselves, for a great many of their reports are undoubtedly exaggerated." The tone was light, but her disgust with missionaries in the Congo was severe. "Many missionaries are mixing far too much with polemics, and seem more devoted to police service than church work," she lamented. Missionaries and other critics were not only misplaced in their concern, according to French-Sheldon, they were disruptive and posed a potential danger to all that had been accomplished thus far by "the white man" in the Congo. "One thing they are doing," she warned, "they are certainly helping to destroy the prestige of the white man in Africa, and if that prestige is once lost it will, indeed, be difficult to replace it. The improvement in the condition of the native races is remarkable, for whereas murders of white men used to be frequent, one seldom or never hears of such things at the present day." She went on to attribute great gains on moral grounds to Leopold's soldiers noting that colonial oversight had quelled internecine fighting among "tribes," suppressed the liquor trade in the Congo and made "Arab slave raiding" a thing "of the past."[44]

As these passages disclose, French-Sheldon was not about to relinquish the philanthropic field to the CRA and other critics of the Congo; instead she sought to redefine the parameters of philanthropy in light of what she believed to be the harsh realities—and the greater good—of the civilizing mission. She ended her lengthy letter to the *Times* with a reminder to the reader that only Leopold, of all the "signatory powers" gathered together at the Berlin Congress in 1885, was willing to take on the "burden" of the Congo before it was clear that the region would prove profitable. "To the contrary," she pointed out, "no country would take upon itself the Congo or be held responsible financially, and magnanimously allowed the entire burden to fall upon the shoulders of his Majesty the King of the Belgians."

French-Sheldon was not simply voicing her opinion. She wrote her letter to the *Times* in early 1905 when the public was still awaiting news of the International Commission sent down to investigate Roger Casement's report of the year before. Letters to such an important organ of the press received a wide domestic as well as international audience. By invoking the authority of the reputable paper, French-Sheldon hoped to reverse the tide of public opinion, which in general was not amenable to Leopold or his position. In a personal letter to a friend, French-Sheldon expressed her certainty that a *Times* editorial had "a marked effect on public and private opinion."[45] Certainly French-Sheldon was overly optimistic, but it is true that the *Times* was a powerful institution of the day. Historian Charles Miller argues, "[T]he letter column of that newspaper, while certainly not as influential as a Cabinet post or a seat in Parliament, nonetheless had a modestly commanding political voice. Even an abbreviated paragraph of praise or dissent by an ordinary citizen could sometimes have a part in shaping public opinion or, just possibly, in guiding official policy."[46] French-Sheldon had high hopes that, with enough exposure, her logic and the charming force of her persona could shape public opinion in favor of Leopold and permit him to continue his policies of rubber extraction unimpeded.

In addition to letters to the *Times* and a lengthy interview conducted by the *Journal of Commerce,* French-Sheldon held at least one *conversazione pictorial* (a presentation with slides or "magic lantern" show) on the topic of the Congo controversy for a spectacular gathering of influential and important figures in London.[47] In the audience of five hundred or more were the American and Italian ambassadors, the Japanese minister with the entire Japanese legation, the Chinese minister, the Austrian Court chamberlain Count Lutzow, and numerous other foreign dignitaries and members of Parliament. Though Lord Lansdowne, the foreign secretary, sent his letter of regret, Sir Alfred Jones, the consul for the Congo in Liverpool, was present. Also present in the audience was W. T. Stead, who could not have been very pleased to see his former secret agent emphatically and effectively pronouncing the Anti-Congo campaign a pack of lies.[48]

French-Sheldon and those committed to defending Leopold and Belgian administrations in the Congo probably succeeded in somewhat dampening the spirit of reform in mid-1905, during what was already a lull in the controversy. However, she and others who found common cause with the Belgian monarchy could not dispel for long the unease fomented by the Protestant missionaries, Roger Casement, and the CRA. With the publication in late 1905 of the damning report of the international commission appointed by Leopold himself to investigate Casement's accusations, the British and American publics exploded with outrage. Even the Belgian public began to demand that Leopold yield his personal hold on the region and agree to allow formal control to pass to the Belgian state. By the fall of 1906, Leopold bowed to pressure and agreed to negotiate the transfer, although he managed to stall its completion for another two years, almost until his death in 1909.

Although it cannot be determined with absolute certainty whether French-Sheldon had united with Leopold before reaching the Congo or swung to his defense as a result of her honest appraisal of conditions as she found them to be, certainly her decision to desert Stead and the CRA and side with Leopold and the rubber plantation owners aligned with her personal affinities. The former explorer's personal sense of importance was anchored to a continuation of the colonial project and untrammeled entrepreneurship in Africa. It was one thing to claim to have superceded her mentor in her approach to Africans as she had in *Sultan to Sultan,* but it would have been an act of personal treachery for the "Lady Stanley" to disown Henry Stanley's most glorious achievement and to throw her own accomplishments as an imperial scout into doubt by casting a pall over the entire project of colonial penetration of the Congo region and capitalist exploitation of the continent.[49] Furthermore the grandiosity of the Belgian monarch, the importance of being his emissary and the possibilities of being his business associate spoke to French-Sheldon's desire for *gloire* far more than (what she likely saw as the unreliable) railings of a low-level colonial official or some presumably misdirected missionaries. Whether French-Sheldon deliberately concealed the labor conditions of Africans in the Congo from European and American publics or simply did not perceive them as atrocious, the aging adventuress had her own interests to consider as her plan to create her own colonization company in West Africa began to take shape.

French-Sheldon's travels from late 1903 through December 1904 through what Joseph Conrad described in these years as a "heart of darkness" put French-Sheldon in touch with the European commercial interests that would inspire her to seek out a more concrete role in the colonization of Africa.[50] As a result of the contacts she made and the lessons she learned about rubber production in the Congo, French-Sheldon set her sights on Liberia and on an entrepreneurial colonization plan to rival that of Belgian concessionaires. In the next chapter I explain how French-Sheldon's aborted plan for an Americo-Liberian Industrial Company illustrates her ability and her willingness to weave philanthropic concerns, national interests, and racial preoccupations together in the hope of achieving the international influence and the personal authority she imagined a White Queen such as she was due.

SEVEN

A Plantation Mistress in Liberia

Mrs. French-Sheldon expressed the sentiments of an
enlightened public opinion in the Anglo-American
world at the close of the nineteenth century. . . . [H]er
opinions were a forecast of things to follow in the first
half of the twentieth century, and this interpretation
of colonial government has since become the goal
of all believers in national self-determination.

Harold E. Hammond, "American Interest in the
Exploration of the Dark Continent," 1956

In December 1904, after a long fourteen months of observing rubber, mineral, and timber harvesting and being hosted by district commissioners and rubber plantation owners throughout the Congo Free State, May French-Sheldon returned to Britain armed with the information and the contacts she needed to establish her own development corporation— the Americo-Liberian Industrial Company.[1] Her plan was to capitalize on the personal contacts she had made in Africa and exploit the advantages that her American citizenship might afford her in nearby Liberia to carve out a more profitable niche for herself within the imperial economy being forged in this period by European and American investors. While acrimonious public debate over the proper stewardship of the Congo Free State raged around her, French-Sheldon parlayed her foray into Central Africa into an opportunity to develop plans for a colonization company that, if successful, could have transformed French-Sheldon from an influential observer on the sidelines of empire-building to an industrialist with a major economic stake in the colonizing of Africa. The company she set about organizing amounted to an enormous plantation for rubber harvesting and the collection of ivory and other minerals using labor supplied by landless black American émigrés she intended to import from the American South.

Although French-Sheldon's scheme failed in the end, the complex weave of political maneuvers and public-relation strategies she employed in her endeavors to establish herself as the mistress of a colossal colonial plantation in Africa provides a window onto the material factors linking the rhetorical practices of exploration with the violence engendered by the capitalist expropriation of resources in colonial Africa. As the epigram above avers, French-Sheldon's rather minor roles in African colonization were less important than the exemplariness of her perspective on colonial relationships and processes—a neo-colonialist perspective that became foundational to American foreign policy and conducted throughout the twentieth century.

Even before French-Sheldon arrived in Africa for the second major excursion of her life, she harbored more than a vague hope that her sojourn in the Congo Free State as an unofficial observer of Leopold's administration would permit her to reanimate the colonial ambitions that had been curtailed by the premature death of her husband following her first trip to Africa over ten years before. A letter from French-Sheldon to Liberia's president, written on the SS *Burutu* off Sierra Leone, constitutes incontrovertible evidence of this intent. The letter is dated October 12, 1903, just at the time of French-Sheldon's departure for the Congo Free State, and is addressed to G. W. Gibson, the president of the Republic of Liberia. In it French-Sheldon frames her desire to purchase an enormous tract of land from the relatively small West African nation as part of a commitment to help thwart "the schemes of those who are jealous of, and inimical to, the influence of Liberia in African affairs, and wish to exploit the country both materially and politically in their own narrow and selfish interests."[2] To distance herself from such malefactors, French-Sheldon's initial overture to the president of this struggling republic stressed several factors that would become the core of French-Sheldon's defense of her actions, once they had come under critical scrutiny by those who questioned the integrity of her proposal. Among those core elements were her American citizenship and Liberia's political and economic dependence on the United States, her endorsement of a work ethic and capitalist economic development as the most reliable form of racial uplift, and her altruistic love of Africa and black people "separated from their ancestral lands" in the United States.

The establishment of herself as unaffiliated with European business interests and nationalist developers, if not a veritable "friend of the black race," was the key to French-Sheldon's ability to project the reliability that a plan such as hers hinged upon. Knowing this, French-Sheldon in her letter drew heavily on the international reputation of neutral observer and defender of Africans that her earlier expedition and writings on Africa had produced. "Long before Miss Kingsley undertook her noble work, which has thus far borne such good fruit," French-Sheldon reminded the Liberian head of state, "I had travelled alone among the natives of East Africa to study the country and the people, with the result that I became more deeply convinced of the wrong and injustice which the so-called civilised and christian [*sic*] world has inflicted upon the Negro race."[3] The "wrong" French-Sheldon refers to consists both of enslavement and colonial subjugation. The partial solution to this doubled historic crime French-Sheldon identifies as the "repatriation" of American blacks to Africa coupled with the economic re-organization of Africa along industrial models of development that, she argues, would produce true independence and national self-determination. In her initial communication with President Gibson, French-Sheldon presented this plan as partly "educational" in its effects and aimed at the "development of the material and other and higher interests" of the people of Liberia. As part of her assurances that her intentions were beneficent ones, she added that the "money for this purpose will all be raised in the United States from white and black." With this introductory letter, French-Sheldon prepared President Gibson for her visit in January, February, or March of 1904 as part of her return from her investigations in the Congo. French-Sheldon signed her letter, "Yours most respectfully in the interests of your country and race, (Mrs.) May French-Sheldon, F.R.G.S.,"[4] adding both the honorific to clarify her respectability as a married woman and the initials indicating her status as a member of the Royal Geographic Society of London.

French-Sheldon did not visit Liberia on the way back from the Congo in early 1904 as she planned. Instead her trip to the Congo region lasted over a year, during which time she learned much about the concessionaire system that was netting enormous profit for Belgian investors in the Free State and acquired general information about the rubber business in Africa that would prove helpful in her plans to obtain her own concession from the Liberian legislature.[5] Her return was too hurried, apparently, to include a trip to Liberia, but that was no indication her interest in the project had waned. French-Sheldon spent the better part of 1905 attracting investors and establishing the American origins of the company by organizing its legal incorporation in Oklahoma in late summer of that year. She arranged to return to Africa in November to seal the deal with the Liberian legislature. Just as the International Commission's report affirming atrocities committed by the administration of Leopold II in the Congo Free State was being released to the public in Europe, French-Sheldon arrived in Liberia to obtain its legislature's approval for her plan. In her letter to Gibson in preparation of her impending visit, she introduced herself as a former explorer of Africa, as a philanthropist with a special interest in the uplift of Africans, and as an authority on the Congo controversy, hoping to command the legislature's attention and smooth the way toward a negotiated contract. "My reports re the Congo have been received, and in some instances solicited by the American President—by Lord Lansdowne of the English Foreign Office—by the President of France and by the Emperor of Germany," she boasted. "So I feel," she proceeded, "when I move in the hope of presenting an opportunity for the Liberians, in which, if it is accepted, they will, as the population of Liberia individually and collectively, participate and benefit thereby—prompt and active attention is my due." With vague references to her earlier writings and presentations as well as her most recent involvement in the Congo controversy, she ended this letter by affirming that her "credentials go without saying, being a record of my indefatigable work, for all oppressed people—and particularly for the Negro Race."[6]

French-Sheldon omitted stating the content of her "reports re the Congo" in this letter. Her stand on Belgian atrocities might have proven alarming to some Liberians. However much she needed to establish her importance, French-Sheldon did not wish to appear a controversial figure. She hoped to convince the Liberian government and the U.S. embassy in Liberia that her intentions were in the best interests of all. In her correspondence French-Sheldon argued that her plan to develop and exploit the forest products of Liberia would benefit Liberians and Americans alike. She often drew on her public image as a model explorer and humanitarian colonizer of Africa. In her various appeals to the Liberian state and to the U.S. State Department, French-Sheldon defined her relationship to Liberia and to black Americans in ways that she believed would appeal to them both.

Above all, May French-Sheldon put her national origin to use in her negotiations with both the Liberian government and with her own. In her 1903 letter to President Gibson she alluded to the history of Liberia as a struggling haven for oppressed black Americans and as an outpost of U.S. civilization and influence. She portrayed Liberia as besieged on all sides by European perfidy. In this drama French-Sheldon played the role, not of White Queen, but of white knight coming to the aid of former slaves and fellow countrymen.

> It is possible that you have heard my name. I am a native of the United States of America and have from my youth been impressed by, and have always born testimony to the unparalleled services which the Africans have rendered to the white people of the United States of America and especially to the South. I am anxious, therefore, that the Negro shall have in his own Fatherland the opportunities which owing to circumstances there, he cannot have in America, and which if European projects succeed, he will not have in his ancestral home, in spite of the benevolent and philanthropic intentions professed by many individual Europeans.

French-Sheldon banked on the paternalist relations between the U.S. government and Liberia, and an interpretation of racial uplift more in line with white American perspectives than with black, to ground her claims to the mutuality of her proposal. To lend urgency to the matter, she also invoked the threat, very real at the time, of European encroachment on Liberian territory as well as the specter of indebtedness that loomed over the Liberian economy. "I have reason to believe that there are in Europe deep laid schemes," she warned,

> to rob Liberia of her Independence and of the integrity of her territory by involving her in pecuniary enterprises and obligations, which owing to inexperience she cannot understand and will not understand until the appearance of the full development of those schemes. This is a prospect seriously threatening the Republic which the best citizens of the United States view with the deepest concern.

The United States' relationship to the republic of Liberia was a close, though not a consistently supportive, one. In 1819 Liberia was founded through the auspices of the American Colonization Society as a refuge for free black Americans and Africans escaped or rescued from slave ships. However, the motives of supporters of the American Colonization Society, like French-Sheldon's nearly a century later, were not wholly humanitarian. In addition to the usual evangelical designs, pressure for a "repatriation" of Africans (many of whom were not only born in the United States but whose lineage in the Americas consisted of many generations) came from white Americans who hoped to rid themselves of a disturbingly free black community, as well as from blacks who hoped for more autonomy and a fresh start in a place they imagined as a genealogical homeland. Just as importantly, the United States government was happy to establish a base and maintain a friendly port along the west coast of Africa where its ships could dock temporarily.[7]

Yet through the nineteenth century the U.S. government did little to ensure the survival of its only outpost in Africa. The lack of commitment to a viable black American settlement in Liberia is reflected in the neglect that the U.S. government showed to the colony throughout the century. Colonists did not possess even their own site for the first ten years until, as legend has it, a naval surgeon appointed by President James Monroe negotiated a land deal between indigenous Africans along the coast and surviving colonists by holding a gun to the head of a local potentate until he agreed to "sell" them a site around Cape Mesurado. Unlike the British colony of Sierra Leone to the north, the American settlement at Monrovia remained small and unfunded as a result of the deliberate decision of the State Department and the U.S. Congress to ignore its existence as much as possible (delaying recognition of its status as an independent republic from 1847 to 1862, for instance). The United States rarely chose to intervene in Liberia, even in the face of the encroachment of the French and British along Liberia's borders. Only in rare cases, such as when Commodore Matthew C. Perry burned several villages to avenge the deaths of some American colonists at the hands of Africans in 1843, did the U.S. government take notice of the warfare that continued to plague the inhabitants. For the most part the United States issued platitudes in support of the small republic without ever committing itself to Liberia's survival as a nation.[8]

In spite of this fact, French-Sheldon knew that there were many forces within Liberia and within the United States determined to keep Liberia's connection to the United States intact. Black American churches held the settlement in special regard and African-American leaders such as Booker T. Washington insisted that black men be appointed to important positions in the U.S. embassy in Liberia. The black Americans who survived the hardships of settlement and colonization were in need of economic investments as well as military aid periodically. They were deeply suspicious of the European powers that had periodically added Liberian territory to their own without any effective protest ensuing from the United States. The Liberian government was anxious to draw American capital to prevent itself from coming under the control of Britain or France by default. This threat became paramount in 1903, just as French-Sheldon was preparing for her trip to the region.

In 1903 the United States, through its Liberian minister Ernest Lyon, began to increase pressure on the government of Liberia to pay off its mounting debts. The strapped nation had fallen behind in its payments in support of the anti-slave trading clauses of the Brussels Act, to which it had been a party as a result of U.S. sponsorship. For that and other reasons, Liberia was desperately in need of cash in 1903–1904. So desperate was the republic that it grudgingly agreed to the re-negotiation of a British wild rubber concession, renaming it the "Liberian Development Company" in return for a half-million-dollar loan at 6 percent interest.[9] The following year, when French-Sheldon appeared waving her American citizenship and a proposal for the Americo-Liberian Industrial Company, also worth half a million dollars, the newly elected president of Liberia, Arthur Barclay, received her graciously in his home and the American legation held a social function in her honor.[10]

French-Sheldon proposed that the Americo-Liberian Industrial Company (or the "Big Company" as she referred to it in private as well as official correspondence) be allotted twelve hundred square miles for the harvesting of timber and all forest products within the area for a term of no less than fifty years, and that she personally receive one thousand acres for her own use.[11] In addition, her contract with the Liberian legislature listed colonization, or the settlement of "deserving coloured people selected in America," as an important aspect of the company's plan to develop the resources of the interior.[12] The treaty between Liberia and the Americo-Liberian Industrial Company passed the legislature with no difficulty. It granted French-Sheldon's company the twelve hundred square miles of land she requested for the proposed period of fifty years. The privileges the treaty accorded to the company included

> the sole right to cut timber and sell same from said selected areas, erect saw mills, planting plants, stone making plants, and sell products, and all things, manufacturing at same or manufactured from timber or other products of the soil, whether they be vegetable or otherwise, erect stone houses, warehouses, and all other buildings, machinery and all other plants necessary and desirable for the successful prosecution of the business enterprises and interests of the Republic and the Company. To gather cocoa-nuts, manufacture copra, cultivate and grow palm trees, manufacture palm oil, to export all such timber products, merchandise, trade goods, to colonize lands with immigrants acceptable to the Republic, provide homes and farms to such immigrants, carry on the business of agriculturists, to establish, conduct and maintain banks, build and operate telegraphs, telephones, cables, submarine and otherwise, install water works, water-power, heating and lighting plants, build and operate railways, tramways, ships, steamers, lighters boats and do all things necessary or expedient for the successful conduct of the business.[13]

Several of the articles of this treaty made reference to the importation of labor and the settling of colonists under conditions highly favorable to the company. Subsections (c), (d), and (e), of Section 6 of the agreement reveal the intentions of the company to leave imported workers in a perpetual state of dependency by restricting to the company control over land allotments to immigrants and over the conditions of repayment. These subsections entitled the company:

> (c) To encourage, assist, and promote the immigration into Liberia of persons, acceptable to the Republic, as citizens, Government to protect the Company by refusing to grant other lands after allotment by Company.

> (d) To allot lands or plots to settlers or colonizers for terms of years.

> (e) To advance to settlers or colonizers money, seeds, tools, implements, and other things as may be necessary, and to receive payment from settlers or colonizers for said advances in cash, produce or otherwise as may be arranged

for between settlers and the Company until said settlers or colonizers have
settled their indebtedness to the Company in full and then the Company
shall advise the Secretary of the Treasury of Liberia that the debt as aforesaid
have been settled, and the said Secretary shall at once have drawn up and
hand to each settler or colonizer who has thus settled his indebtedness to the
Company as above described, a deed in fee simple giving such settler absolute ownership of the land or plot of land he has thus purchased and paid
for.[14]

Subsection (c), while purporting to be concerned with the "acceptability" of
individual immigrants to the republic, in effect granted the company total
control over land distribution. If this rule was adhered to, laborers for the
Big Company would have no way of purchasing land except through the
Company. Subsection (d) ensured that the Big Company could make the
terms of the repayment stretch out over an indefinite number of years. Finally, subsection (e) put all authority over the settling of colonists' debts in
the hands of the company. The treaty arranged between the Americo-Liberian Industrial Company would have effectively put in place a system of debt
peonage and sharecropping that would have seemed tragically familiar to
black Americans fleeing similar conditions in the southern United States.

French-Sheldon's plan centered on her belief in the availability and de-
sirability of importing black Americans as laborers or "colonists." Unfortu-
nately for her, she miscalculated the attractiveness to Liberians of encouraging black American migration in two ways. First, she underestimated the
concerns of the more affluent members of the American community in
Monrovia regarding the character of the lower-class laborers whom French-
Sheldon intended to transform into future colonists. Much of this concern
derived from the prejudices of the (American-born) Liberian elite who
blamed some of Liberia's problems on the influx of unskilled laborers into
an unstable and often shrinking economy. The failure of Liberia's export
economy had resulted in large numbers of unemployable workers residing
in Monrovia who then became targets of an aggravated bourgeoisie.

French-Sheldon compounded her mistake by misreading the antipathy
sometimes expressed by the primarily black American-Liberian elite for
their poorer fellow expatriates. Though affluent Liberians disdained the society of indigent laborers and partly blamed the economic situation on their
presence, many viewed the problem as systemic and pointed to the maldis-
tribution of property as the source of the problem rather than to the character of the newly arrived American émigrés. These Liberians did not
vouchsafe plans to magnify a system that had already resulted in an idle,
landless labor pool to gather in the streets of Monrovia. French-Sheldon especially incurred the wrath of the American minister, Ernest Lyon, by sug-

gesting that the profits of the company be ensured through a practice of charging the costs of importing future sharecroppers to the émigrés themselves, payable through labor over a period of years, and "depriving them of the usual allotment of land gratis."[15] Lyon, like most black American officials in Liberia, believed in the project of "repatriation" as a solution to the mire of impoverishment and systematic disenfranchisement blacks Americans experienced in the United States. He bristled at French-Sheldon's blatant attempt to indenture new arrivals permanently. Apparently, to Lyon, the "Big Company" seemed too much like an overseas, post–Civil War substitute for the "Big House" of southern American plantation life.

Despite these issues, French-Sheldon's contract initially met with little resistance from Lyon or other governmental officials. French-Sheldon's problems with Lyon, along with other nagging issues, surfaced late in the negotiation process, after the Liberian legislature had ratified the treaty with the company on January 6, 1906, and French-Sheldon had left to return to England. In the two months that French-Sheldon spent in Liberia at the end of 1905, the American legation, including Minister Lyon, and the Liberian government under the guidance of President Barclay warmly welcomed French-Sheldon personally and seemed to have viewed her proposal with optimism. In January 1906, French-Sheldon left Africa firm in the belief that her newfound friends, President Barclay and his wife, would facilitate the implementation of her plans in her absence. However, after her departure, and before Barclay had signed the treaty into law, serious questions arose. The realization on the part of Lyon and Barclay that French-Sheldon's plan hinged on intensified immigration and a redoubled exploitation of immigrants as sharecroppers in ways that would leave them entirely dependent on the company was only a small part of the problem. This feature of the contract was likely to be true of any concession the legislature might grant and was more or less business as usual in the game of colonial capitalism in Africa. Of more immediate concern to government officials, both Liberian and American, were the rumors surfacing that French-Sheldon had little or no capital of her own and that the Americo-Liberian Industrial Company was a front for European businessmen. High on the list of those persons who might be backing French-Sheldon's plan were the former members of what was known a few years earlier as the "London Liberian Rubber Syndicate."[16]

It is difficult to say whether the rumors were true that the company was backed primarily by Europeans. French-Sheldon vehemently denied the fact, and no evidence ever surfaced to support the contention. French-Sheldon's relationship with Stead and the Congo Reform Association may have reached the ears of the Liberian elite, and her role as a secret agent for them as well as a double agent for Leopold II may have produced uneasiness about the lack of transparency in her international dealings. Or her long residence in London may have been responsible for the impression that she did not represent American investors. Though French-Sheldon listed her sister's residence at 195 Huntington Avenue in Boston as her American home, all who knew her were aware that she had only journeyed to the United States for brief visits in the dozen years since her appearance at the Chicago World's Fair in 1893. Even more fishy were the identities of her investors. Though French-Sheldon listed U.S. congressmen and a financier whom she claimed represented "Rockefellar" [*sic*] among them, few of these men could be confirmed as investors in the company.[17] By the end of 1906, the Liberians began to doubt not only who the money was coming from but how much of it there really was. More and more, French-Sheldon's company had begun to look like a shady deal.

Shady deals, especially shady rubber deals, were burgeoning in the United States in the first few years of the twentieth century. This was largely a function of the encouragement rubber industrialists were receiving from a federal government that wanted to see private investors secure valuable holdings around the world that could keep the supply of cheap rubber flowing into the United States. French-Sheldon's old ally, Secretary of State James G. Blaine, and the McKinley administration vigorously promoted rubber companies' investments overseas, especially in the Philippines and Southeast Asia. They also encouraged the planting of rubber trees in the United States. With the rise of industries that relied on rubber, the resin became one of the most valuable of raw materials, and the U.S. government urged American businesses to make procurement of inexpensive resin a top priority. Although the United States looked to South America and Southeast Asia for rubber, rubber from Africa was not exempt from American commercial development strategies. When in 1906 Leopold bowed to public pressure to relinquish his personal hold on the Congo Free State, he invited American rubber magnates Tom Ryan and Senator Nelson Aldritch to form the American Congo Company with him in order to exempt a portion of his holdings from the terms of the treaty with his own government.[18] Neither was American interest in rubber confined to big business or big money, according to historians Howard and Ralph Wolf, "the craze to invest in rubber farms struck all classes."[19] The sudden American interest in rubber resulted in hundreds of stock companies being formed in the United States between 1899 and 1907, a number of which were fraudulent.

In 1905 and 1906 many of these frauds came to light and erupted in notorious scandals. One of the most sensational was that of the Ubero Plantation Company, whose supposed backers outwardly resembled the Americo-Liberian Industrial Company's impressive but vague list of investors. According to the U.S. Post Office, the branch of government charged with investigating the matter, Ubero's plan was to "secure the names of prominent men to create an appearance of stability, and then by alluring literature and fraudulent dividends, to give the scheme the appearance of a profitable enterprise. The development work done was solely for the purpose of misleading visiting directors and investors. All the funds of the company were diverted to the pockets of the promoters through the medium of selling companies."[20] Between 1906 and 1908 failures and bankruptcies and the loss of millions of dollars resulted from hundreds of such fraudulent enterprises in the United States alone.

Barclay's administration in Liberia, perhaps in light of the rubber scandals surfacing in the United States and in view of the debt Liberia had recently incurred to Britain, became nervous about the integrity of French-Sheldon's proposal. If the Americo-Liberian Industrial Company was not as solvent as French-Sheldon claimed, and its investors were not as American, then default might put hundreds of acres of central Liberian land in the hands of Europeans. American minister Lyon warned Secretary of State Elihu Root, and most likely President Barclay, that even if the company remained viable, and French-Sheldon's initial investors were all American, it might be composed of "mere speculators, in league with some English syndicate, and who will sell their rights to the highest bidder as soon as the Agreement between them and the Government is ratified."[21] In light of these fears, Barclay decided not to sign the concession to the Americo-Liberian Industrial Company in 1906 as expected, and in early 1907 the Liberian legislature overturned their earlier decision concerning the treaty with French-Sheldon.

French-Sheldon and the company's representative in the United States bombarded the office of Secretary of State Root with letters of indignation and protest in the wake of the Liberian legislature's decision, to no avail.[22] French-Sheldon had used several different approaches over the past year in her efforts to persuade President Barclay to sign the agreement and U.S. minister Lyon to act on her behalf in Liberia,[23] including warning President Barclay that his actions were showing "the impotence of the negro to successfully govern himself or others in an administrative way."[24] Now she turned to petitioning the Liberian legislature, threatening Barclay's administration with public exposure, and insisting on intervention by the Roosevelt administration. Once again, she relied heavily on her American affiliation and the European threat to make her case. She claimed that Barclay's refusal to sign the treaty into law was evidence of the presence of "certain influences, favourable to Europeans, but antagonistic to the introduction of American capital into Liberia, and therefore, inimical to the best interests of

Liberia and dangerous to its independence, have been powerful with President Barclay to direct him in his strange and unprecedented action." French-Sheldon added the threat of "giving publicity" to her experiences with the legislature in ways that would undermine Liberia's ability to do business with investors in the future. She pointed out that many Liberian churches and schools enjoyed the support of Americans and implied vaguely that news of Liberia's intent to "discriminate against Americans" could cause American support to dwindle. Much, if not all, of this was bluster and did not produce a reversal of the Liberian legislature's decision. French-Sheldon resurrected her arguments favoring the influx of black American labor for the purpose of working for the Big Company as part of a dire picture she drew of European perfidy and invasion. "Whether Liberia is to remain an independent state," she warned,

> absolutely depends upon her success in adding to her civilized population, and that without delay. She can be successful in that direction only by inducing an influx of immigrants from the United States. This Company's most particular object . . . is the establishing of deserving coloured people selected in America, upon farms in Liberia, the putting into the Republic a large number of really desirable citizens. Of course the representatives of the commercial nations of Europe now operating in Liberia, are not in favour of a scheme of this kind and, doubtless, have used such influence as they could to bear, in order to prevent the signing of the Agreement with this Company, and thus defeat this Company's first, and most important object.[25]

None of these arguments outweighed the fear of Liberian politicians that the Americo-Liberian Industrial Company was founded on speculation and supported by insufficient and possibly foreign capital. Her appeals to the U.S. State Department fell on Root's dull ears. With news of fraudulent rubber deals exploding in the press at home, the Roosevelt administration found no reason to support this longtime resident of London's claims of "discrimination" against Americans in Liberia. French-Sheldon continued to protest the treatment she received by the Liberian government and the treachery (as she saw it) of Lyon by bombarding Root's office with extensive letters demanding aid in holding Liberia to the contract she had initially negotiated, but by 1909 she was forced to give up her plans for a "Big Company" in Africa in addition to the personal plantation of one thousand acres the treaty had "set aside for her own use." Permanently dashed were French-Sheldon's hopes of ever becoming a major industrialist or (like Isak Dinesen/Karen Blixen a few years later) of owning a farm in Africa.[26]

CONCLUSION: FRENCH-SHELDON'S
LEGACY IN CONGO AND LIBERIA

> If the United States had happened to possess in
> Darkest Africa a territory seven times as large and
> four times as populous as the Philippines, we, too,
> might find good government difficult and come in
> for our own share of just or unjust criticism.
> —Former U.S. secretary of state, Elihu Root, 1938[27]

In an interview held during his retirement years, Secretary of State Root laid bare the self-serving mindset of the Roosevelt administration in the years 1903–1905, when his office was besieged with demands by Protestant churches and progressives that the president act against Leopold in the matter of the Congo.[28] Moreover this perspective was not confined to the White House. The *New York Tribune,* for instance, agreed with the secretary of state's cautious view of the matter, querying that if the United States asserted the right to intervene in the Congo then what was to stop Belgium from claiming jurisdiction over cases of lynching in the South?[29] Apparently Ida B. Wells-Barnett's American and European campaign against lynching in the 1890s had hit a nerve—even if the response of defensive whites was only to insist that the United States refrain from taking a moral stand on international issues.[30] Yet in spite of the *Tribune's* recognition of American hypocrisy and the potential backlash that moral stands abroad might inspire against race relations at home, the United States did play a central role in the international movement to deprive Leopold of the Congo. Under pressure from Protestant missions; progressive reformers; and in the words of Root, "many good women [who] were wild to have us stop the atrocities in the Congo,"[31] the Roosevelt administration finally added its voice to that of Britain and France to compel the Belgian monarch to relinquish personal possession of the Free State. Gender-specific progressive reformist attitudes did not, however, mandate radical changes in the power structures governing rubber production in the Congo. The terms of white solidarity, however internally contradicted by opposing commercial and national interests and a gendered discourse of global humanitarianism, did not allow for that possibility.

The U.S. government was both un-involved enough in African colonization to support French-Sheldon's shaky development schemes and too implicated by its own history of enslavement, repression, and exploitation to demand a restructuring of economic and political relations in Leopold's Congo Free State. As Root pointed out years later, the United States did not "happen to possess in Darkest Africa a territory seven times as large and four times as populous as the Philippines." But it did have some overlapping interests with Europe in Africa. American businessmen with close ties to the Roosevelt administration and Capitol Hill capitalized on the change in government in the Congo even as the U.S. State Department and Congress began to declare themselves officially aghast at the atrocities.[32] In 1906, before Leopold had agreed to the terms of the transfer of the Congo Free State to the Belgian government, he managed to hide a portion of his holdings within the newly formed American Congo Company. Leopold hoped to vest American business interests in the status quo in Central Africa, so he could be allowed to continue to exploit the rubber and peoples of Central Africa and in addition offset the wrath of those who viewed Leopold's policies as cutting the rest of Europe out of the profits.[33]

The international reform movement that coalesced around reports of atrocities in the Congo could appear to be in opposition with the colonial ideologies of the moment. Yet the "open door" demands made by the members of the Congo Reform Association (that control of the Congo go to the government of Belgium, that the system of Leopold's private concessions halt, and that the principle of free trade permit access by non-Belgian companies) were hardly designed with the best interests of Central Africans in mind. Much as reformers and missionaries insisted that the effects of such changes would alter the treatment of African workers, they did not lay aside national and denominational interests to advocate a wholesale abandonment of the colonial project in the Congo. The discourse of philanthropy enveloping the international dialogue on the Free State was paternalist at best—at its worst, in the case of French-Sheldon for instance, it was a weak echo of the disingenuous philanthropic pronouncements obscuring commercial greed and avarice that had inaugurated Leopold's arrogation of the Congo for himself in the first place.

As in the international anti-slavery movement, philanthropic language covered a multitude of selfish interests. Following Leopold's lead, French-Sheldon used the language of philanthropy as it emerged from the debates on the Congo to cloak her intentions in Africa to Stead and then to the Liberian government, and likely, to cloak them to herself as well. As I have shown, French-Sheldon never conceded the principle of humanitarianism to the reform movement. Instead she insisted that the civilizing mission was necessarily a painful but worthwhile program: that one could not be too squeamish about the details of its operations. In the end her loyalty to Leopold would inspire her to compose a lengthy history of Belgium, in which Leopold appeared as an Atlas figure supporting the heavy weight that was "the white man's burden." French-Sheldon's history of Belgian colonialism in Africa, variously titled *Belgium: Little Mother of a Giant* and *A Tribute to Belgium Little and Great,* never reached publication despite the encouragement its author received from Leopold's successor and nephew, Albert I.[34] Albert provided her with unrestricted access to the palace archives and the personal papers of his uncle. In a note Albert personally wrote to French-Sheldon in May 1921, he acknowledged the propagandistic value of French-Sheldon's work. "I am convinced it will help to better knowledge of our Colony," he wrote, believing her book about to be published, "as well as of Belgium's steady efforts to develop it and to allow the natives to reap the benefit of civilization."[35] The king's personal letter is signed simply "Albert." The personal familiarity of the signature was a result of a voluminous correspondence campaign waged by French-Sheldon to gain the recognition of the nephew of Leopold II. French-Sheldon spent a large part of her time in the 1910s imploring the young monarch to publicly recognize her loyalty to his deceased uncle and to his country. In 1921 she was finally granted her wish when Albert agreed (after a year of particularly heavy bombardment by French-Sheldon through the mails) to make her the first woman to be awarded the Belgian equivalent of knighthood, *la Croix de Chevalier de l'Ordre de la Couronne.*[36]

The flow of rubber, profits, and philanthropy came full circle when Albert invited French-Sheldon to hang her portrait and deposit photos and artifacts she took on both her African expeditions at the Belgian Royal African Museum at Tervuren, a small city just outside Brussels. Built with money Leopold gained through his Congo concessions, the museum's purpose was to promote the Belgian public's interest in Africa and to encourage investment specifically in the Congo. Through the years, the objects French-Sheldon donated to the museum, like all of its exhibits, have helped to confirm and promote a relationship of exploitation between metropole and colony even while they have purported to be expressions of humanitarians' concern with the preservation of African culture.[37]

Just as the museum at Tervuren has stood as a monument and a materialization of Leopold's so-called philanthropic sentiments, so has May French-Sheldon's historical reputation perverted the story of the scramble for Africa at the turn of the twentieth century. In direct disregard of the imperial mechanisms upon which French-Sheldon depended and helped to construct, her legacy has been construed to be that of a great humanitarian. The obituary editor for the *New York Times* in 1936, for example, credited French-Sheldon with being a defender of Africans, and in this, an anomaly of her times:

> Mrs. French-Sheldon was not only a pioneer among women explorers in Africa but one of the few of either sex who in her generation returned with kind words for the natives. In a day when they were described as treacherous and bloodthirsty she insisted their white exploiters were more guilty. . . .
>
> For many years she argued the cause of blacks, and decrease in the cruelty with which natives were handled was in some part attributed to her championship.[38]

The glowing portrait that the *New York Times* painted of French-Sheldon, in contradistinction to the role she played as a defender of Congo atrocities and as ambitious colonialist in Liberia, reappears in scholarly treatments of her throughout the twentieth century. Harold E. Hammond, the respected historian of Africa and U.S. foreign policy, wrote an article for *The Historian* in 1956 praising French-Sheldon as a model to be emulated. He asserted that, unlike pernicious others, French-Sheldon had not "gone to Africa as a stunt," but instead had gone "in the interests of her philanthropic work there in which she had already expended a small fortune." Hammond echoes the praise of former years when he congratulates French-Sheldon for "civilizing" Africans not with force but by "providing natives with the tools and equipment which they were so eager to learn about and utilize." Quoting the *New York Times*'s obituary, Hammond uncritically assesses French-Sheldon's efforts as illustrating the belief that "natives" should be allowed to "develop their own civilization rather than 'force the bitter pill . . . down unwilling throats.'"[39] More than a half century after her initial expedition to Africa, French-Sheldon's accomplishments were viewed as presaging a theory of cultural and economic development that was unabashed in its assumptions concerning the superiority of Western civilization and capitalism:

> Mrs. French-Sheldon expressed the sentiments of an enlightened public opinion in the Anglo-American world at the close of the nineteenth century. Although these views were not popularly accepted in that day, her opinions were a forecast of things to follow in the first half of the twentieth century, and this interpretation of colonial government has since become the goal of all believers in national self-determination. . . . In bringing such people as Mrs. French-Sheldon before the Society, the American Geographical Society made a unique contribution to American public opinion by providing a sounding board for diversified theories on the best methods of developing the African continent.[40]

Hammond's uncritical reliance upon *Sultan to Sultan* and French-Sheldon's 1936 obituary in the *New York Times* doom his analysis to the same liberal discourse that infused and informed his sources in ways that preclude a critique of neocolonialism as yet another expression of a racialized discourse on civilization that inevitably places Africans in the position of needing Western tutelage. As we shall see in part 3, this same liberalism that helped propel French-Sheldon into the controversy surrounding the Congo Free State and that framed her negotiations with the Liberian legislature over a rubber concession of her own also undergirded her reincarnation in the United States in the 1920s as a foremother of the modern American woman and normative feminism.

Part III

FEMINIST FOR
A NEW GENERATION:
MASTERING FEMININITY
IN 1920S AMERICA

EIGHT

Taking Feminism on the Road

"My dear," she said, "people thought I was mad.
I was unsexing myself. . . . However, things
have changed considerably."
—May French-Sheldon, quoted in the
Brooklyn Daily Eagle, April 12, 1915

Although a cursory glance at the resuscitation of May French-Sheldon's career as a public pundit in the 1910s and 1920s might suggest that little had changed in her self-presentation and in the American public's perception of new women since the 1890s, such a conclusion ignores a significant shift in the ideology of new womanhood experienced by a new generation of Americans coming of age in the early twentieth century. It also elides the nuanced ways that the aging French-Sheldon responded to the challenge of relating to audiences filled with women and girls who were thirty, forty, even fifty and sixty, years younger than she. French-Sheldon's continuing success on the public circuit in these later years was due to the fortunate confluence between the persona she had earlier crafted, the sorts of attributes valued in the new woman of the 1920s, and the new forms of mass media that French-Sheldon would draw from to make her public appearances readable to a new generation of auditors.

Whereas once French-Sheldon had struggled to present herself as an exception to the rule that woman's place was in the home, in the World War I–era the rule of thumb by which exemplary American womanhood was measured had changed sufficiently to make positioning herself at the center of mainstream nationalist discourses on womanhood a far simpler task. In the 1920s adventurous women who traveled to the most remote and exotic places of the planet, no less than those who broke worlds records in athletic competitions from which women were once banned, were celebrated rather than puzzled at and argued over, and viewed not so much as curiosities as national heroines. Women like French-Sheldon, presenting themselves as "unusual people doing unusual things," were less controversial; in fact they had come to represent a new norm for American women rather than, at worst, a challenge to the natural order of things or, at best, an alternative ideal to a national norm.

Clearly, not all the versions of new womanhood sustained in an earlier era were deemed worthy of the modern women of a new generation. The ideal that French-Sheldon exemplified in the 1890s—what I have been calling the White Queen—won out over other competing ideals of unconventional womanhood, particularly those that depended heavily upon political organizing for social reform measures, involved combativeness with men or male institutions, advocated homosociality or sex-segregation, or smacked of androgyny or sexlessness. While I would not argue that the more politically activist and reformist elements of new womanhood entirely died out, they certainly were nearly drowned out by the newer features of the "modern gal" so loudly touted in the rapidly developing mass media of the age. Depictions of the modern woman in the 1920s sheared off these features of the older ideals deemed no longer relevant or repulsive and added elements such as sexual expressiveness, a heightened valuation of heterosociality, and an excessive ardor for leisure, adventure and feats of physical achievement and daring. Such refinement rendered the label of new or modern womanhood more vague inasmuch as it was related less to particular reforms such as suffrage or temperance or voluntary motherhood and became more a matter of sensibility, demeanor, and—a new word signifying the new importance attached to surface and image in this period—*lifestyle*. Negative images of politically active women who "ranted" about particular political causes appeared alongside a newly hegemonic ideal of the emancipated woman as the exemplary American girl who was always already liberated—the evidence for which, of course, lay with her manner more than with explicitly political commitments. The irony that the emancipation of the latter grew out of the efforts of the former was lost amid the general celebration of the liberated American girl as an outgrowth of the liberatory nature of her national culture. Indeed, despite the publicity and controversy that arose around the suffrage movement in the late 1910s, by the mid-1920s the idea that American women's liberation was indebted to political organizing violated the ideology of "new" new womanhood. Instead of crediting women who had organized collectively to insist on political equality, economic opportunity, or legal protection, the individualist ethic underpinning new womanhood in the 1920s lent credence to the conclusion that gains had been won purely as a function of the innate character of American women. The presence in the nation of strong-willed and courageous individual women who daringly refused to be hampered by unjust ideas or societal pressures evinced the character of a nation that would not vouchsafe inequality before the law or the undermining of its meritocratic institutions. Thus was new woman-hood, even as it grew more vague and broad in connotation, narrowed in these years to suit the ideologies underpinning American national identity formation.

As new womanhood was robbed of association with specific political commitments and was more closely tailored to serve the function of evinc-ing national identity, the nation-, ethnic-, and race-specific connotations surrounding representations of new women became more significant. Some of the most effective backdrops for the display of an American woman's lib-eratory nature naturally became that of foreign locales or situations deemed "exotic"—ethnic or racialized settings where "primitive" or otherwise infe-rior women could be portrayed alongside a plucky, independent, and strong-willed American girl whose individuality, spiritedness, and direct-ness would be offset by the degraded submissiveness or evil craftiness of women belonging to foreign, non-white, or ethnic cultures. As the char-acter of the nation more and more became the subtext for depictions of modern American womanhood, and with nativist sentiment in the nation reaching a violent peak in the early 1920s, the significance of new women as emblems of both national superiority and racial and ethnic purity over-whelmed other aspects of feminist identity in popular representations and discourse.

The key to whether an independently minded woman might be held up for emulation or sneered at as either too shrill or too "masculine" lay not only with her ability to distance herself from particular political agendas but also with her effectiveness at harnessing the dichotomy of modern/primi-tive in ways that threw her Americanness and her whiteness into relief. More than anything in particular that the new woman of the 1920s might advo-cate or even do, the contrast between herself as a "modern" and women who were imagined as "traditional" or even "primitive" assumed critical impor-tance in the construction of emancipated womanhood not as an *alternative ideal* to the norm as it had for previous generations but as a new national norm in itself. Thus what I have identified as the White Queen elements of French-Sheldon's public persona—the exotic setting that her African ad-ventures provided, her insistence on her authority over the primitive as flow-ing naturally from her status as a white, middle-class American woman, the focus in her writings and presentations on African gender relationships, and her claims to having helped "modernize" Africans and the colonial relation-ship between black Africans and white colonizers—placed her in an ex-tremely advantageous position to assume the mantle of "new" new woman-hood as it emerged in the popular culture of the post-suffrage era.

SPEAKING OF WOMEN

Mrs. M. French Sheldon,
explorer of the Congo and friend of many famous men
will speak today at 5 p.m. in Carroll Chapel on
World Celebrities I Have Known
A Wonderful Opportunity
Price 35c, to students 25c[1]

French-Sheldon's lengthy residence in London was interrupted in October 1914, when she and her longtime companion Nellie Butler left England on emergency-issue passports to escape the turmoil and alarm of a country already plunged into war. The couple based themselves in southern California where they had many friends and acquaintances. French-Sheldon arranged to give a few interviews and lectures that winter, a portion of whose proceeds were donated to the Belgian Red Cross. In 1919, once the war was safely over, French-Sheldon and Butler sailed back to England to take up permanent residence again in London. But it would not be long before they returned to the United States. During the war French-Sheldon discovered that there was a good deal of public interest in her African adventures and unconventional career, even though it had been many years since she had been to Africa and the war superceded all other topics. Once again French-Sheldon had found a way to contribute to public debate as an established authority on many questions relating to race, gender, and international relations. The sunshine of the American Southwest and the lucrative nature of the lecture circuit likely added to the allure of the spotlight. The two women gladly arranged to spend most of the winters of the 1920s stateside.

Since French-Sheldon's inspirational appeal lay less in her notes than in herself, it is not surprising that the experienced and engaging lecturer beguiled and invigorated her audiences in this period less and less with prepared lectures and more and more with charming anecdotes, impromptu question-and-answer sessions, and candid autobiographical sketches. Flyers advertising French-Sheldon's versatility and flexibility as a speaker made it clear that French-Sheldon could speak on "any ethical and general subjects as required." Her range, her flair, and her fluid speaking ability combined to make her a popular speaker on the lecture circuit. But it was her "woman's point of view" that was her most valuable asset, and this, combined with the exoticism of her African experiences, were the features that permitted her to carve out a professional niche in the 1920s. Clearly, considering the age of her ethnographic research by this time, French-Sheldon's experiences in Africa only held significance in light of a feminist "point of view" on woman's abilities. She accented the gender angle whenever possible by, for instance, including a caveat at the bottom of her flyer that read: "She is especially interested in the achievements of women and counts her unique experiences chiefly valuable from that point of view." French-Sheldon included this statement, despite her fears of being branded a feminist, because feminism gave her a position from which to have "experiences" and "points of view" and provided the stages on which she stood to share these views with others. In fact, her status as a White Queen and her role as an exemplary new woman and feminist could not be separated. While in the 1890s French-Sheldon had carefully constructed a new woman persona that utilized the conflicting discourses of true womanhood to shore up her claims to authority over the colonization of Africa, a generation later her authority on Africa wholly comprised her claim to being a representative modern American woman. Whereas once the need to be a certain kind of woman to be permitted to have views on colonization predominated, now French-Sheldon needed the colonial backdrop that Africa provided for her views on women to have significance. While Africa was no less crucial to her ability to attract an audience, the point of her presentations in this period dramatically shifted as new womanhood became more and more a vehicle for expressions of national identity. The evidence from this period of her life makes it clear that her views on colonialism, on Africa, and on the sciences of ethnography and geography were enthusiastically processed by her audiences as views on American feminism. As a living testament to "A Woman's Power," as one headline put it, French-Sheldon's reminiscences of her caravan trek through Africa thirty years before delivered a message of nation-specific feminist agency and exemplary new-woman activism to the white and middle-class female audiences that gathered to hear her speak.

In the post-war period, French-Sheldon spoke mostly before schools, colleges, YWCAs, and women's clubs. On February 26, 1923, the respectable and affluent women of the City Federation of Women's Clubs in Pasadena charged fifty cents to persons attending French-Sheldon's lecture in the Raleigh Hotel Ballroom. French-Sheldon also arranged to speak at bookstores and galleries. One of her largest audiences gathered in San Francisco on April 8, 1924, at the posh Paul Elder's gallery. Hundreds of people paid a dollar that night to hear French-Sheldon's tales of adventure and feminine resourcefulness. Later that spring French-Sheldon accepted 40 percent of the proceeds from an engagement that cost spectators a dollar each to attend. In the summer of 1924, fifteen hundred students in attendance at the University of California's summer session were treated to a slideshow by French-Sheldon. Though one of her most well-attended engagements, this lecture only netted French-Sheldon twenty-five dollars in speaker's fees.[2] Lectures at colleges could be profitable, but all too often they were among the least remunerative for French-Sheldon. Still, presentations to colleges were probably the most thrilling for the former explorer given how significant institutions of higher education were to her vision of female emancipation as well as how large and unstinting in their praise college audiences tended to be. French-Sheldon overwhelmed college-age audiences merely with her stage presence, producing exaggerated reviews in college newspapers. In 1925 a college newspaper reported that French-Sheldon's appearance there rendered the university "richer in her possession of genius than she has ever before been." The author of this article dramatically proclaimed the seventy-three-year-old speaker to be "a gust filled with such vigor of thought, choice of diction and achievement fairly throbbing to be related." This "gust," according to the writer, "stood in the English rooms before an audience which filled chairs, doorways, hallways, windows and standing space." The paper reported that "Madame May French-Sheldon came into the rooms to the accompaniment of bursts of welcoming applause from the huge audience which stood as one man before the small woman who was entering for another triumph," The article gushed further,

> It has been said she was the friend of men and women long since gone the long trail. Her vivid magnetism of bearing belied the fact. Her flashing eye, her mobile lips, her every motion filled to the brim with vibrant power declared her the most vitally alive person in the entire hall and such a thing as age falls from her as evil perishes at the sign of the Cross.[3]

French-Sheldon's audiences, both collegiate and non-collegiate, seemed to welcome French-Sheldon's overblown self-presentation. No longer muting her claims to accommodate the expectations and standards of academics and specialists, French-Sheldon had a free hand to invent herself anew. Her expedition in 1891 took on definitive scientific worth in articles, such as one appearing in Sunday edition of the *Los Angeles Times* that claimed she "had a deeper purpose in her trips into South Africa than mere adventure" and went on to attribute to her anthropological discoveries, botanical experiments, even "medical studies that threw light on many questions that had puzzled the medical profession for years."[4] Lake Chala fell deeper and deeper into the bush as the years passed, becoming "one of the most inaccessible parts of Africa."[5] French-Sheldon's circumnavigation of Chala was deemed to have "amazed the scientific world."[6] Reports on French-Sheldon's lectures typically received large write-ups in the Sunday editions of such respectable and widely read newspapers as the *San Francisco Chronicle*, the *San Francisco Examiner*, the *Los Angeles Daily Times*, the *Boston Herald*, the *Boston Globe*, and the *New York Press*. The media eagerly accommodated French-Sheldon's tendency to inflate her accomplishments. Not only did journalists faithfully record French-Sheldon's favorite stories of adventure in Africa verbatim,[7] but the 150 porters she employed on her 1891 expedition turned into 350, and one paper put it at 500.[8] The one "blood brotherhood society" French-Sheldon claimed to have been initiated into in *Sultan to Sultan* mushroomed into 35 by 1910.[9] The admiration she claimed Africans showered on her manifested itself in sixty marriage proposals according to one obituary of French-Sheldon in 1936.[10] In an article in the *Los Angeles Sunday Daily Times,* reportedly such admiration had resulted in the offer of "$150,000 worth of ivory for the capture of a white wife" from a "Sheik."[11] Of course, she never ceased to claim that she was the "first" woman to be accepted into the Royal Geographical Society, despite the fact that fourteen other women were included in the induction that welcomed French-Sheldon into that society. Finally, French-Sheldon made much of her "knighthood"—the conferring of the Belgian *la Croix de Chevalier de l'Ordre de la Couronne* upon her in 1921.[12] French-Sheldon received the award following an intense bout of lobbying of the Belgian monarchy to recognize her lifelong support of Belgian interests in Africa. She left American audiences and the press with the impression that the award, and the button from King Albert I's coat French-Sheldon proudly exhibited to audiences, had been spontaneously bestowed. With such exaggerations and padding of the record few women could match French-Sheldon as a symbol of feminine achievement, even in an era known for its accomplished heroines and "women-firsts."

French-Sheldon had never completely abandoned her public-speaking career and was able to pull out speeches prepared earlier for audiences in Britain, Canada, and the United States without effort. Such presentations, even when their titles purported to focus on "Africa's Burden of an Irrevocable Civilization and Enlightenment," or "Belgium, Little Mother of a Giant," inevitably foregrounded the figure of French-Sheldon, as her presentations always had. However, new talks also appeared on her lecture list explicitly offering the lecturer herself as the main exhibit. Giving presentations primarily to audiences filled with young women, she relied more and more in the 1920s on lectures with titles such as "Spurs Won as a Woman Pioneer Explorer," "Women as Brilliant Opportunists," and "Women Scientists? Explorers and Other Public Workers," as well as her old standbys: "Thrilling Adventures of a Lone White Woman in Savage Africa," "A White Queen in Africa," and "Ten Thousand Miles Through Africa on Foot." Fascination in this period with fame for its own sake shines through lectures such as "The Anvil of Destiny—How Fame is Forged" and "Celebrities I Have Known." The female educational context French-Sheldon typically found herself in prompted talks on "The Value of Travel as a Post-Graduate Education" and "Vocational Education as The Keynote to Success." French-

Sheldon seemed to offer a woman's manual for life in the public sphere, with which she meant to instill in young women aspirations of fame, professional careers, travel, and adventure.

French-Sheldon's at best paternalistic and at worst brutalizing attitudes toward Africans made her no less a gentle hero to her white audiences in the early twentieth century than she had been to audiences thirty years earlier. The lectures she gave, boasting titles such as "Modern Methods of African Civilization," "Possibilities of Native Africans," and "Commercialization Rules the World," promoted a convenient and comforting view of black people as malleable if intellectually limited. This perspective coincided with segregated America's psychic needs and a white New South's economic plans for African-Americans. French-Sheldon's favorite quotes and aphorisms often couched white-supremacist principles in the paternalist rhetorics of uplift and social engineering. One of her favorite quotes was that of Louis Franck, the Belgian colonial minister, who wrote in a 1920 communication to her, "[W]e do not believe in the process of manufacturing some third or fourth class black copies of the white man. We wish to help the native to become, on his own line, a better African."[13] His statements neatly sum up French-Sheldon's lecture "The Faults of the Attempts to Reconstruct the African." Such views correlated well with the conservative "Bookerism" espoused by many liberal whites at the time.[14]

Though demeaning and patronizing, French-Sheldon's depictions of Africans were relatively sympathetic as compared with more vitriolic expressions of race hatred rife in the white-controlled press of this period. Her often favorable portrayal of African customs, along with her consistent indictment of German colonialism in East Africa for its violent nature, lent a humanitarian tone to French-Sheldon's orations and presentations, as they had for some time. If in 1904 these statements had seemed credible enough to persuade W. T. Stead and the Congo Reform Association that French-Sheldon would make an effective friend of the Congolese and exposer of colonial abuses, in the 1920s her "anti-imperialist" imperialism satisfied post-war audiences that they were receiving a balanced and sensitive view of Africans.[15]

Even French-Sheldon's ardent and unrelenting defense of King Leopold II in the first decade of the twentieth century did not diminish her public image as a compassionate observer of Africa and a critic of colonial abuses of power. In fact, her devotion to Belgium, that most appealing underdog of World War I, translated into a humanitarianism of distinctly feminine heroic proportion when she raised money giving lectures during World War I for the Belgian Red Cross. For her efforts on behalf of Belgian refugees, a columnist for the *New York Eagle* argued that French-Sheldon be placed "on a plane alongside Florence Nightingale."[16] While French-Sheldon's relatively minor contributions to the Red Cross could hardly be compared to Nightingale's service in the Crimea (1854–1855) and her crusade to establish nursing as a profession, the comparison between French-Sheldon and Nightingale fit on deeper levels. Both women had made their reputations as national heroines through activities in support of British colonial penetration, in the Crimea and East Africa, respectively. Like French-Sheldon, not only had Nightingale made national service on the colonial frontier seem compatible with the duties of respectable British womanhood, her larger-than-life image exceeded her personal politics and resulted in her eventual reinvention as a feminist foremother in the same period French-Sheldon embraced this identity. Mary Poovey explains how, though Nightingale was not successfully incorporated into women's rights campaigns during the nineteenth century, by the end of the Victorian era, Nightingale's image "so dwarfed the bedridden woman that most people in England were shocked to learn that Nightingale was still alive." "In a very real sense," Poovey goes on to explain, "it had ceased to matter that she was: her image had become far more powerful than anything she could say or write, and it had long escaped her control. . . . Nightingale could not single-handedly determine the ends that her efforts and her image would serve." "Yet precisely because she was displaced by her own image," Poovey concludes, "the name of Florence Nightingale could be enlisted in the feminist cause the woman herself refused to support."[17]

Like that most admired heroine of the nineteenth century, French-Sheldon's feminist persona overwhelmed her self-presentation and designated her a symbol of feminist triumph in the first quarter of the twentieth century despite her avoidance of feminist politics in any specific sense. As Poovey argues so forcefully, this idea should not be dismissed as merely a puzzling irony of history. An avoidance of feminist politics per se, combined with a deft utilization of the intertwined discourses of modernity, colonialism, race, and nationalism succeeded in establishing the positive feminist identity of a "pioneer" for women far more effectively than overt organizing on the behalf of womanhood could have. French-Sheldon met with far more success as a larger-than-life figure of vaguely feminist achievement by concentrating on the image of herself surrounded by African savages than she might ever have by espousing a particular reform or set of feminist demands. Without hope of achieving the iconic status of a Florence Nightingale, French-Sheldon nevertheless enlisted the cooperation of the press in exaggerating the sexual and racial politics of her African experiences to reproduce herself as a minor popular heroine of the day and an American feminist foremother for a new generation.

THE HEROINE IS THE MESSAGE

> Before the feminist had been made one of the issues
> of the day a woman explorer had found her way
> into the heart of Africa.
> —*New York Press*, April 4, 1915

The construction of French-Sheldon as a modern woman, as a feminist role model, and as a national icon in the process, was as much a result of journalists' decisions as French-Sheldon's. The lengthy feature articles reviewing her public appearances frequently took up whole pages in the Sunday editions of newspapers, but during the week she was more than likely sandwiched between stories just as emblematic as hers of modern life, women's advancement, or U.S. supremacy. For example, in the *San Francisco Chronicle* on February 21, 1924, she was squeezed between an article on aviation and an advertisement for an automobile exhibition. The brief article declared, "Mrs. Sheldon is American born, although having spent most of her life thus far in carrying American civilization to other lands." (Whether "other lands" meant Africa or England is unclear.) Once her national allegiance had been established, the *Chronicle* had no problem acknowledging the accolades "crowned heads" had paid to French-Sheldon. Finally, the paper confirmed a new norm for American woman, honoring French-Sheldon as "one of the most remarkable of women" specifically for her distinctly unwomanly behavior: the journalist ended the piece by offering the paper's sincere reverence to French-Sheldon "to whose accomplishments in lines not usually considered within woman's sphere it is a pleasure to pay this tribute."[18]

Even if a report on French-Sheldon's public lecture declined to celebrate French-Sheldon's transgression of gender boundaries so overtly, her association with specifically feminist reforms (such as suffrage) was ensured by the frequent juxtaposition of articles relating to women's activism next to articles about her. Less than two weeks prior to the appearance of the *Chronicle* article cited above, the "Around the Lobbies" section of the *San Francisco Examiner* (April 19, 1924) grouped an article on French-Sheldon's circumnavigation of Lake Chala with an article on prohibition and one concerning female voters. The latter was written with the intention to provoke American readers by taunting them with the claim made by an English society woman that British women made more use of suffrage than American women did. The writer of the article on French-Sheldon put her ahead of the greatest of male explorers and grouped her with other philanthropists of the day by announcing that French-Sheldon, though "possessed of great wealth . . . spent of it lavishly to explore and penetrate into wild regions of Africa which neither Livingstone, Stanley nor Du Chaillu were able to enter." The article clearly wrapped her in the mantle of feminist (not just feminine) heroism when it justified her "bold, even brutal frankness" that "stood her in good stead when attempts were made to impose upon her or refuse her just honors because she was a woman."[19]

In the 1910s and into the 1920s, French-Sheldon was assumed to be a feminist, accused of being feminist, and directly asked if she was one. She responded by distancing herself from certain forms of feminism, in a slightly altered version of the stock rejoinder, "I'm not . . . but . . ." When a member of the faculty at Baylor University in Texas made the mistake of referring to French-Sheldon as a feminist without qualifying the term, French-Sheldon wrote a letter to the professor and made sure the college newspaper quoted from it as an addendum to its next article about her. The *Daily Lariat* reported, "Madame French-Sheldon . . . says she is 'strongly averse to working feminism. I am in favor of ability. I advocate no favor but that resting on ability and efficiency. Girls must face the acid test just as you men do.'"[20] Though French-Sheldon's qualifier, *working,* obscures more than it explains, her answer was not the result of lack of preparation or misquoting. The same sentiments almost verbatim were attributed to French-Sheldon six months earlier, apparently in response to the question of a San Francisco reporter who interviewed French-Sheldon in August 1924. That article reported, "She is not a feminist, but demands the same standard of excellence in work from women and men."[21]

French-Sheldon's emphasis on "the same standard of excellence" and her statement advocating "no favor" suggest that she sought to disavow the protectionist legislation (predominantly aimed at working-class women) that many female reformers favored in this period. French-Sheldon, a proselytizer of individualism and capitalism, could hardly be expected to have endorsed any political position that could be perceived to undermine individuality, personal ambition, or free market principles. More pointedly, her vociferousness on this point perhaps indicates the threat that special considerations or "favor" could pose to the legitimacy of women's accomplishments. A public perception that accomplished women, such as she, were being held to a different "standard of excellence" would diminish the impressiveness of her achievements and undermine the very masculinist nature of her claims. Something akin to this position was held, in fact, by Alice Paul and the "equality" feminists of the National Women's Party who worried that special legislation for working women would undermine the principle of women's equality. French-Sheldon's rejection of a feminism that called for different standards for women and men could have been heard as an endorsement of the Equal Rights Amendment advocated by the

NWP. French-Sheldon's response invited such speculation even while it eliminated the need for her to commit to a political position. By disclaiming only a certain kind of feminism, French-Sheldon kept the option open that she was *some* kind of one. In any case, by employing a modifier rather than shunning the label entirely, French-Sheldon rhetorically demonstrated a desire or a need to sustain a connection to feminism as a set of ideas and images that explained the significance of her public life.

The term *feminism* entered into American popular discourse around 1913, according to scholar Karen Offen.[22] Unlike most changes in language, *feminism* was always self-consciously stylized, overtly seen as in-the-making. Often embedded in rhetorical expressions such as, "What is feminism?" or "What feminism means to me," the term appeared most often in newspaper and magazine articles seeking to define it. Many Americans' first introduction to the word itself, therefore, foregrounded the debates over its application and its integrity.[23] The term's indefinability seemed to defy all efforts to confine it to specific political figures or even an undisputed set of reforms. Instead it soon came to indicate inexactly a desire or ability of a woman to "liberate" herself from the "traditional" domain of Woman—the domestic sphere. Its ambiguity meant if one were a woman and one were acting "modern," feminism must be what one was acting out or advocating.

Despite this purely individualist connotation, the term never successfully detached itself entirely from the combativeness associated with the political organizing of an older, blue-stockinged generation. As Nancy Cott has argued, "Feminism and 'militance' were not the same thing, but common parlance linked them."[24] Modern women's breaking of taboos and rejection of unequivocal male dominance in the public realm suggested a rebellion against masculine prerogative and, therefore, could not be divorced absolutely from political radicalism, or "agitation." Though the popular heroines of the 1920s, along with the professional women and flappers who idolized them, denied almost to a woman that they were feminists, they were obliged to participate actively in the discourse of women's advancement by a media that consistently and often explicitly associated them with feminist struggle for women's equality. Younger women who fancied themselves liberated from traditional views of women but disdained the need for continuing political action or bellicose rhetoric tried to tailor the feminist label into a shape that suited them by attaching qualifiers to the word. They decried *militant, political,* or *radical* feminism. Rejecting language that smacked of special political considerations or organized rebellion, and often affirming the value of marriage, motherhood, heterosexuality, and adornment, young women in the 1920s often chose to embrace the identity of the emancipated woman without positioning themselves as outside the mainstream of society's norms. The difficulty of embracing an identity that at its core consisted of triumph over convention and prejudice without evoking dissension was demonstrated by popular heroines' frequent recourse to the ambivalent phrase (one that has echoed hauntingly in every succeeding generation since) "I'm not a feminist, but . . ."[25]

Claiming to be the "truly modern ones," and confident that "the worst of the fight (was) over," "new-style" feminists, such as *Harper's Magazine* columnist Dorothy Dunbar Bromley, gladly accepted the gains of the past but threw away the political analyses of gender as a social system that had permitted them.[26] In an article published in 1927, Bromley vilified "sex-conscious" feminists for thinking of themselves in terms of the group rather than of the individual, but appropriated an extra-domestic vision for the modern American woman nonetheless.

> Feminist New-Style proclaims that men and children shall no longer circumscribe her world, although they may constitute a large part of it. She is intensely self-conscious whereas the feminists were intensely sex-conscious. Aware of possessing a mind, she takes a keen pleasure in using that mind for some definite purpose; and also in learning to think clearly and cogently against a background of historical and scientific knowledge.[27]

At stake for Bromley as well as for French-Sheldon and other "modern gals" in this period was not feminism as political practice but feminist liberation as the signaling characteristic of a superior woman, one with privileged access to "historical and scientific" knowledges. Such access demonstrated that she was a full-fledged member of a modern society. But this discursive positioning could not be established without recourse to the language of feminism. The final statements of Bromley's article excoriating women who "rant about equality when they might better prove their ability" disclose the ideological yoking of the bourgeois discourses of feminism, nationalism, and modernism. "Feminist New-Style," Bromley exclaims,

> aspires to understand *the meaning of the twentieth century* as she sees it expressed in the skyscrapers, the rapid pace of city life, the expressionistic drama, the abstract conceptions of art, the new music, the Joycian novel. She is acutely conscious that she is being carried along in the current of these sweeping forces, that *she and her sex are in the vanguard* of change. *She knows that it is her American, her twentieth-century birthright* to emerge from a creature of instinct into a full-fledged individual who is capable of molding her own life. And in this respect she holds that she is becoming man's equal.[28]

Feminism in this view is imagined as part of the "sweeping forces" of change. A central element of progress, women's equality belongs to the modern era and the new generation of American women who personify that era. Bromley's assertion that equality and the realization of a fully subjectified self (a "full-fledged individual" rather than a "creature of instinct") constituted her "American, her twentieth-century birthright" reveals the progressive mechanism by which a liberal notion of feminism, emptied of explicit political content, had become a defining national characteristic by the mid-1920s. The evolutionary paradigm implicit in Bromley's celebration of modern woman's transgression of "outmoded" codes of domesticity set American women apart from women of other times. It also distanced them from women of other lands, imagined as non-contemporaneous with the modern era or industrialized world. As a marker of modernity (the "meaning of the twentieth century"), feminism was ineluctably bound to the presumed superiority and contemporaneity of industrialized civilizations, and to the United States as the leader of such in particular.

French-Sheldon did not endorse women's capacities in general as much as she declared herself to be an exceptionally independent woman. A headline that appeared often proclaimed her radical individualism more than any other. It read, "Mrs. French-Sheldon Would Take No Woman Companion Because 'I Might Have to Take Care of Her' and No Man Because 'He Might Want to Take Care of Me.'"[29] By the 1920s, as emancipation came to seem less a matter of political positioning and more of a matter of personal style, the independent self-portrait French-Sheldon projected was all it took to designate her a feminist. While the term *feminist* occurs often enough in interviews with French-Sheldon held in the 1910s, by the 1920s reporters ceased asking for clarifications on this point and concentrated on imagistic assertions of the inspiring role she had played in "opening doors" for women. They and French-Sheldon saw little distinction between her acting as a feminist and other women's advocating feminist reform of society. French-Sheldon privately imagined herself on a par with Susan B. Anthony, whose portrait she drew in chalk and placed in a scrapbook next to an unidentified woman's face remarkably resembling her own younger self that, she claimed, had come to her in a dream.[30] In keeping with her individualist and apolitical vision, French-Sheldon claimed that her personal successes had helped change public perceptions of women's abilities. French-Sheldon pointed most frequently to her induction in the Royal Geographical Society in 1913 to demonstrate how her accomplishments had helped integrate previously sex-segregated institutions. (She obfuscated this point somewhat by failing to mention that women were soon barred from membership by a reinstatement of the rule excluding them in 1892, and subsequently were welcomed again to the society in 1913. Such evidence would have gone to show that French-Sheldon's induction could not have affected the permanent lifting of the injunction. Journalists cooperated in crediting French-Sheldon with opening up the society to women by further blurring over the time lag. One journalist writing in 1915 granted, "[T]he innovation in her case has led to the admission of many other worthy explorer-women in recent years—since the change in the society's constitution three years ago.")[31] French-Sheldon's point was that she had accomplished what most women could not "long before the feminist had been made one of the issues of the day," as another journalist put it.[32] French-Sheldon located feminist struggle and her role in it in the recent past and urged women to simply follow her glorious example now that the doors were opened for them.

Mostly French-Sheldon thought that women in the 1920s suffered from little other than lack of aspiration or purpose. As far as structural barriers, she believed that the current generation of women was constrained by nothing more substantial than the "pessimism" of some who doubted their abilities. Her assertion that such pessimism "should only be a stimulant to uncrowned heroes" reflected French-Sheldon's reliance (and, indeed, that of all feminist heroines in this period) on such "pessimism" or prejudice to justify the public acclaim she received. Since individual achievement was French-Sheldon's preferred method of dismantling the "galling" and "unjust" "proscriptions of former days," she saw the inspiration she was able to supply as providing the final touch necessary for the achievement of women's advancement. French-Sheldon's politics in the 1920s denied any need for an oppositional stance vis-à-vis American society, now that her own struggle with male authorities and institutions (such as the Royal Geographical Society) had cleared the way. She often contrasted the 1920s with the 1890s to demonstrate the progress that her actions had instigated. Recasting her personal history, French-Sheldon contended, "Things have changed considerably since I made my first trip . . . now I am praised for the very thing that the general public condemned at that time." French-Sheldon ignored the nearly universal accolades she received as a new woman in the 1890s to construct a history of feminist struggle, the need for which was over. Presenting herself as a veteran of the previous struggles against "prejudice," French-Sheldon pointed to women's lack of "will" as the only issue left to consider. She lamented, "Woman are likely not to have a strong purpose in life, . . . and a great purpose is the greatest force in life. With a strong purpose and an indomitable will one can triumph over anything, over disease, discouragement, despair, obstacles of every kind." French-Sheldon did not list "men" or even "prejudice" among the obstacles women might meet with; she implied that the only gender barrier left lay in women themselves and offered her personal example as the best remedy for that predicament.[33]

CONCLUSION: A WOMAN'S POWER

Madame French-Sheldon knows by now the vastness of her
sway over our hearts but not even she can estimate the
projecting influence of her contagious personality upon
the future adventurous undertakings of her . . . auditors.
— *Baylor Towers,* March 1925

College newspaper reports and letters written to French-Sheldon by young
fans reveal the extent to which young middle-class women accepted her
construction of herself and shared her version of feminism. French-Sheldon met some of her greatest triumphs in the 1920s on the stages of
women's colleges, in front of audiences filled with young, middle-class
female admirers who eagerly embraced French-Sheldon and her views. The
Baylor University "coeds" in Waco, Texas, were among her most enthusiastic admirers. Apparently, French-Sheldon gave a stunning performance
there in February 1925. Her lecture was widely extolled in local papers with
articles about her that ran for weeks. The praise of the university newspaper, the *Daily Lariat,* knew no bounds. In keeping with French-Sheldon's
(strangely cross-dressed) charismatic persona, the paper awkwardly acknowledged that she "grasped her audience like a new father juggles his first
born," and went on to say that her audience, "like that same new heir," im-
pressionably hung on every word and "every variation of mental suggestion" she offered. "In such a presence" and "before such a power" as French-
Sheldon's, the *Lariat* declared itself speechless—claiming that words "are
not even symbolic" and cannot adequately convey the effect upon her auditors.[34]

The collegiate hyperbole displayed in this amateur journalist's account
of French-Sheldon's talk at a Texas college was not merely a reflection of
youthful irrepressibility. A headline in the *Waco News-Tribune* the following
Sunday confirms that a "Lone Woman Who Quelled Rebel Caravan in
Heart of Africa (Held) Baylor Audience Spellbound."[35] The female students at Baylor seemed to have been among the most affected by French-
Sheldon's lectures in the 1920s. They asked French-Sheldon to write a special message for the second issue of the *Baylor Towers,* a "magazine for and
by and about Baylor women," which was slated for publication that month.
French-Sheldon contributed a congratulatory message for the second issue
that, along with the coverage of her in the college and local press attests to
her utilization of, and inescapable association with, a public discourse of
feminism. French-Sheldon praised the establishment of the *Baylor Towers,*
calling it "an extensive forum to propound the work of girls today!—A
forum from which may be heralded the accomplishments, the progress, the

fulfillment of splendid opportunities women have without old proscriptions of former days which were so galling so unfair and unjust."[36]

The student editor of the magazine introduced French-Sheldon's article by reminding readers that French-Sheldon had "swept Baylor women into a spontaneous paean of praise with her electrifying address some weeks ago, and into an overwhelming pride of their own sex so magnificently displayed." She acknowledged French-Sheldon's effectiveness as a role model who inspired her female audience to translate that "pride of their own sex" into personal ambitions in the public sphere. The power of French-Sheldon's "projecting influence" seems to have rested partly in French-Sheldon's manner and partly in the attractiveness of the liberal feminist content of her address.

French-Sheldon's congratulatory message assured her female readers that their education, "if preparing for some vocation,—it matters not in what sphere," would afford them "an enlargement of understanding, and expansion of character, with an asset of attributes from which to draw at all times." She comforted them with the idea that "developing the 'Limbs of the Mind' through the instrumentality of education just as have the boys taken pride in the developing in sports their physical limbs . . . [was the surest way to personal success, for the] day will come when the stars and winners in sports must retire. Yours will be a perpetual advance, greater excellency, larger vision, more extended influence throughout life."[37] In French-Sheldon's message, the outside world was there for the educated woman's taking and there was no mention of becoming better wives or mothers.

Still, French-Sheldon did not mention political struggle, collective organizing, or simple rebelliousness either. Though she acknowledged that "disturbing elements of pessimism" (presumably the voices of those who lacked confidence in the inherent abilities of women) did exist and implied that lack of opportunity had hindered the achievements of women in the past, she counseled that the best response to this situation was individual assertiveness rather than political resistance. For inspiration, she quoted the following lines from the preeminent nineteenth-century guide to individualist self-realization, Ralph Waldo Emerson:

> Not in the clamour of the crowded streets,
> Not in the shouts and plaudits of the throng,
> But in ourselves are triumphs and defeats

The tools of self-improvement, professional aspirations, and sufficient inspiration apparently were all that women lacked. After all, according to French-Sheldon, the "rusty bolts of prejudice" already had been forced and the door flung open.

French-Sheldon's significance as a public feminist lies in the way that her audiences constructed her as a foremother and a renegade who had helped fling that metaphorical door open. The young women in French-Sheldon's audiences felt themselves on the cusp of a new era, one that did not bar women from public roles, political influence, or economic independence. And they saw French-Sheldon as their guide to the modern woman's liberated future—even as the metaphorical door itself leading to it. A poem of adoration written to French-Sheldon by one of the Baylor students posits her as such:

> To Mrs. French-Sheldon:
> As often as I read so have I felt
> The touch of minds and men: so have I known
> A yearning to behold men who have grown
> Into such colossal size. My spirit knelt
> In homage: then in fancy it would melt
> And recreate itself into tone
> All hopeful that, at least, it might blown
> Into their banquet hall. My mind had dwelt
> On means of entrance by some magic key:
> And then a Jewelled door swung wide for me
> And through this scintillating door I see
> The answer to my innate yearnings call.
> And while I love the view within the hall
> Shall I not love the door disclosing all?[38]

Here one can see the romantic lens through which French-Sheldon's young fans viewed her.[39] Also reflected in this fan's vision of the popular heroine is French-Sheldon's longstanding theme of her initiation into the public sphere and pantheon of great men and historical deeds—only now French-Sheldon appears as the vehicle for other women as well.

Female audience members fairly swooned at the thrilling sight of French-Sheldon relating her experiences in Africa. "I have told many of my dearest friends of my experience that magic afternoon," a young woman named Valerie Rochen wrote to French-Sheldon. "For was it not an experience to sit for three quarters of an hour before the living embodiment of the Spirit of all that is good and true and Beautiful in Womanhood? I will forget many geometric theorems, yes, but never, never some of the things you told me that afternoon." Rochen pleaded with "Madame" at the end of her letter to acknowledge her in some way. "Madame," she begged, "will you accept all the prayers and thanks from the heart of an eighteen-year old girl, given in utter sincerity please?"[40]

Another young woman, a high-school teacher of girls, expressed a similar confidence in French-Sheldon's ability to impress herself on students.

Exhilarated by French-Sheldon's speech at a local YWCA in northern California, yet sorrowful that a favorite student of hers had not been able to attend the lecture, the high-school teacher respectfully beseeched French-Sheldon to treat her city to a repeat performance so that her student might be directly inspired by French-Sheldon. Addressing herself to "Madam French-Sheldon," Cobby de Stivers pleaded with the renowned explorer to pardon her "impertinence" in expressing all that the presentation had meant to her. De Stivers explained her need to reach out to French-Sheldon as a consequence of being moved not only by someone whose life evinced "accomplishment and success" but by someone whose "whole personality so inspired" her as to have left a "genuine and lasting impression" upon her life merely through the "contact" that French-Sheldon's speech had provided. De Stivers expressed gratitude specifically for the "intimate" nature of the event, entirely apart from the fact that the presentation was made in a large lecture hall at a YMCA and had been attended by many dozens of people. The aim of the young teacher's letter was not only to thank French-Sheldon for the inspiring effect of her presence but also to beg her to make herself available for the high-school girl who had been absent that day and who, de Stivers strongly believed, would benefit in untold ways if only she had the opportunity to be "near enough to you to feel that she had received a portion of your invincible courage and will." De Stivers explained her desire that this young friend be exposed to French-Sheldon by saying, "I dream great things for her, and I want the memory of you to be one of the good things that I have been able to bring to her life." She signed her letter, "From a sincere admirer."[41]

Such admiration was characteristic of young women's responses to French-Sheldon, but older women felt the thrill also. In a letter to French-Sheldon, the president of the League of American Pen Women praised French-Sheldon highly and passed on a compliment that she believed summed up the club's appraisal of French-Sheldon's lecture. Instead of paraphrasing, she wanted to convince French-Sheldon that she was not exaggerating by quoting a member as saying, "I regard Mrs. Sheldon's talk as one of the star events of my life."[42] Men, also, recognized French-Sheldon's effect on her audiences and often acknowledged her inspirational impact. One chairman of a publicity board wrote to French-Sheldon: "I cannot refrain from saying that I consider your visit to Baylor University the most heartening and stimulating to high intellectual achievement I have known. That your work will be a constant ideal to our women no one can doubt."[43]

Without a doubt French-Sheldon, although eighty years old in 1927 with her "adventures" in Africa more than thirty years behind her, moved her auditors deeply. Certainly French-Sheldon's charting of new territory for women overlay her stories of charting Africa, as it had since the 1890s.

But letters and journalistic comments from the 1920s reveal that French-Sheldon's presentations suggested a bit more to audiences in the period following the passage of the Nineteenth Amendment. With the emergence of a feminist discourse and its dissipation of the woman movement down to a celebration of individual women's defiance of separate-sphere ideology sufficient to produce a new norm of feminist achievement, French-Sheldon became an emblem of feminism without hardly being its advocate. Moreover, as these letters from female admirers attest, the story of French-Sheldon's achievements took on a distinctly erotic cast that lent themselves to a homoerotic relationship developing between the "spirit that is all good and true and Beautiful in Womanhood" and her young auditors. As I will explore in the next chapter, it was not just French-Sheldon's dramatic style, notable accomplishments, and pleasing deportment that made her a representative of feminism and an inspiring role model. The imperialist images French-Sheldon had always invoked in her writing and presentations in the 1920s took on fetishistic significance and helped to position her as a (hybrid sexual) subject of a historical narrative. Through a process of identification engendered by such new mass cultural phenomena as Hollywood's "star system," French-Sheldon's presentations extended the promise of subjecthood to those female spectators who shared the "modern gal's" nationality, race, and class. I shall explore in the next chapter how French-Sheldon, as the walking, talking protagonist of her own story of empire, found herself perfectly positioned in the 1920s to play the part of the White Queen, by that point a star persona of nearly cinematic proportion.

NINE

Masquerading as the Subject of Feminism

Am I not a Boy? Yes I am—Not!
—Headline, *Boston American,*
July 14, 1913

The rhetorical and psychological contortions of identity performed publicly in the 1910s and 1920s reveal some women's conflicted desire to align themselves with feminist liberation as demonstrably modern American women while maintaining distance from the denial of sexual difference that a popular understanding of radical or militant feminism might appear to warrant. Such contortions are clearly in evidence in French-Sheldon's presentations and in her intense relationships with her audiences in these years. In this chapter, I examine the social practices and psycho-sexual processes presenting French-Sheldon's female audience members with opportunities to construct a feminist subject position based on their identification with her as a *Bebe Bwana* or "Woman-Man." The oscillations, reversals, and hybridic formulations converging in these years to create an exclusively white American feminist subject position reproduced French-Sheldon as a "feminist fetish"[1] for audiences who once simply admired her as a novelty. Feminist theorizing of the female spectator and film, along with psychoanalysts' formulations of fetishism, have informed my analysis of the effect French-Sheldon had on audiences in the 1920s and have shaped my thoughts on the relationship between the emergence of the White Queen as an archetype and the development of twentieth-century American feminist identity and subjectivity.[2]

American newspapers possessed significant power to determine which modern women were appropriate as popular role models and which were not.[3] For May French-Sheldon and most of the popular heroines of the

1920s, the introduction of the daily newspaper with mass circulation was crucial to their ability to market themselves and fashion a career out of their unconventional lifestyles or accomplishments. The film industry turned others into *stars,* a new word used to describe those individuals catapulted to the pinnacle of fame. Whether disseminated in print or on film, new feminine idols brought the "new" or "modern" woman to the forefront of the American conscious in the 1910s. The class- and race-specific feminine ideal French-Sheldon had helped to launch two decades before was sustained by the growth of a mass media and proliferated in its glare. This ideal reached full maturation in the post-suffrage 1920s, once a mass culture had firmly established itself as arbiter of American popular culture and once a vision of modernity that included an endorsement of women's advancement had achieved a distinct degree of hegemony as evidenced by the passage of the Nineteenth Amendment in 1920.

The inception and ascendancy of mass culture in the 1920s spoke to emergent gender ideologies on several levels. According to cultural historian Billie Melman, "[W]hat distinguishes the twenties from the previous decades is not only the unprecedented volume of writing on the contemporary young female, but also the development of forms classified as 'feminine,' and the modulation of 'masculine forms' into 'feminine' ones."[4] As Melman suggests and other cultural theorists have noted, the relationship between mass culture and "the feminine" was an overdetermined one. The "modern gal" was a creation of a mass media obsessed with the issue of feminine sexuality and the female role; the mass audience-member was most frequently visualized as a young, impressionable, and pleasure-seeking woman; and mass media itself was deemed a degraded, "feminine" cultural form by its harshest critics.[5] Thus, the influence of mass communications on popular notions of femininity was of a material nature as well as a textual one. New ideals of femininity were erected and new psychic relationships to them and to their images were manufactured by technologies that purported merely to broadcast them. Moving the "liberated" or "emancipated" modern woman from the margins to the center stream of American popular culture involved new forms of identity formation and subject constitution as well as new ideas about Woman.

Just as French-Sheldon's attractive and ultra-feminine appearance had preempted a dismissal of her as a violator of true womanhood in the 1890s, the lavender dress and white lace scarf she frequently donned for public presentations in the 1920s pleased audiences and undermined any critique of her as "mannish" for her masculine achievements.[6] French-Sheldon was an expert in negotiating this tricky ideological terrain. By 1920 she could draw on almost thirty years of experience playing the female embodiment of the adventure narrative while dodging an association with that desiccated apparition, the eccentric, spinster adventuress. Even considering her charming and congenial manner, eluding the dismissive label of *eccentric* was no mean feat for a woman in her seventies who had been widowed half her life and boasted of traveling through Africa unaccompanied by any white man—and in a tiara, no less. To the contrary, French-Sheldon betrays no tendency to downplay the more gaudy elements of her White Queen persona that might have permitted a dismissal of her as ex-centric or unrepresentative of a national norm of womanhood. Indeed, the tiara and the other excessive signs of fashion accessorization that had long accorded this unconventional woman protection from the charge of "mannishness" became even more pronounced in the last stages of her public career. Sensationalist written material, a tendency toward hyperbole in person, and a dramatic toilette had served French-Sheldon well in her career from the beginning. The lessons she took from her earlier success stood her in good stead three decades later, as she faced audiences primed by the cinema to enjoy women who represented glamour, adventure, and excess for its own sake.

MASTERING FEMININITY:
LONG LIVE THE WHITE (DRAG) QUEEN!

> The Queen is dead. Long live the Queen!
> —Dorothy Dunbar Bromley, "Feminist
> —New Style," *Harper's*, 1927

> You don't think me unwomanly even if I have
> explored the wilds of Africa. I don't look so, do I?
> —French-Sheldon, quoted in the
> *New York Evening Sun*, February 15, 1915

> One cannot conceive of a more womanly woman.
> —Excerpt from French-Sheldon's promotional flyer

French-Sheldon was excessively feminine in more than just her accoutrements. Not merely a "Woman-Master" as the sobriquet *Bebe Bwana* proclaimed her to be, she was a "Master Woman," too. But French-Sheldon was not alone in her construction of masterful femininity. The ubiquity of the fantasy that one personified womanliness, even as one claimed masculine prerogative and authority on the basis of such, caught the attention of psychoanalysts in the period. A body of scholarship emerged in response to their witnessing of professional white women acting out what seemed like a newly discovered neurosis. Before the end of the decade, psychiatry had developed a name for the masterful art of super-womanly women: *masquerade*. Joan Riviere's essay "Womanliness as a Masquerade," first published in the *International Journal of Psychoanalysis* in 1929, asserts that a woman "whose aim is to obtain 'recognition' of her masculinity from men" will claim possession of "the penis" indirectly in order to conciliate while dominating and, according to Stephen Heath's reading of the essay, "guard against retaliation of her victory by the self-sacrifice she makes for weaker women."[7] Riviere was talking about an ultra-feminine analysand who gave very scholarly presentations as an avowed intellectual and professional academic, but her formulation of the masquerade applies equally well to the public persona French-Sheldon had cultivated. As an exceptionally feminine heroine participating in the typically masculine realms of Victorian exploration and travel writing, French-Sheldon appears to fit the notion of the masquerade as it was conceptualized by Freudian analysts in her own time and since.[8]

As material presented in preceding chapters has shown, French-Sheldon strove to engage in what theorists of the masquerade have identified as "a public discourse with men" in many ways. Among the more obvious is her infiltration of elite and virtually male-only geographical and scientific societies as a result of an expedition meant to put her in dialogue with colonial policy makers. Her 1885 translation of Flaubert's *Salammbô* and dedication of the orientalist novel to Henry Morton Stanley provides another example of her attempts to triangulate masculine and masculinist public discourses, as does her interventions in the controversy surrounding the Congo reform movement. Yet for all of the efforts she exerted in the direction of men and masculinist space, French-Sheldon reveled in a super-femininity that explicitly and implicitly proclaimed her mastery of the sphere of Woman. If Riviere and other theorists of this inter-subjective state are right, *masquerading* as Woman effectively saved French-Sheldon from the confining experiences of *being* a woman on the level of the Subject. Her masquerade, involving the perverse logic of a woman cross-dressing as Woman, did not just buffer her from accusations of usurping male prerogative, it enhanced the power of her self-representation by demonstrating her ability to appropriate the feminine like a man. She was a woman, but she performed her femininity as a man playing a woman might, with the ultra-feminine gestures and excesses of a drag queen.[9]

"Drag," to quote Alisa Solomon, "changes meaning depending on who's wearing it" and "which way the vestments are crossed."[10] In other words, assuming male authority and status is not as simple as adopting male dress or mimicking men. French-Sheldon, like most of her generation, always avoided any hint of masculine attire, not simply from the desire to temper an unconventional image but from a recognition that attempts to appropriate the masculine in dress usually wound up highlighting the very inability of a woman to "wear" or perform masculinity. As a woman who forged her public identity in the 1890s, French-Sheldon would have been sensitive to the danger of an unsuccessful attempt to authorize oneself by taking on a masculine appearance.[11] A September 1891 *Punch* cartoon, entitled "The Sterner Sex!" exactly illustrates this point. The cartoon features two women, both in full-length skirts, one with a racquet in her hand (denoting athleticism) and the other in a man's blazer and fedora. The caption has the woman in the fedora asking her friend's opinion about her decision to wear "Fred's" hat and coat. The response: "Well—it makes you look like a Young Man you know, and that's so Effeminate!"[12] The cartoon gives expression to the anxieties of new women regarding the adoption of gender ambiguous or ambivalent attire, even as it ventilates fears that the current generation of developing manhood was being effeminized by such women. In fact, although many of the debates surrounding new womanhood in the 1890s were of far more substance, few subjects elicited a more acidic response from Anglo or American pundits than new-woman fashion. As a result most women of French-Sheldon's generation took pains to avoid the ridicule generated in response to middle-class women's infrequent but conspicuous attempts to cross-dress in these years.

On the other hand, as Mary Russo puts it, "[T]o put on femininity with a vengeance suggests the power of taking it off."[13] "Precisely because 'man' is the Universal Human and 'woman' the gussied-up other," an ultra-feminine mask can suggest the power to create a feminine self over which one's inner "human" will has control.[14] Many feminist theorists, among them Luce Irigaray, Nancy Miller, Mary Ann Doane, Linda Kauffman, and Judith Butler, have conceptualized "drag" or the "hyperbolization of gender" along these lines.[15] French-Sheldon's adoption of a White Queen costume as described in her primary text *Sultan to Sultan* and in her appearance at the 1893 Chicago World's Fair, for instance, took advantage of the cultural logistics of drag. Thirty years later French-Sheldon still invoked the image of herself in full-length ball gown, tiara, and long blonde wig to hyper-realize a larger-than-life feminine persona for new generations of American women. The contrast that her sweet grandmotherly appearance in the 1910s and 1920s made with the images she projected of herself in her presentations—that of a sexually alluring femme fatale, a super-macho queller of rebel soldiers, and a shooter of rapacious sheiks—amounts to a performance of femininity even more internally conflicted than did her previous middle-aged incarnation. Though most journalists commented approvingly on French-Sheldon's true-woman demeanor throughout her early career, thirty years later they seemed to take delight less in her acquiescence to normative femininity than in the extravagance of her contrasting selves.

While journalists in the 1890s had found it difficult to criticize a speaker who made her audiences feel "as though they were being entertained by some genial, kind hostess,"[16] the press of the 1910s and 1920s positively reveled in the gender duality that the "Noted Woman Explorer . . . who penetrated Darkest Africa" exhibited while "sitting at the daintily appointed breakfast table in the Woman's Athletic Club, dressed in a black frock, a lace shawl over her shoulders."[17] Journalistic emphasis on her appearance took on a decidedly ironic tone in these years. One journalist chortled, "she owns a shawl, too!" which indicates a slight but significant shift from mere relief at French-Sheldon's appearance to a perverse fascination with it.[18] For instance, despite the ultra-conservative attire perfectly suitable for an aging middle-class woman in the 1920s that French-Sheldon is wearing in all the photos accompanying the many write-ups about her in the newspapers, journalists' copy tended to linger on the image of the "dainty things" that French-Sheldon told them she had brought with her to the "jungle."[19] French-Sheldon encouraged the press with coquettish banter and flirtatious references to herself as a target of African lust. Indeed, the banner she had broadly waved in the 1890s emblazoned with the phrase *Noli me tangere,* or "Touch Me Not," she had waved so purposely thirty years before was little in evidence in these accounts. When journalists did mention the banner, their commentary on it only served to heighten the image of French-Sheldon as an emphatically sexual being who had been placed in a highly charged sexual context.

The press's sexualization of French-Sheldon countered any hint of "blue-stocking" that her age otherwise might have brought to mind, given the widespread portrayals in the 1920s of the first generation of new women as bitter, ranting, and sexually repressed man-haters. Stereotypes appearing in the mass media, such as the "Mannish Lesbian" and the aged "Lady in Lavender" both of whom "taught young girls to reject men and repress their own sexuality," tarred French-Sheldon's generation of women-identified women and reformers with being the "enemies of liberated women," according to Carroll Smith-Rosenberg.[20] Though, in many ways, French-Sheldon constituted a classic example of this first generation of new women even down to her childlessness and the presence of a woman-companion at her side, the elderly explorer was taken for the muse of modern woman, not her enemy. French-Sheldon, though dressed as a typical woman of her generation in "all lace and violet-tones," escaped the outmoded asexualism of the Lady in Lavender and avoided the stereotype of the eccentric spinster despite the many qualities she shared with both figures. The set of erotically charged images and narratives that the African context invoked located the elderly woman well within the purview of a "new" new womanhood that depended so heavily upon exotic situations for the sexual expressiveness that was the signal characteristic of a modern woman's liberation.[21]

The cooperation of the press was crucial in helping French-Sheldon create an elderly persona that appealed to younger, flapper tastes. Indeed, reporters' affection for French-Sheldon and eagerness to ascribe youthful qualities to her were unrestrained. One can only wonder if the journalist was joking when describing French-Sheldon as a "dyed-in-the-batik bohemian bubbling over with the gay, pushing spirit of Parisian Bohemia," since the accompanying photo showed her encased in the somber and respectable black overcoat, sensible black shoes, substantial hat and spectacles, of a prototypical elderly woman.[22]

A section of the *New York Press,* entitled "Feminine Views, Reviews, and Interviews of Interest to Men and Women," gleefully countered their readers' expectations to report,

> No, she isn't a stalwart, muscular person, with a somewhat mannish air and appearance, as you or I, hedged about with the traditions of the past as regards woman, might expect, but it is instead a slender, little woman, with gracious manner and gentle voice, and wears the daintiest of collars.[23]

Journalists came to adopt a distinctly playful, slightly flirtatious tone with French-Sheldon, even hinting at a libidinous nature beneath her eminently respectable black frocks, lavender dresses, and lace scarves. The consistent and sincere celebration of French-Sheldon's vivacity and allure despite her advanced age and wholly conservative attire indicates that journalists and audiences were reacting to something far less straightforward than beauty. Somehow French-Sheldon's ultra-conservative exterior, combined with her tales of mastery and imperial adventure, attracted and stimulated audiences in the 1920s on an erotic level. Certainly, the erotic-tinged adulation lavished on the near octogenarian by some of her youngest female fans is evidence of the sexual magnetism her contradictory persona inspired in this period.

THE ROSY TULIP OF OPPORTUNITY

"Baylor Beauty Fails to Land Kiss From World-Famous Explorer At Reception," a Texas college newspaper provocatively bemoaned in 1925. At the "Colonial reception" given by a chapter of the Daughters of the American Revolution in Waco, Texas, according to the student writer of this article, one "Baylor beauty" named "Ouida," missed "becoming the most envied woman on Baylor University campus" by neglecting to take seriously French-Sheldon's promise to kiss "the next young girl" who came to greet her. According to the highly titillating article, "Ouida felt magnetism in the air" emanating from "the most electric human document that has ever turned its current on Waco" and rushed to join the "privileged few avidly lingering within this powerful influence." The article rushed on to report that, unlike the other young girls present, "Ouida evidently used her eyes to good effect. For Madame Sheldon leaned forward in her inimical impetuosity and, holding Ouida's hand a cherished instant longer, exclaimed, 'My dear, the next young girl who comes I am going to say, "Yes, I know you are so happy to meet me. Lean down, my dear and kiss me!"'" The college newspaper tantalized readers with the image of Ouida and French-Sheldon in an embrace only to conclude on a note of regret: "Ouida's fate trembled in the balance. Quick as a flash she replied, 'Then I'll go back and come in again!' But she didn't go. And . . . the rosy tulip of opportunity was lost."[24] The double floral metaphor leaves no doubt as to the homoerotic feelings the seventy-eight-year-old French-Sheldon produced in young women in these years.

The "rosy tulip" that French-Sheldon held out to her young female audiences was not so much the promise of a kiss as it was the gender-blending possibilities that she personified. The charm that captivated and thrilled Ouida and others in the 1920s issued from French-Sheldon's seemingly masterful handling of Africans as well as herself, indicating that a virile "will" lay within her womanly figure. Another article in the same college paper that month (mentioned in a previous chapter) utilized a distinctly paternal metaphor, oddly enough, to describe the power of her persona when it raved that "she grasped her audience like a new father juggles his first born and the audience responded like that same new heir to every variation of mental suggestion." The article went on to associate "Madame Sheldon" with Christ by claiming that frailty and age fell from her as she began to speak, "as evil perishes at the sign of the Cross."[25] Paternal metaphors to describe French-Sheldon's performances typically appeared in juxtaposition with effulgent praise of her ultra feminine deportment and sensuality; such a set of contradictory messages constitutes a case of what Marjorie Garber calls "unmarked" cross-dressing.

Garber cautions scholars not to overlook the "unconscious of transvestism as a speaking symptom, a language of clothing which is, tacitly, both dress and address" even if, or especially if, this "address" is unmarked or "latent."[26] Some entertainers who do not overtly claim to be 'female impersonators,'" she argues, "may in fact signal their cross-gender identities onstage, and . . . this quality of crossing—which is fundamentally related to other kinds of boundary-crossing in their performances—can be more powerful and seductive than explicit 'female impersonation' . . . [which] may in fact merely literalize something that is more powerful when masked or veiled—that is, when it remains unconscious."[27] Garber points to several famous (male) personalities, such as Elvis Presley and French-Sheldon's contemporary Rudolph Valentino, as illustrative examples of the power of an "unconscious" transvestism. The unmarked or unconscious transvestism is not a presentation of a man explicitly cross-dressed as a woman, but instead invokes the logic of drag through expressions of excess and mimicry that are open to both women and men. Following Roland Barthes's thoughts on fashion, Garber is even more interested in the "rhetorical or latent signified," all the more powerful because it is "received" rather than consciously "read." Building off of Lacan's reading of Freud, Garber has argued that the "seemingly feminine" constitutes a "virile display" of the possession of the phallus. The hyper-realization of femininity, therefore, can signal the possession of the phallus in women as well as men.[28]

Similarly, Esther Newton maintains in *Mother Camp: Female Impersonators in America* that "drag says, my 'outside' appearance is feminine, but my essence 'inside' is masculine."[29] French-Sheldon's written texts and personal presentation "said" much the same. She vigorously defended her outward femininity and explicitly directed her exceptionality amorphously away from her body to locate it in her determination, her spirit, her "will." Seen in this light, the press's concentration on French-Sheldon's excessive femininity embedded within articles that authorized her to speak on a wide range of domestic and international concerns is less puzzling. Her hyperbolized performance of femininity set her audiences to wondering subconsciously not whether they could see the "lack" that lay beneath such manly accomplishments, but rather, whether they might catch a glimpse of some truly phallic potential poking out from under her skirt. Audiences attributed masculine authority to French-Sheldon and eroticized her as ultra-feminine, marking French-Sheldon as a woman who was successfully, though unconsciously, cross-dressed as Woman.

The fact that French-Sheldon's audiences and fans were overwhelmingly female in these years, that write-ups about her in college journals and major newspapers mostly appeared on the women's pages and special subsections written by female journalists, and that the eroticism expressed in fan letters and in media representations was notably homo-, rather than hetero-, in character, lends further credence to the notion that French-Sheldon occupied the "third space" of the transvestite.[30] This space often figures as homosexual within queer theory and frequently as the terrain of the lesbian in the work of French feminist theorists. French-Sheldon's invoking of lesbian desire in her female auditors and her relationship to lesbian identity further secured her symbolic location in this space.

While in 1915 French-Sheldon never publicly characterized her relationship with Nellie Butler as sexual or romantic, French-Sheldon's performances inevitably hinged on the homoerotic desire she seemed to inspire in her audiences. As the evidence of the previous chapter discloses, girls wrote poems laced with romantic metaphors confessing their admiration for the aging explorer. One, for instance, likened her to a "jewelled" and "scintillating door" through which the poem's narrator could see "The answer to my innate yearnings call /And while I love the view within the hall / Shall I not love the door disclosing all?" Letters begged French-Sheldon to accept thanks for a "magic afternoon," "from the heart of an eighteen-year old girl, given in utter sincerity." Girls wrote of swooning before one who "stood there born to command, like a queen"; they imagined other girls "turning green with envy" at the thought of their luck to spend time with "the living embodiment of the Spirit of all that is good and true and Beautiful in Womanhood." College students at Baylor University supposed that Ouida "must have experienced a wisp of regret as she offered up her daily gratitude" the night she missed the "rosy tulip of opportunity" to receive Madame French-Sheldon's kiss.[31] According to the editor of a college publication, French-Sheldon, "that bewilderingly captivating author" mesmerized her young devotees no less with expressions of her "indomitable will" than with her "magnetic pen."[32] Though there was never the suggestion that French-Sheldon was herself a "mannish lesbian," French-Sheldon's independence and public relationship with Nellie Butler "cited the [lesbian] persona," to use a phrase found in the work of Judith Mayne.[33] Such citation could have been enough to lend French-Sheldon an intangible aura of sexual availability to her young female fans. While I do not feel we can say for sure what the nature of French-Sheldon and Butler's relationship was, the public's awareness of Nellie Butler as French-Sheldon's primary companion may have affected the message French-Sheldon communicated to her audiences in ways that heightened the homoerotic effects of her self-presentation.

Butler acted as French-Sheldon's social secretary while on tour, making arrangements as to lodging and taking orders for tickets from friends and acquaintances. She never appeared on stage, nor is there any evidence that French-Sheldon ever referred to Butler in one of her presentations. Only on rare occasions was Butler mentioned in the society pages announcing French-Sheldon's arrival and intention to deliver a public lecture. Even in these cases, she was never identified further, nor was her relationship to French-Sheldon ever specified. Though their relationship was not foregrounded by the press, nor made a matter for discussion by French-Sheldon, having Butler at her side may have added another layer to "Bebe Bwana's" projection of herself as a "Woman-Man." Lightly passed over by the paparazzi and common enough to women of French-Sheldon's age cohort, such information could have added only slightly to the impression that French-Sheldon inhabited a position of masculine responsibility and prerogative but was never highlighted enough to become a substantial factor in her audiences' estimation of her identity. Still, the lovesick fan letters and articles filled with sexual innuendo suggest that French-Sheldon's performances in the 1920s were, as Judith Mayne might say, "informed by the lesbian desire" of her auditors. Her activation of "lesbian" or "homoerotic" desires in women so much younger than her requires some explaining given the intergenerational tensions of this decade with its intensified celebration of the young, its emphasis on heterosexuality and heterosociality, and its gender-specific rejection of older women as sexless bluestockings. How is it that French-Sheldon, aged seventy-four in 1921, not only captured the respect of a new generation of young women but also climbed into their hearts and erotic imaginations?

EXTRA-CINEMATIC SPECTATORSHIP AND FEMALE FETISHISM

The worship-from-afar quality of young women's regard for French-Sheldon parallels both the relationship of star to fan (discussed in more depth in the next chapter) and a pattern of courtly love particular to cases of what some feminist psychoanalysts and cultural theorists term the "female fetish."[34] Feminist film theorists and cultural historians, in attempting to think through the nature of the enormous outpouring of women's desire for cinematic and extra-cinematic images (such as those rife in fan magazines and newspapers, and consisting of public appearances of celebrities) of other women in this period have constructed arguments that hinge on psychoanalytic readings of filmic desire. Their analyses often take up the relationship between sexual desire and the Subject and engage with ideas about the construction of subjectivity most forcefully articulated in the writings of French psychoanalytic theorist Jacques Lacan. Though Lacan never commented on the possibilities of a female fetish explicitly, in his view the "perversions" of lesbian desire (the patterns of "courtly love" that the homosexual(ized) woman inspires) emanate from the fact that the lesbian "excels in relation to what is lacking to her" (i.e., the phallus).[35] Like Judith Mayne, who sees the lesbian as a space marked out for subjectivity by virtue of its ability to produce a desiring subject, Marjorie Garber postulates further that it is, then, "the lesbian, and not the straight woman, who follows the path of something analogous to fetishism."[36] Neither Garber nor Garber's reading of Lacan's theory restricts this pattern of desire to lesbians defined as women who have or have had sex with women; instead *lesbian* in this case should signal the woman constructed in reference to lesbian desire, whatever her sexual history. This is an important distinction and one that allows us to further interrogate the significance of the homoerotic response to French-Sheldon's persona and the reproduction of her as a female fetish

—the object of women's fetishistic fantasy and that which might give rise to a privileged subjectivity—in this period quite apart from the question of the nature of her private relationship with Nellie Butler.

At stake in the question of female fetishism is the ownership of desire, or the creation of a female desiring subject, as opposed to the usual position of woman represented as desired object. Traditional Freudian theory does not recognize the possibility of women's fetishism, anymore than Lacanian theory imagines the possibility of a female subject. However, Sarah Kofman has reread Freud's discussion of the male fetish. In Freud's view, the fetish is a substitute for the penis that the little boy believed the mother once had, permitting him to deny the reality (that is, illusion) of her castration. By permitting the fantasy of the phallic mother, fetishistic behavior relieves male anxieties regarding castration.[37] Kofman argues that Freud may have neglected to notice a similar denial of the mother's castration in girls' psychological development. The recognition that the mother is "castrated" (that is, that she does not have a penis or, rather in a world of sexual difference, the phallus) could provoke a parallel anxiety in girls who conceivably would wish to deny and repress such a realization as much as boys although for different reasons. Acknowledgment of the mother's castration would compel girls to acknowledge their own evident castration as opposed to the mere threat of castration that boys face. Presumably, as with boys, the "castration anxiety" girls experienced would cause a split in ego and similar form of denial. Like men, women might sexually fixate on an object or image as a reassuring substitute for the maternal phallus that they are unwilling to acknowledge does not exist. Like boys, girls might also experience fetishism or a nostalgia for "wholeness" in the form of a maternal phallus that could lead them to experience fetishistic desire.[38] This theorizing of girls' need for and fixation on the maternal phallus may explain the excessive and erotic character of young women's intense and erotic admiration for French-Sheldon in this period.

If the young women in French-Sheldon's audiences yearned for (a return to) the phallic mother, they seemed to find it in public representations of French-Sheldon as a pioneering foremother of the modern gal. French-Sheldon's position as a mother figure was firmly established as a result of her status as a source of inspiration and an appropriate female role model. As often as the media utilized authoritative paternal metaphors to describe French-Sheldon's mastery of the stage and audience, writers of fan letters paid obeisance to French-Sheldon as an eroticized maternal figure. Employing a few words in French to lend a sense of intimacy and romance to the exchange one female fan, though fully adult and president of the League of American Pen Women at Berkeley, addressed her letter to "Cheri Mere Adoptione" and signed it "Devotedly your adoring fille adoptione."[39]

French-Sheldon's ability to satisfy her female audiences' wish for a mother who would not deny her child's need for originary wholeness further reveals itself in the "indian" name that the Campfire Girls of Waco, Texas, conferred on "Madame." They gave French-Sheldon the title *Wi-to-no-hi,* which the troop translated for French-Sheldon as "She-who-withholds-nothing." A small certificate in French-Sheldon's papers at the Library of Congress explains that this name was meant for the woman who "gives all—herself, her heart, her joy and sorrow she holds out, reaching towards the world. The figure in the centre of the diagram is the heart. On either side are little flames of joy, directly above is a cloud of sorrow, and nearly encircling that are the arms of love."[40] As *phallicized* mother, French-Sheldon represented a deeper (even more primitive considering the originary associations with which whites imbued American Indians) ideal of motherhood than even the nineteenth-century notion of true womanhood that she sometimes outwardly resembled. The maternal ideal of the woman who "gives all" presumes that she already is in possession of, but is not reducible to, the phallus and thus represents what, according to Lacanian theory, the child most longs to identify with.

The source of young women's adoration of French-Sheldon in this period lies in French-Sheldon's successful mastery of the phallus and overcoming of Woman's "lack," as her unmarked cross-dressing as a White Queen tended to suggest. As the "seemingly feminine," French-Sheldon could speak for woman without appearing to be confined to the category of Woman. Press reports confirm French-Sheldon's ability to represent a "both/and" rather than "either/or" of gender polarity.[41] Evidence of this abounds in the press's treatment of French-Sheldon and fans' letters to her. All in the same sentence, the *Brooklyn Daily Eagle* found French-Sheldon's "fearlessness and determination" to be nonetheless "charmingly feminine."[42] One fan exclaimed over "how charming a picture [French-Sheldon] made in a costume of richness with its violet-tones and white-lace touches . . . designed to express mentality in her appearance—all mind and not anything less."[43] Feminine accoutrements such as lace did not typically signify "all mind and not anything less" in popular conceptions of intellectualism or knowledgeable authority. Such puzzling statements require that we pay attention to the underlying layers of meaning they suggest. These contradictory statements and juxtapositions resemble the "oscillations" of the female fetish as theorized by Sarah Kofman, Naomi Schor, Jane Marcus, and Marjorie Garber. Garber figures the fetish as a "metonymic structure" but also sees it as a metaphor for "the undecidability of castration," which she goes on to describe as "a figure of nostalgia for originary 'wholeness'—in the mother, in the child. Thus the fetish, like the transvestite—or the transvestite, like the fetish—is a sign at once of lack and its covering over."[44]

French-Sheldon betrays the traces of the female fetish as theorized by Garber on multiple grounds. First, as an example of "unconscious" or "unmarked" cross-dressing, we have seen that her excessive and theatrical displays of the "seemingly feminine" communicated a thoroughly virile "will" that lay beneath a womanly figure without anyone actually "reading" her performance explicitly as cross-dressing. The oscillating character of the feminine fetish, Garber's second point, is also evident. French-Sheldon simultaneously professed to be different from most women yet representative of "a woman's power." Thirty years earlier French-Sheldon's desire to identify herself as exceptional confused sympathetic journalists such as Fannie C. Williams, reporter for the *Chautauquan* at the 1893 Chicago World's Fair. Williams struggled to explain French-Sheldon's ambivalence on this point, reporting that the explorer had "made one or two astonishing admissions during the conversation, one of which was her belief that exploration is not the *forte* of woman, because it requires too much self-sacrifice and too great a power of command. And yet she made a success of her own undertaking."[45] By the 1920s positioning herself as exceptional even while declaring herself representational produced no such confusion or frustration. A new subject position that refused either polarity was now available. Italicized headings in newspapers that quoted French-Sheldon's most tantalizing of quips ("I would take no man with me because he might want to take care of me, and no woman because I might have to take care of her!") signifies at once the "lack and its covering over" that Garber and others find central to the feminine fetish.[46] The invocation of "unmarked" transvestism and the oscillations associated with the female fetish are not, however, the only formulations of female fetishism that fit with French-Sheldon's White Queen performance.

Garber's notion of simultaneity ("undecidability" or the "sign at once of lack and its covering over") is borrowed from Kofman who argues, "[W]hat is pertinent to women in fetishism is the paradigm of undecidability that it offers."[47] Kofman believes that women, "by appropriating the fetishist's oscillation between denial and recognition of castration," can "effectively counter any move to reduce their bisexuality to a single one of its poles." She sees female fetishism as "not so much, if at all, a perversion" but rather describes it as a "strategy designed to turn the so-called 'riddle of femininity' to women's account."[48]

If we view French-Sheldon's oscillations regarding her announcement of difference from most women (even from those of her same race and class) and her sameness to them (evident in her intention to "show what a woman could do") in light of Kofman's formulation of the female fetish, French-Sheldon's seemingly paradoxical politics become visible as strategies designed to turn the "riddle of femininity" to her own purposes. French-

Sheldon's political stance as at once a representative of an always/already formerly embattled sisterhood and as a repudiator of a sisterhood based on her refusal of a shared subjection, closely resembles the refusal "to reduce [her] bisexuality to a single one of its poles" that Kofman believes the female fetish permits. Likewise, Naomi Schor's encapsulation of the female fetish as "neither a turning away from femininity, nor even a feminist protest against woman's condition under patriarchy, but rather a refusal firmly to anchor woman . . . on either side of the axis of castration"[49] fits French-Sheldon's pattern of avoidance/alliance with feminism.

What I have so far described as French-Sheldon's versatility and ambivalence did more than simply aid her in an avoidance of controversial political positions; they conferred on her an ability to "embody the lack, as well as the covering over of it." Viewed from such a perspective, French-Sheldon's ability to "cite the [lesbian] persona" enough to become the subject of girls' desires in the 1920s becomes more intelligible. If considered apart from a psychoanalytical understanding of subject constitution, the lack of fear invoked by French-Sheldon's homoerotic effects on girls makes little sense. As Kathy Peiss and others have shown, during the 1920s women of French-Sheldon's generation were being vilified for their influence on young women as part of a deliberate celebration of heterosociality and the repression of women's homosocial relationships.[50] However, when situated within a psychoanalytical model of subject constitution, the contradictory nature of the evidence on French-Sheldon's popularity in this period reveals significant changes in how women became positioned as feminine heroines and feminist icons in the years that stretched between the end of the Victorian era and the beginning of the Jazz Age.

Elizabeth Berg believes Kofman's formulation of the female fetish presents feminists with a new way to conceptualize feminist strategic interventions in culture. Berg writes that Kofman "gives us a framework for reconciling two tendencies of feminism which have tended to remain in apparently irremediable contradiction: the claim for equal rights and the claim for acknowledgment of sexual difference."[51] Berg enthusiastically endorses performances of the phallic woman, whom she also calls "the third woman—the affirmative woman—the woman who affirms, in spite of everything produced to persuade her to the contrary, that the penis is both there and not there, that the question is undecidable, that she may be both active and passive, both masculine and feminine." "It is essential," Berg concludes, that "feminists refuse the castration that has been attributed to them and affirm their double implication in masculine and feminine universes. The phallic mother—or the phallic woman—is not a fantasm to be dismissed, or simply the product of the child's imagination; she is the reality of the woman who is beyond the "truth" of castration."[52]

Taken in the abstract, Berg is able to ignore the complexities of the female fetish that a historical examination of its deployment might uncover. Jane Marcus, in her analysis of British suffragists' subversion of woman-as-commodity fetish through fetishistic feminist iconography provides a much-needed historical illustration of the potential and the limits of a "deliberate feminist fetishism."[53] Berg's admitted misgiving about the phallic woman, that such a "hazardous enterprise . . . opens the door to all sorts of masculine appropriations," is borne out by Marcus's example of suffragist images of phallic heroines that morph into reinscriptions of patriarchal repression during World War I.[54] In view of the uses to which a "feminist fetish" could be put, Marcus cautiously concludes that feminists carefully "interrogate our own plots as we generate them."[55] But neither she nor Berg acknowledge hierarchical axes other than gender that are affected by the female fetish as a strategy of cultural intervention.[56]

Similar to the British suffragists' use of phallicized imagery, French-Sheldon's "undecidability" stemmed from her ambivalence over "whether or not to depict (and therefore call down upon [herself]) representations of [her] own victimization."[57] Though French-Sheldon throughout her career as a public speaker explicitly "count[ed] her unique experiences chiefly from the point of view" that they were achievements of Woman, she also consistently and persistently denied the continuing existence of a fundamental oppression in order to appear undefiled by the subjugation that she imagined characterized Other women.[58] Like other "new-style" feminists in the 1920s, French-Sheldon's answer to the puzzle was to locate male supremacy in her race's and nation's recent past. Her self-presentation positioned her as a heroine who had "opened the doors" to a masculine world of power and prestige and universal human subjecthood for other exceptional women who might excel at typically masculine pursuits. Younger women who resembled French-Sheldon in terms of race, class, and national affiliation were positioned in French-Sheldon's performances as daughters poised to receive the patrimony (the phallus) long denied them and now made available by a phallic mother, "She-Who-Withholds Nothing." But what of those Others?

The feminist fetish may be considered tantamount to fixation on what Irigaray calls "mimicry," in which "the woman plays with 'her' image (the fetishistic masquerade), putting it on so as to signify it is a put on, and can easily be taken off [while] the woman is also 'elsewhere.'"[59] But where is "elsewhere"? Homi Bhabha, who also discusses mimicry, the third space, and the "ambivalence of colonial discourse," informs us that the realm of the masculine, the Symbolic, is a colonial space not only in terms of gender but also in terms of race, class, and nation. Bhabha warns us to consider the extent to which the fetish, "gives access to an 'identity' which is predicated as much on mastery and pleasure as it is on anxiety and defence, for it is a form of multiple and contradictory belief in its recognition of difference and disavowal of it. The conflict of pleasure/unpleasure, mastery/defence, knowledge/disavowal, absence/presence, has a fundamental significance for colonial discourse." In trying to explain the significance of the role that the fetish plays in the construction of a mastering colonial imaginary, he reminds us of how fundamental gender is to the operations of colonial ideology when he notes that "the scene of fetishism is also the scene of the reactivation and repetition of primal fantasy the subject's desire for a pure origin that is always threatened by its division, for the subject must be gendered to be engendered, to be spoken."[60]

Carole-Anne Tyler echoes Bhabha's warnings, arguing that the fetish, as a defense against castration, can only succeed in a white imaginary if difference can be located away from the self in an Other who "is just the same as, just the opposite of, or just the right complement and supplement to the white self, whether that other is romanticized (as whole, closer to nature, more fully human) or reviled (as lacking, uncivilized, less than human)."[61] If the operations of colonialism and of gender are considered together rather than left as independent variables, French-Sheldon's seeming inconsistencies concerning the relative patriarchalism suffered by or egalitarianism enjoyed by "the African woman" reveal themselves to be a part of the necessary ambivalence belonging to a strategy of Othering and displacement. Berg may celebrate "the penetration of women into the masculine world and the order of the symbolic."[62] But my reading of French-Sheldon's White Queen performance suggests that if white Western feminists are able to "penetrate" that realm, they often do so as *imperial* feminists, since their admittance into this sphere is often dependent not only upon their conscious ability to invoke a nationally and racially specific sense of authority but also upon the unconscious fetishism that marks the feminist as well. In a world marked by imperialism and white supremacy as well as capitalism and patriarchy, the phallus cuts across several lines of domination at once.

CONCLUSION:
MASTERY AND THE MASQUERADE

As Mary Ann Doane has noted, Joan Riviere's analysand, the original "masquerading" woman, had a number of sexual fantasies linking black men with sex, power, and degradation.[63] Just like French-Sheldon, Riviere's patient thought of herself as a daughter of the Old South and structured her fantasies along lines of eroticized racial dominance to accord with fantasies of plantation life.[64] In ways similar to French-Sheldon's depictions of East African sultans who desired her but could not possess her, Riviere's analysand interwove comments regarding the sexuality of black men and their power struggles with white women within her reports of her sexual fantasies. Riviere did not recognize the importance of her analysand's racial fantasies as evidence of the other axes of hierarchy at work in the masquerade, but she did pinpoint the "megalomaniac character" of the masquerading woman, nonetheless. Riviere argues that, through the pose of womanliness and the assertion of manliness, the masquerading woman could "gratify her id-impulses, her narcissistic ego and her super-ego at one and the same time. The phantasy was the mainspring of her whole life and character, and she came within a narrow margin of carrying it through to complete perfection. But its weak point was the megalomanic character, under all the disguises, of the necessity for supremacy."[65] Because Riviere assigns little weight to considerations of race, or any other relations of power besides gender, she overlooks how "the necessity for supremacy," clearly the crux of the masquerade, may have been satisfied at least in part in terms of white supremacy and class privilege. Arguably it was the politics of white supremacy, and colonialist relations, that allowed for the masquerades that Riviere identified in her white middle-class clients' performances of gender. Such "womanly women," as much as they appeared to have overcome their gender even while hyper-realizing it, comprised a veritable "race" of "Master Women" in the 1920s.

Certainly, the mastery of Others lay at the heart of ultra-feminine masquerades such as French-Sheldon's. Like Marlene Dietrich who paraded as a camped-up gorilla surrounded by Afro-ized chorus girls in black face in *Blonde Venus* (1932), or Mae West who enhanced her personal power and mastery of femininity by surrounding the characters she played with submissive mammy figures played by black actresses, French-Sheldon conjured up images of tyrannized and degraded Africans and Arabs to throw her triumph over subjugation into relief.[66] In an effort to appear whole, French-Sheldon as imperial and feminist fetish held out the promise of sameness by redrawing the line of difference to include some women who were able to own their desire for her image. Such displacement, I argue, may be central, even essential, to the practices of masquerade. Other feminist theorists agree that the key to this configuration of subjectivity and fetishism lies with hierarchical axes such as race and class.[67] This perspective helps explain how French-Sheldon's fantasy of herself in Africa and the fantasy she provided for those auditors who identified with her reaffirmed race and national distinctions as a way of compensating for violations of gender hierarchy. French-Sheldon's masquerade displaced the notion of femininity qua subjugation onto racialized Others, specifically Africans but also by extension other people implicated by her discourses on the colonization of Africa such as black Americans. The experience of empire provided a structure and a language for middle-class white women's displacement of defiled femininity onto these Others and thereby permitted the masquerade underpinning the archetype of the White Queen to be performed. The technologies available to French-Sheldon in her pursuit of this strategic positioning, and the mechanisms she drew upon to forge a female fetishistic persona, are further elaborated in the next chapter.

TEN

The Queen, the Sheik, the Sultana, and the Female Spectator

Madame French-Sheldon knows by now the
vastness of her sway over our hearts but not even
she can estimate the projecting influence of her
contagious personality upon . . . [her] auditors.
—*Baylor Towers,* March 1925

As I have documented in earlier chapters, French-Sheldon had an immediate and often profound effect on her young female audiences in the 1920s. In part, the reception she received in these years was a continuation of the rave reviews her public speaking had garnered as far back as 1891. However, the bombastic nature of the press coverage had changed somewhat. Not only was French-Sheldon's effect on audiences in the 1920s more erotic in nature, but the overwhelming impression one gets from reviewing public commentary on French-Sheldon over the years and examining her private fan mail is that a closer, more personal identification existed between French-Sheldon and the young women in her audiences in this period. The fact that French-Sheldon now received "fan mail" at all, for instance, testifies to this. Personal letters addressed to French-Sheldon from perfect strangers, letters from young women who poured out their hearts on paper in order to imagine a more intimate bond with the popular speaker, do not appear in her papers until the early 1920s, once the twinned concepts of the "star" and the "fan" had formed in American popular culture. In this chapter, I continue my discussion of French-Sheldon as feminist role model and female fetish by situating her career in reference to the mass cultural texts and social practices of the period that created the female "star" and produced, en masse, women as spectators of other women.

The influence of the invention of cinema on women's lives in the 1920s would be difficult to overstate and the gendering of mass media a mistake to overlook. New mass media technologies and a mass audience were often associated with a feminine and therefore degraded realm of cultural production.[1] The female spectator became the prototypical image of the (presumed to be, passive) consumer of mass cultural texts. Vast numbers of American girls and young women attended the movies several times a week in the 1920s. Most Hollywood films were romances or melodramas focused on sexual relationships and women's negotiation of them. The "crucial link in this female cultural chain," Mary P. Ryan argues, was the "star." According to Ryan, "the star was a unique cultural phenomenon, an actress whose personal style enlivened a multiplicity of familiar but fictional roles, blending the real with the imaginary in one glamourous individual."[2] Ryan describes female movie stars in the 1920s as the "vivid embodiments of the new womanhood, known to contemporaries as 'the moderns.'" Films in the 1920s gave precise details on how to become correctly modern; above all, she argues, the "new movie women exuded . . . a sense of physical freedom."[3] Though Ryan makes no attempt to problematize the racial and imperial set of meanings that hinged on "being modern" and being "free" (beyond the imperatives of a prescripted heterosexuality), her succinct summary nevertheless encapsulates the ideological function of the female star.

Female stars were material manifestations of the perception that a direct correlation existed between modernity and women's emancipation, characterized as the "freedom" to be flagrantly (hetero)sexual.[4] The female movie star was, by virtue of her public success and careerism, a liberated woman in "real life," too. Recognizable to audiences as individual women playing many different characters, the movie star embodied a commitment to uniqueness and individuality, even as the phenomenon encouraged conformity to an image. Indeed, Stanley Cavell describes the star as an "individuality [that] projects particular ways of inhabiting a social role."[5] "Blending the real with the imaginary," movie actresses quickly surpassed all other public figures as role models for girls. They evoked feelings and fantasies in their female fans which then carried over into fans' perceptions of themselves and of non-cinematic figures. French-Sheldon's success with young female audiences in the 1920s is one example of the extra-cinematic effects of the industry. French-Sheldon was re-produced as a female role model in the 1920s by the young women in her audiences who had grown accustomed to viewing cinematic female protagonists as "modern" projections of aspects of their own ideal selves.[6]

Throughout her career French-Sheldon had been praised not only for her achievements but also for the way she presented herself on stage. In the 1920s, as the self she offered became valued as image per se, the performative aspect of her public self became even more central to her success. French-Sheldon's "gift" both in the sense of her "talent" as well as her "contribution" to women's advancement consisted of her unique ability to embody the idea of feminine achievement. Many professional women of French-Sheldon's generation could look to past accomplishments, but it was French-Sheldon's effective contemporary *performance* of success onstage that was inspiring to a younger generation. Whereas French-Sheldon had been careful in the 1890s to distinguish herself from entertainers by mastering the language of social science (readers should recall the dryness of the anthropological lecture French-Sheldon gave while dressed as a White Queen at the 1893 Chicago World's Fair), in the cultural milieu of the 1920s in which actresses were preeminent role models, such distinctions meant little. French-Sheldon to a great degree dropped her formal pose and gave full vent to her performative skills. Consequently, for the first time, French-Sheldon was likened explicitly to famous nineteenth-century actresses. The *Wasp,* the organ for the Berkeley branch of the League of American Pen Women, commented in 1924, "[I]n her . . . desire to achieve the unusual and outstanding she reminds one of Mme. Sarah Bernhardt, Mme. Modjeska and other dauntless women who took up the challenge of life and set their indomitable wills to work to conquer."[7] What these actresses were conquering with their "wills" was not only the stage, of course. Like French-Sheldon, actresses were contravening the limitations of a feminine bodily presence, the stage being a premier space of transvestic transgression. For reasons that my discussion of camp in the last chapter makes clear, the ability of actresses to "put on" a feminine self implied the ability to remove it by or at their "will." French-Sheldon was likened to nineteenth-century actresses not just because they were her age cohorts, but also because these were women "pioneers" of the stage and thereby the foremothers who had first perfected the technique of travesty and camp that had become so central to the cinematic performances of the "moderns" in the 1920s.

SUBJECTS OF FEMINISM:
FRENCH-SHELDON AND THE FEMALE SPECTATOR

> [W]hen [they] saw her (in those gorgeous clothes) they thought she was a goddess and almost worshipped her.
> —*Evening Sun,* February 15, 1915

Famous cross-dressed personalities in this decade constructed an atmosphere in which gender and sexual hybridity was celebrated. The almost tangible phallic self not quite peeking out from under French-Sheldon's demure lavender dress suited the tastes of audiences' attracted to macho/prissy "She-Males" like Valentino and "female 'female' impersonators" like Mae West. Such a cultural landscape made French-Sheldon's performance as a *Bebe Bwana* and a White Queen easily readable and newly appreciated. Audiences may not only have "read" French-Sheldon as "star," they may have also viewed her performances much the way they viewed classic Hollywood cinema. Although cinema has distinct codes especially in terms of editing, such as the "point of view" shot not readily applicable to French-Sheldon's live performances, narrative cinema shares certain key features—its narratives, its "star" system, its spectacle—with French-Sheldon's public representation. Annette Kuhn explains that the "specificity of cinema as representation," lies "in its construction of spectacle—of a larger-than-life image which nonetheless also often claims if not actually to reproduce reality, at least to suspend the spectator's awareness of the artifice of the medium.[8] French-Sheldon's performances also projected an imaginary "larger-than-life" image—that of the white woman in Africa with French-Sheldon acting as camera, projector, and voiceover as well as living artifact to prove the tale was a true one. The thrill French-Sheldon's young audiences experienced stemmed from the way they received her performance as a real, live manifestation of the hyper-real "sex-goddesses" young women otherwise encountered in two-dimensional form on the screen. This slippage between French-Sheldon as "goddess" in Africa and the "sex-goddesses" of the movies was facilitated first and foremost by the glamorous image of herself as a White Queen that French-Sheldon hyped more and more with each passing year.

Journalists unconsciously reified the connection between French-Sheldon and actresses by recapitulating her exploits as if they were plots of a recent movie. In the process, they tended to position their readers as spectators of an imaginary French-Sheldon in (a fantasy of a thoroughly subjugated yet still savage) Africa. The parenthetical colloquialism in the *Evening Sun* excerpt forming the epigraph to this section—"[W]hen natives saw her (in those gorgeous clothes) they thought she was a goddess and almost worshipped her"[9]—discloses a psychological conflation between Africans as viewers of French-Sheldon and the white female audiences who adored her. My replacement of "natives" with "they" in the epigraph begs the question: Who are the "natives" who would describe French-Sheldon's apparel as "those gorgeous clothes"? As I mention in the first half of this chapter, journalists and fans never failed to express not only Africans' but their own delight in French-Sheldon's attire: her lavender dresses and lace scarves; and earlier, her "ball gown," blonde wig, and tiara. Not only was sumptuous women's clothing among the most ubiquitous of the commodities that Hollywood films intentionally and unintentionally advertised, "up-to-date" fashions were the quintessential mark of the modern gal of the 1920s. Though her actual clothing in no way resembled that of a "sex-goddess," French-Sheldon's imagined clothing certainly did. In a gesture of extra-cinematic significance, the phrase, "those gorgeous clothes" as a phrase alone cued the "modern" feminine consumption practices that readers of the *Evening Sun* were familiar with and thereby served to place French-Sheldon in the same sphere as the far more famous modern "goddesses" of the screen.

The preoccupation with imperial themes in early Hollywood cinema, magazine fiction, and novels—among the most ubiquitous and powerful forces shaping public representations of liberated American women— helped to secure French-Sheldon's overdetermination as "goddess." British Victorian imperial fiction was among the first genres Hollywood producers and directors mined for stories and Rider Haggard's novels were among the most revered of stories that made for successful adaptation to film. According to Kenneth Cameron, Haggard's novels of forty years before, especially *She, Allan Quartermaine,* and *King Solomon's Mines,* together comprised the "single source" that quickly came to dominate "cinematic ideas of Africa."[10] Of all Haggard's novels, *She,* filmed five times before 1925, served as a blueprint for Hollywood's early racialized depictions of Africa. *She* told the story of an Englishman's quest to find a mythological but no less "real" two-thousand-year-old White Queen named "Ayesha: She-Who-Must-Be-Obeyed." As legend had it, Ayesha resided deep in the jungles of Africa, though her origins were "lost in the mists of time." Through a mixture of sorcery and superior intelligence, Ayesha ruled tyrannically over servile or beastly African male soldiers and servants, and to look at her just once would drive a man mad with desire for her. The popularity of narratives based along the lines of *She* demonstrates the extent to which the "problem" of Africa as well as blacks at home loomed large in a white imaginary.[11] However, the importance of *She* in the history of film and U.S. popular culture should not be confined to the issue of the cinemagraphic representation of Africa, or of race considered apart from other axes of power such as gender.[12] Early filmed versions of *She* helped format the conventions of the White Queen and thereby informed a racialist construction of white movie actresses as the "goddesses" of Hollywood cinema. On the other hand, neither should the issue of gender overshadow the fact that it was through the displacement of Africa (and the erasure of the black woman as African "queen") that the Anglo-Saxon woman was re-imaged as spectacle, as fetishized star, and most importantly in my view, as a liberated white woman. Cameron's description of movie-goers' experience of watching *She* illuminates the film industry's heavy reliance on the Othering of Africa and things African to create the aura of empowered white womanhood and is worth quoting at length for the ways in which it illuminates the appeal of White Queen performances such as French-Sheldon's in this period.

> The lights go down, the shrill voices of children still, and to the throbbing of drums, a woman takes shape on the screen of the neighborhood movie house. Her nature—magic, erotic, powerful—defies all sense, but the movies make her real.
> *The White Goddess is a key filmic archetype of the white idea of Africa.* However much we patronize her, however much we see her as a cliché and not a myth figure, she is in the consciousness and the unconsciousness; in the very worst sense, she is in the blood. Beautiful (by white standards), magical, powerful, she is a goddess to be sought through the horrors of movie jungle and desert: *ruler of hordes of black people by virtue of her whiteness—itself her magic and her power*—she is the embodiment of a gut-level racialism. Whether she is the wild woman of Trader Horn or the white-robed Vestal of Jungle Queen, she is a proof of white might in Africa, and she descends from a single female ancestor: Ayesha, She-Who-Must-Be-Obeyed, the immortal white beauty of *She.*[13]

Significantly for my analysis of the facility with which French-Sheldon was able to contrive a splashy if unlikely comeback in the mid-1920s, according to Cameron, after the last film version of *She* in 1925, the stereotype of a more British-inflected "White Goddess" in Africa gave way to an all-American "White Queen"—the "one female archetype," he claims, "which has dominated American fiction films about Africa ever since."[14] Less vampish than Ayesha, Cameron finds that the all-American White Queen retained her most defining characteristic, "her separateness from black Africans . . . and her dominance of them."[15] Likewise, French-Sheldon's separateness from and domination of black Africans and Arabs is the most prevalent topic of *Sultan to Sultan* and in all of the accounts, whether written or performed, of her travels in Africa. As we saw in my discussion of *Sultan to Sultan* in Part I, her lectures and stories were full of confronting bully "sultans," de-spearing defiant Masai warriors and subduing rebellious Zanzibari porters, that is of subjugating Africa so firmly and yet charmingly that Africans themselves begged her to stay and rule over them as their White Queen. French-Sheldon's career in the 1920s was strongly affected by the development of a "cult of the female star" which was, in part, shaped around the fantastical figure of *She*. French-Sheldon, an otherwise maternal figure ("She-Who-Withholds-Nothing"), was made glamorous and star-like as a direct result of playing the role of White Queen and macho dominatrix ("She-Who-Must-Be-Obeyed") in Africa.

Laura Mulvey touches on the "cult of the female star" in her ground-breaking essay, "Visual Pleasure and Narrative Cinema" (1975). In that article, Mulvey maintained that the codes of classic Hollywood cinema (particularly the films of Hitchcock) dictated that only male spectators gain pleasure through an identification with the camera and the male hero, and that the female performer could only connote a "to-be-looked-at-ness." As objects "to be looked at," female stars were fetishized, but only by male (or masculinized) spectators. According to Mulvey, "[T]he woman as icon,

> displayed for the gaze and enjoyment of men, the active controllers of the look, always threatens to evoke the anxiety it originally signified. The male unconscious has two avenues of escape from this castration anxiety: preoccupation with the re-enactment of the original trauma . . . or else complete disavowal of castration by the substitution of a fetish object or turning the represented figure itself into a fetish so that it becomes reassuring rather than dangerous (hence over-valuation, the cult of the female star.)[16]

In this early essay, Mulvey does not imagine the possibility of a female or feminine fetishism resulting from female spectators' feminine castration anxiety as others since have posited it. In Mulvey's explanation, there is no possibility of the female star experienced as other than a male or masculinized fetish in narrative cinema because, through specific filming and editing procedures, female spectators are dispossessed of "the gaze" permitting spectators an unconflicted identification with the mechanism of fetishization, the camera or "the Look."

Since the publication of "Visual Pleasure and Narrative Cinema," and in response to a deluge of feminist film criticism concerning the possibilities of a "female gaze," Mulvey has reconsidered the problem of pleasure and the female spectator. In "Afterthoughts on 'Visual Pleasure,'" Mulvey begins by asking the questions, "What about the women in the audience?" and "What happens when there is a female character occupying the center of the arena?"[17] Mulvey's characterization of the female protagonists of such films in which "a woman central protagonist is shown to be unable to achieve a stable sexual identity, torn between the deep blue sea of passive femininity and the devil of regressive masculinity" resembles the oscillations that lay at the heart of the female fetish as described by Naomi Schor ("neither a turning away from femininity, nor even a feminist protest against woman's condition under patriarchy, but rather a refusal firmly to anchor woman—but also man—on either side of the axis of castration").[18] Unlike Kofman's and Schor's writings, "Afterthoughts" does not take into account the possibility that such oscillation may act to suspend the recognition of women's lack of the phallus, allowing the female spectator to "own" the fetish. Instead, as Janet Walker characterizes it, Mulvey views the instability of the female spectator's position as a "dilemma" that "echoes the predicament of the female spectator who must accept 'masculinization' to identify with a male hero."[19] Without seeing the subversive potential of transvestic oscillation, Mulvey concludes that pleasure for the female spectator must involve "temporary masculinization."[20] According to Mulvey, though the female spectator tenuously occupies the position of a masculine viewer as a result of identification with the male hero (compelled by the editing that characterizes dominant narrative cinema), she is unable to "own" the desire for the fetishized female star that the camera prompts because of her inability to achieve a sufficient distance from this objectified figure of Woman. Hollywood's forcing of female spectators into identifying with a male fetishizing "look," without allowing them to disengage from identification with the fetishized female star, results in women's masochistic identification with the female star as male fetish, even in film genres that assume a primarily female audience.[21]

Many feminist theorists have taken issue with Mulvey's monolithic masochistic female spectator and masculinist model of female subject constitution.[22] My purpose here is not to debate these issues in terms of film spectatorship but to interject the example of French-Sheldon in the discussion to shed light on Hollywood's historical production of female desire and the extra-cinematic cultural and political uses to which that desire was put in the 1920s.

French-Sheldon's performances in the 1920s not only shared many common elements with the oft-filmed story of *She,* but her lectures in that decade also cited the film genre that constituted the most important popular film phenomenon of the decade—the desert romance. As many cultural historians of the 1920s have argued, Rudolph Valentino's films (among them *The Four Horsemen of the Apocalypse, The Sheik,* 1921; *Blood and Sand,* 1922; *Son of the Sheik,* 1926) may have generated more, and more intense, female desire than any other set of films ever produced.[23] As such, Valentino's films comprise important texts for the study of the relationship between cinematic pleasure and the female spectator generally and for the relationship between sexuality, spectacularity, and new womanhood in the 1920s specifically. Miriam Hansen has observed that, following the release of Valentino's films, "for the first time in film history, women spectators were perceived as a socially and economically significant group; female spectatorship was recognized as a mass phenomenon; and the films were explicitly addressed to a female spectator, regardless of the actual composition of the audience. . . . Never before was the discourse on fan behavior so strongly marked by the terms of sexual difference, and never again was spectatorship so explicitly linked to the discourse on female desire."[24] Various, related elements of Valentino's films conspired to elicit the intense response of his female fans and his primarily male critics to his performance. Among the most salient features operating to trigger female fans' sexual fantasies were the exotic racialism of the orientalist context in which most of the films were set; Valentino's "to-be-looked-at-ness"; and the sadomasochistic character of much of the editing and action. *The Sheik,* for instance, was set somewhere in "Araby" (a vague reference to various areas in the vicinity of the Eastern Mediterranean, North Africa, East Africa, or Southwest Asia), Valentino was filmed as a sexual object of desire, and the plot revolved around his character's abduction and violation of a white woman.[25] The film was adapted from the novel of the same name, published in 1919 by E. M. Hull (a pseudonym). In the mid-1920s sales of this novel surpassed those of all other contemporary best-sellers taken together. The phenomenal success of the novel and the film inspired untold numbers of formulaic works in the genre of the "desert" or "Eastern" romance. Among the predominant features of this genre are ethnological description, topographical splendor, travel, and a white woman's exploration of the oriental Other as a way of establishing her own autonomy.

French-Sheldon's autobiographical presentations in the 1920s resembled the pattern of the typical desert romance as described by, for instance, literary historian Billie Melman. Again, the commonalities between the construction of a female protagonist in these narratives as summarized by Melman justify quoting at length. "In this pattern," she explains,

> an aristocratic Englishwoman, economically and socially independent but sexually unawakened, embarks upon a voyage into the heart of the Sahara desert. . . . The narrative typically begins at an oriental coastal town, or at a garrison town, which symbolizes the junction of East and West. It is here, where the two cultures meet, that the heroine cuts herself off from the "civilised" Western world and its restricting conventions to explore the symbolic desert. The Sahara romance concludes in an oasis . . . and the beginning, for the heroine, of a new life. . . .
>
> The desert novelist seeks to validate her fantastic fabrications by an almost obsessive attention to scenic actuality. Accuracy in geographical and ethnographical details is the primary requirement of the genre. The wilder and the more fatuous the fantasy, the greater the pain that is taken to authenticate it. . . . Sometimes these passages fit into the narrative. But more often they are flamboyant and extraneous tours de force whose sole purpose is to impress the reader with the writer's knowledge of her subject matter and to establish her as the omnipresent traveller-narrator.[26]

Given that women of all ages in the mid-1920s voraciously consumed abundant written and filmed versions of such a scenario, it should come as no surprise to find French-Sheldon easily slipping into the role of heroine of the "desert love story" in her lectures to the public.[27] Indeed, it would have been difficult for audiences not to be reminded by the heroine of *Sultan to*

Sultan of the character of Lady Diana, the female protagonist of *The Sheik*. French-Sheldon sealed the conflation between herself as this character by adding the one element missing from her performance as heroine of the 1920s desert romance—a scene of abduction. Luckily, she had one already written to draw upon.

French-Sheldon had long made it her practice to excerpt entire passages from either her travel narrative or her anthropological essays, incorporating these anecdotes into her public lectures. Reading aloud from her many works of short fiction, in addition to extemporaneous speaking, more and more characterized the content of her presentations during and following World War I. But it was not until the mid-1920s that French-Sheldon included two short stories she had written over twenty years before and made reading them aloud the centerpieces of her public appearances. "The Sultana's Pearl" and "A Night of Peril" appear in published form in a collection French-Sheldon authored and published through her own Saxon and Company in the mid-1890s.[28] Though both "Pearl" and "Peril" were clearly fanciful embellishments on French-Sheldon's original travel narrative, by the mid-1920s French-Sheldon presented (or journalists heard or both) the stories as non-fiction accounts of actual incidents. My interest lies in the stories that her immediate audiences heard (read directly from the published text) and in the abridged version that many newspapers printed the day following one of her appearances, which mirrored each other and followed the published version closely. "The Sultana's Pearl" and "A Night of Peril" caused observers to liken French-Sheldon's lecture material to that long-standing source of Western knowledge about the "East," "A Thousand and One Arabian Nights."[29] Both titillated her sheik-mad audiences with the suggestiveness of the "barbaric" sexuality of dark foreigners and the "degraded" sensuality of the harem. Though both these stories contain elements of the desert romance, the plot of "A Night of Peril" most closely mimes the conventions of that genre.[30]

In an article in the March 11, 1923, Sunday edition of the *Los Angeles Daily Times* entitled, "Real Life 'Sheik' Adventure," a journalist quoted at length "A Night of Peril," which French-Sheldon had relayed to the Hollywood chapter of the Daughters of the American Revolution the night before. The story stemmed from and served to further enhance French-Sheldon's claims that as many as sixty "sheiks" (or "chiefs," in some instances) had proposed marriage to her while on her trek. "A Night of Peril" told of "her narrow escape from being captured by an Arab for a Sheik's harem," saved, as the paper recalled, by the shout of a companion of the Arab abductor just soon enough to give French-Sheldon enough time to pull out her guns and shoot her assailant. The paper explained that the remorseful companion of the assailant, a "half-Italian," was struck with the "memory of his mother [which] deterred him." The article went on to note that this man "remained with Mrs. Sheldon who later bought for him an olive plantation in Sicily, where he made enough to pay her back." Published accounts of French-Sheldon's retelling of this story faithfully record its key desert love-story elements: the title of the article utilizes the word *sheik* (as compared with French-Sheldon's usual use of the term *sultan*); the female protagonist is usually simply referred to as "the white woman"; the story is set vaguely in Northeastern Africa among "Arabs" as well as Africans; and the scene of the attempted abduction occurs late at night while the heroine lay asleep in a tent. Moreover, the male protagonist/rapist is revealed by the end of the story to be of European extraction, that is, at least half white. The conventions of the desert love story foreground the sexual tensions that French-Sheldon thirty years before had only hinted at euphemistically. As the paper recorded, her abductor "advanced toward her with quick sinuous movements of his whole body"; his body language revealed that "it was her he wanted not her treasures"; and with a gun in each hand, French-Sheldon shot the Arab "through both hands."[31] *Noli me tangere!*

While at least a surface reading of the film and book versions of *The Sheik* could be viewed as bearing out a view of the female spectator of Valentino's movies as essentially masochistic in nature, French-Sheldon's version of the story and the pleasure it seemed to inspire in her audiences suggests the possibility of a female pleasure and female fetishism that does not rely upon masochistic identificatory processes. With the lynching of black men peaking in Southern states, "A Night of Peril" maintains that (white) women are not vulnerable to any real "peril," certainly not from black men or those who loomed largest in white American minds as congenital rapists and the main scourge of vulnerable white womanhood. The only sadism in this desert story is practiced by French-Sheldon herself who shoots her attacker through the hands for trying to touch her.[32] This fantasy is not one of masochism but of maternal mastery—recall that the memory of Mother prompted voluntary obeisance to Bibi Bwana.[33] Not only does the plot obviously negate feminine submissiveness, but the cinematic imperative which dictates that female spectators identify with a "masculine" look (assuming Mulvey is correct regarding dominant cinema) is undercut by the absence in this case of any such mechanism as a male narrator or a camera, though the story is, in fact, structured by the economy of (what film theorists and Lacanian psychoanalysts term) "the gaze" or the "Look."

The female protagonist, or Bibi Bwana (the spelling of this term shifts a bit here as Swahili is becoming standardized in texts), is the bearer of the Look throughout the published text of "A Night of Peril." However, in contrast to Mulvey's analysis, she is not masculinized by assuming this position. French-Sheldon represents Woman, as the rest of her lecture material forcefully maintained, yet she is empowered in this version of the desert love story to defy her lack as well as her womanly subjugation to men. Significantly, her alter ego, Bibi Bwana, remains feminine throughout the narrative inasmuch as she remains the object of frustrated male lust and retains the potential to be raped. The published version depicts French-Sheldon as Bibi Bwana lying vulnerable in a tent in a strange place with no (white, male) protection and an Arab man's face poking through her tent. At first, her gaze falters:

> Half dozing Bibi Bwana's sleepy eyes unable to gaze about any longer, riveted themselves upon the opposite side of the tent facing her palanquin. In a vague way she saw down close to the ground a slight swaying movement of the canvas. In a stealthy fashion it increased; soon, at the point where the canvas swayed the most, the Arab's head was cautiously thrust beneath; his eyes gleamed with wicked intent, as the flickering light from the watch-fires at the entrance danced fitfully upon them.
>
> . . . With the vision of the Arab's face still before her, Bibi Bwana's eyelids so heavy laden with sleep, closed, and her poor distracted brain grew dizzy in the lightning changes of the hideous nightmare, so hideous, that the terror, or possibly a faint, shrill, prolonged whistle without, summoned her back to consciousness.
>
> . . . [W]ith startled eyes, she cast a swift glance about the tent, but never moved.
>
> Behold! there, directly in front of the palanquin, back towards her, cautiously listening, stood the Arab! He held in his hand Bibi Bwana's rifle. Danger was imminent. This rallied Bibi Bwana, who was essentially above all else one for emergencies demanding quick action.
>
> A pair of woman's hands stole quickly under her pillow and drew resolutely forth two loaded revolvers. As she cocked them, the metallic click of the trigger attracted the ear of the alert Arab, who wheeled round like a flash, to find himself covered by two pistols. His surprise and terror caused him to waver; not so the woman, who called out clearly, "Who goes there?"—no answer! Then she cried out, "Askari (guard), help!" and shot at the rascal. . . . the rifle fell out of his disabled hand. (*HB:* 106–107)

The gaze is an important framing device for this story of thwarted rape. French-Sheldon only flirts with the idea that she is not in control of it briefly, to establish that she can by willpower alone regain possession of it. Just as the infant's game of peek-a-boo delights by reassuring, in "A Night of Peril," first Bibi Bwana experiences a lack, only to cover over it reassuringly in a show of her triumph over feminine vulnerability. The Arab here is phallic in his snake-like ways ("down close to the ground," "slightly swaying movement," "stealthy fashion," "his eyes gleamed with wicked intent").

Rape is clearly the intent here; in fact, the physical act of rape symbolically occurs when "at the point where the canvas swayed the most, the Arab's head thrust beneath the "folds" of Bibi Bwana's tent. Male sentinels outside the tent cannot ensure Bibi Bwana's safety. But, though her "poor, distracted brain grew dizzy" (in that quintessential way that feminine brains seemingly will), Bibi Bwana's control of the plot returns in the nick of time. Once her "startled eyes" cast their "swift glance about the tent," "Behold!"—her gaze as well as her power over the situation is restored.

Significantly, Bibi Bwana's victory is not a result of the feminization of her Arab attackers. At the moment of reversal, the assailant holds the stolen rifle in his hands; no longer "close to the ground," he is alert and erect when she confronts him. Later, upon interrogating the member of the Arab band who betrayed his co-conspirators to warn French-Sheldon by whistling sharply to waken her, we see that the spokesman for the group of assailants is a worthy (part white, and not the least bit effeminate) adversary. The narrator finds it "strange" that he arose and "stood erect like a white man, instead of crouching on his heels as is the custom of the African when a supplicant before a superior or a white leader. This was significant. It in a way betrayed him. He was not then of pure African origin. Stranger yet instead of an African dialect there came rolling from his lips English words!" (*HB:* 111–112).

Just as being able to see indicates mastery of the scene, using English (the "White Man's tongue") (*HB:* 116), that is, speaking a language that can be heard, is crucial to the articulation of agency in this story. Bibi Bwana's captive is an authorized, speaking subject. Her triumph over him, therefore, requires that she, too, establish her ability to speak as a Subject. The moment of truth, on several levels, comes when surprise causes the original assailant to waver mutely but "not so the woman who called out clearly." When Bibi Bwana's query "Who goes there?" receives "no answer," she fires. French-Sheldon (as a white) does not suffer an inability to speak, or act, as a subject. Likewise, the establishment of the half-Arab's masculinity is dependent upon *his* ability to speak up during the emergency and, later, to speak English in his self-defense to Bibi Bwana. At the trial, when he finishes speaking, he ends his explanation for being half-European (his Sicilian mother was abducted by his Arab father) and his decision to betray his fellow abductor by warning Bibi Bwana ("I . . . resolved to save the White Queen in memory of my mother") by capping off his speech with, "It is true—I have spoken." Thus, the "good" (not entirely black) African has dignity, agency, and moral sensibility only as a consequence of his European heritage as revealed in his mastery of English. French-Sheldon establishes parity between herself and this adversary by ending her story the same way, dedicating the story to him: "Black, unchristianized, but God-like man.

This narrative her testimony to him—it is true—she too has spoken."(*HB:* 120) The parity achieved is not entirely even; Bibi Bwana, by getting the last word in, and as arbiter of his fate, retains the upper hand. Still, the parallelism French-Sheldon establishes in this text implies that neither gender "owns" the phallus exclusively—while all whites, in the presence of blacks, certainly do.

Bibi Bwana (itself a term which in its literal translation as "woman man" refuses to assign French-Sheldon either sex exclusively), though in possession of the phallus, does not relegate femininity to an inferior symbolic sphere. Bibi Bwana is not rendered mute by the "hideous nightmare, so hideous that the terror" compels her to take control even before she hears a "faint, shrill whistle without" that constituted the half-Arab's alarm signal. True, her Arab attacker may have stolen her rifle, but it is expressly "a pair of woman's hands" that reaches under the pillow for two revolvers, "cocks" them, and shoots the rifle out of her attacker's hand, thus "disabling" it. The sexual imagery is obvious. That Bibi Bwana pulls not one revolver out but two, keeps the image at once feminized and phallic: the pair of revolvers echoes the pair of woman's hands which echoes a pair of woman's breasts. If breasts need to be "cocked" before firing, it is Bibi Bwana, a Woman-Man after all, who is capable of doing the cocking. Though Bibi Bwana is clearly in possession of the phallus in this story, her body is still marked by femininity (the folds of the tent, the two-ness of the pistols which dominate the rifle, the feminine allure that drives Arab men to commit foolhardy crimes); nor does she have to become masculinized to resist penetration or punish the perpetrator. Bibi Bwana is able to emerge from a not-so-devastating night of terror, unaffected by the violation that has (already symbolically) occurred. If in this rape scene, a pair of revolvers beats one long rifle, then no rescue on the order of a strong, empowered male is much needed to save the damsel in not-so- dire peril.

Unlike in the Rudolph Valentino movie, in this sheik story, "the white woman" is simply not abductable at all. She retains control of both the narrative and her subject position in the absence of a male protagonist like the one Valentino played. Just as in the encounters French-Sheldon describes occurred between her and the sultans of East Africa in *Sultan to Sultan,* the entirely de-subjectified Othered men in this story desire Bibi Bwana, but their desire never has the power to degrade her; instead it just highlights her value as white. The possibility that, as a woman, French-Sheldon was vulnerable to being rendered an object for exchange between men is wholly disavowed and contained by a story which, in the newspaper version, ends with French-Sheldon playing the part of capitalist investor and patron of an Arab who really turns out to be a half-Italian, obsessed with his mother and eager to return to Italy as a budding entrepreneur of an olive farm.[34] In the

Hollywood film *The Sheik,* of course, the "Arab" turns out to be a Scottish nobleman, the Earl of Glencarryl, and Lady Diana is all the better for his cruel rape of her.

Even in *The Sheik,* arguably a sadomasochistic film about over-civilized women wanting to be raped by a foreigner, the gender reversals provide key moments that serve to destabilize the predominant plot of female subjugation. Marjorie Garber points out that in a famous still from *The Sheik,* Valentino and Agnes Ayres, similarly robed and turbaned, stand parallel, she with a gun pointed directly at Valentino's smaller, effeminate even, cigarette holder.[35] Like French-Sheldon, Rudolph Valentino, too, was a "Woman Man" of sorts, and women loved to watch him for that very quality. According to Miriam Hansen, Valentino's films produced the manic fan response that they did because they utilized cinematic techniques that sutured women into a position of identification with the leading character. Valentino was not merely a man women wanted to be with, his was a feminized masculinity that they wanted to and could imagine themselves assuming. The female characters, often uptight but not submissive white heroines, also provided a point of identification for white female audiences as long as they exhibited the subjecthood marking them as modern, white, and Western—that is as long as their personalities marked them as emancipated women. Whether the female lead was being imperious and defiant or Valentino's character was compelling the heroine to conquer her fear and acquiesce to a naturalized heterosexual sense of sexual abandon, female audiences members had several sexually hybridized subject positions from which to choose.[36] The licentious thrill women experienced as consumers of desert romance narratives was a result not only of a unprecedented or newly "modern" freedom to indulge in sexual fantasy but also of a construction of a fantasy that positioned female spectators "on top," as subjects of their own desire. The mass culture narrative of a plucky modern gal stuck out in the desert with an unrestrained foreign man did not simply allow such desire to express itself—it manufactured it.[37] French-Sheldon built off the desire produced by *The Sheik* and its imitators, but (as Rachel du Plessis might say) wrote beyond the ending to reproduce herself as heroine and reinforce the character as an imperial feminist subject.[38] In "A Night of Peril," French-Sheldon is neither violated, nor is she stripped of her femininity; as the object of African male lust, she is fetishized. But in the absence of a viable male hero and in light of young white female audience members' worship of French-Sheldon, the White Queen is constructed as a female fetish in this story for female readers and auditors who did not have to masculinize her (or be masculinized by their identification with her) to experience themselves as the subjects of their own desire.

French-Sheldon's constant reiteration of "the woman," "the white woman," "the White Queen," as well as "Bibi Bwana" (which, alone, appears forty-three times in the short written text of "A Night of Peril") highlights her gender identity while refusing the hierarchy usually associated with sexual difference. However, as I have explained, the crux of this imperial feminist fantasy lies with the naturalizing of racial hierarchy in ways that act to partly dislodge the hierarchy of gender. This displacement is found in many white-authored feminist texts.[39] Elements within "A Night of Peril" (the childish blacks, the discovery of a half-white speaking subject, etc.) and without the text (the context of French-Sheldon's civilizing mission, the broader social context that was saturated with stereotypical images of black American men as rapists) coalesce to reconfirm hierarchy along racial lines, soothing any gender anxiety her story of feminine mastery may have inspired and reminding readers that her feminist agency was an outgrowth of her racial and national identity. Other stories French-Sheldon told to audiences in this period that featured African women rather than men as French-Sheldon's foils accomplished similar aims with slightly different implications as I explain below.

"THE SULTANA'S PEARL": AN EXCHANGE OF OTHERED WOMEN

> The white woman keeps the pearl if only because her skin is like unto the lining of its shell.
> —*Haunted Bells,* 55

In tandem with "A Night of Peril," French-Sheldon told or read to her audiences in the 1920s the story of "The Sultana's Pearl," the central theme of which echoes the "Peril's" preoccupation with denying sexual hierarchy among whites without eschewing sexual difference. While in "A Night of Peril" French-Sheldon adamantly opposes the notion of her autobiographical protagonist as an object of exchange between men (she cannot be abducted and sold to a harem, regardless of how valuable her race makes her), in "The Sultana's Pearl" the autobiographical protagonist, "the white woman," that French-Sheldon constructs becomes a partner with men in an exchange of African women.

Though "A Night of Peril" received top billing in newspaper headlines that boomed, "Shot a Sheik," journalists reported both "Peril" and "Pearl" at length. French-Sheldon had sketched the basic outlines of "The Sultana's Pearl" originally in *Sultan to Sultan* (*SS:* 97–100). The short story she wrote and published in the 1890s as "The Sultana's Pearl" embellished on her visit to the Sultan of Zanzibar to request his aid in assembling porters for her caravan. To recall my discussion (in part 1) of this visit as described in *Sultan to Sultan,* in the scene French-Sheldon positions herself on a level with the Sultan in strong contradistinction to his "poor, degraded concubines" who are "too many, all alike, and not worth" French-Sheldon's even greeting them as individuals. The sadness displayed by the Sultan's wives, their envy of French-Sheldon, and their collective washing of her foot, speak to French-Sheldon's racial superiority and their gendered and raced inferiority. As a consequence of the strong contrast between French-Sheldon and the Sultana, the story rejects the existence of women's shared experience of subjection. The scene denies gender difference an important role in the constitution of subjectivity, enshrining race in its stead. "The Sultana's Pearl," as the fictionalized version of this episode from *Sultan to Sultan,* results in a similar if even more extreme and explicit impression through its re-presentation of the tragic figure of the Sultana as an object of exchange between the Sultan and French-Sheldon.

"The Sultana's Pearl" actualizes an exchange of Other women in the form of a pearl ring that the Sultan's beautiful wife, named Azwid in the story, is powerless to prevent her husband from giving to "the white woman" (the only name given to the narrator/protagonist in the story).[40] The ring represents Azwid's long, prestigious lineage and her exalted status in the Sultan's household. With expressed disgust for Azwid's feelings and in disregard of her protest, the Sultan commands that French-Sheldon be given the ring, and that the story behind the ring be read to her from a scroll by Azwid herself. At first, the Sultana, in a fit of pique, refuses to read the story. Quickly, however, she changes her mind. Deciding that she could not bear to have her family history drop from the lips of a lowly eunuch servant, the Sultana begs her husband to allow her to relate the story of her patrilineality to French-Sheldon personally, despite the great pain it will cause her to do so.

Evidently the Sultan was willing to give acquiescence, if the white woman expressed the desire to hear from Azwid's lips the story, for no sooner had she bowed her head in sign thereof than by an imperious wave of the hand he dismissed the eunuchs in attendance. After seating the white woman and himself, he pointed to a pile of cushions, upon which the Sultana flung herself, her Oriental beauty indeed enhanced by the setting of the brilliant silk covers of the cushions, as they irregularly puffed all about her.

With unwonted courtesy the Sultan arose, took from the centre-table a couple of glasses of sherbet, handed one to the white woman, quaffed half the contents of the other, then handed it to the Sultana, who ceremoniously touched her forehead with the tips of the fingers of the left hand, and with graceful swing, as she bowed her head, touched first her knee, then her bare toes, as they thrust naked through the jewelled straps of her sandal and turned the ring upon her left big toe twice round, then swallowed the remaining contents of the glass. (*HB:* 49)

This fictional scene positions French-Sheldon and the Sultan on equal planes, in much the same way that the (ostensibly non-fiction) scene in *Sultan to Sultan* does. "The Sultana's Pearl" ends when the Sultana finishes relating the legend of the pearl, "the Soul of the Mountain," and begins pleading with "the white woman" not to accept the gift as the pearl is the sign of her identity—an "insignia of my beauty, loveliness, and faithfulness." The Sultan disdains his wife's protest that giving the ring away would strip her of all dignity or sense of self. He bestows the pearl on "the white woman" in spite of the Sultana's evident distress, declaring that "The White Woman" keeps the ring, "if only because her skin is like unto the lining of the shell" (*HB:* 55). The reader is left with the impression that "the white woman" is moved by the drama of the scene and pities the tragic Sultana, but, nevertheless, is compelled to accept the pearl ring in recognition of the legitimacy of the Sultan's racial rationale and in light of the hierarchical relationship which places whites (whether male or female) on the same level with Sultans, husbands, and masters of Other women. As French-Sheldon complained to one news reporter in the 1910s, "It is only in the West that my sex really matters"; in the colonial context, surrounded as French-Sheldon was by men and women of Other races and colonized status, she did not have to try to renounce her femininity to achieve the mastery associated with her race and class.

In this orientalist scenario, so reminiscent of other "seraglio" scenes counterposing a usually defiant individual Western woman against compliant or demoralized "Eastern" concubines or vamps, French-Sheldon figures as the receiver with the Sultan as the possessor of women, the giver in the exchange. In other texts, at other like moments of a symbolic exchange, French-Sheldon positions herself as the giver of Other women. African women and effeminized men become the currency of exchange in French-Sheldon's partnerships with the primarily male memberships of scientific societies and museums and, later, with her primarily white, middle-class, female audiences. In the text of *Sultan to Sultan* and in her anthropological article, "Customs among the Natives of East Africa . . . with Special Reference to their Women and Children," French-Sheldon describes several occasions when she wrenches from Africans items which either represent sexual power or externalize the feminine identity of their owner in much the same way that the fictional pearl of the Sultana does. These items, (discussed in part 1, they include the metal bands cut out of living African men or dead African women, the beaded apron French-Sheldon wrested from one woman, and the many spears she procured while on her expedition), unlike the pearl, were not fictional but material and "artifactual." As evidence of French-Sheldon's intimacy with Africans, French-Sheldon treasured these items more than any other objects she acquired while in East Africa. By the presentation of them to the male members of prestigious scientific organizations such as the Royal Geographical Society, French-Sheldon was able to prove that she accomplished a feat of exploration and ethnographic research presumed to be the exclusive preserve of Western men. But the items themselves reveal that French-Sheldon's constitution of herself as a subject of equal ontological status with the men of these organizations was based on her willingness to symbolically hand over African women and feminized African men as a gesture of her collegiality with and equality to the men of her race and class. By displaying and distributing such items, French-Sheldon helped create in the minds of her Western audiences a proprietary relationship between Africans and Westerners. Though imaginary this relationship had material effects, of course. The cloth French-Sheldon obtained from her African "sister," unlike the wholly fictional Sultana's pearl, slides outside of French-Sheldon's text. The theft and incarceration of the material symbols of Othered women's very selves, that is, French-Sheldon's physical deposit of these items in European museums, completed one level in a circle of exchange enabling an assertion of Western women's subject status in the twentieth century at the expense of Africans.[41] In this vision of East/West relations, white women do not represent the "dark continent" as Freud said; instead, they share the role of colonial proprietor with white men.[42]

Although it is easy to isolate authorized *male* figures as French-Sheldon's partners in these exchanges (in "The Sultana's Pearl," the fictionalized character of the Sultan, and in her anthropological writings, the elite male members of an Anglo-American scientific community), an imagined exchange of Othered women occurs between French-Sheldon and white *women* as well. It is important to recall that in the 1920s French-Sheldon's audiences were overwhelmingly female and that it was young women to whom she was presented as an appropriate role model in these years. Although French-Sheldon "explored" Africa, "collected" artifacts from Africans, wrote and published "A Night of Peril," and "The Sultana's Pearl" in the 1890s, it was not until the 1920s that the subject position enabled by these colonialist maneuvers was recognizable to a general audience for the reasons and through the mechanisms I have described above. Thus, while in the 1890s, French-Sheldon was chiefly concerned with persuading male authorities and institutions to embrace her as a viable candidate for inclusion among their ranks, by the 1920s when she read her short stories aloud to audiences primed by the mania for desert love stories and cinematic heroines, her part-

ners in the exchange of Othered women were the female audiences attending white, middle-class women's clubs and schools. The young women who
were urged to identify with French-Sheldon were encouraged to experience
subjectivity as the "users" of signs rather than "sign-objects," a subject position otherwise denied to them. In French-Sheldon's presentations, African
women—objectified, sexualized, or just plain robbed of their identifying
emblems—and their castrated or "de-speared" male counterparts became
the objects of exchange between French-Sheldon and her white, middle-
class, female admirers. Thus the Othering of Africa was the textual vehicle
by which young, middle-class white women, through forging an identificatory relationship with French-Sheldon as White Queen, constructed an inherently imperial feminist subject position for themselves as representative
modern American women.

CONCLUSION:
THE WHITE QUEEN AS WOMEN'S HISTORY

> Hardly can we look now at the map of Africa without
> picturing [Madame French-Sheldon] that small dauntless
> figure, revolver in her belt, marching at the head of her
> mile-long line of natives across that land of mystery.
> —*Carmel Pine Cone,* February 16, 1924

If "adventuresses" and "exploratresses" in the Victorian era garnered attention for being unusual novelties, it is important to note that by the 1920s
American audiences were not just fascinated by such women as eccentric or
"odd" characters, they were inspired and elated by them as representative
ideal selves. The historical significance of the avalanche of fan mail an
Amelia Earhart could inspire in the 1930s is not, as Susan Ware argues, that
feminism was "kept alive," even if that is in some small way true.[43] The significant fact about Earhart's popularity was that she became a national heroine, even an icon of national identity on the basis of her distinctly unwomanly behavior. The monumental endorsement of Earhart in the press, even
by the government itself, was staggering for its wholehearted support of a
married woman who flew airplanes for money, glory, and fame. My study
of French-Sheldon suggests that we should interrogate the success women
such as Earhart experienced in terms of its race, class, and nationalist implications. For instance, the backdrop that Mexico, India, Hawaii, and the
islands of the South Seas formed for Earhart's flights helped to throw her
nationality and race into relief and shaped the way that her feminist
achievement would be read as a consequence of race and nationality. The
implicit, and sometimes explicit, contrasts inevitably drawn between Ear-

hart and "swarthy runts" or immigrant populations helped to render her a White Queen even when the context was the United States.[44] Thus, though the "Lady Lindy" may have played second fiddle to Lindbergh to some, for a generation of young women she helped define feminist achievement as forming a central part of what it meant to be a modern, American, and white. French-Sheldon's self-presentation as a White Queen in Africa likewise tied those three attributes together, even if, at eighty years old in 1927, she was unable to take command of the national stage to the degree that a lanky, blonde, young aviatrix such as Earhart could. Still, like the "Lady Lindy," the "Lady Stanley" succeeded in re-presenting herself as the break between an unjustifiably male-dominated past and a feminist present by foregrounding a contrast between herself and racial Others that left feminist identity linked with expressions of American and white supremacy. Her career, spanning two important moments in the construction of a feminist-inflected ideal of modern American womanhood, provides the historical background needed to explain the more well-known phenomenon of Earhart and the other popular heroines of the period.

Marjorie Garber has said, "a fetish is a story masquerading as an object."[45] French-Sheldon not only told mesmerizing stories, as far as the members of her audiences were concerned, she was a living story—a historical artifact—of how feminism in America had come to be. That this story was also, necessarily, a history of the construction of a white racist and colonial imaginary might not occur to some. In this chapter, as in my study of French-Sheldon generally, I have worked to deconstruct the figure of the White Queen so as to disrupt a popular history of feminism that insistently denies its relation to colonial histories and repeatedly attempts to erase its complicity with imperial ideologies from view.

Conclusion:
The White Queen in the Mirror, or
Reflections on the Construction
of White Feminist Identity

It is possible to feel nostalgia for a place
you've never seen.
—Greta Garbo in *Queen Christina* (1933)

Like the wistful longing that Greta Garbo, playing the enlightened white queen of seventeenth-century Sweden, feels for a place where she might live unhindered by restrictions on women, nostalgia for a place and for an experience of power that they had not encountered themselves structured French-Sheldon's audiences' enthusiastic and sometimes eroticized responses to her in the 1920s. Nostalgia suggests a distance structured by time. Africa, the site of the construction of French-Sheldon's feminist subjectivity and historical self, figured nostalgically as an other time as much as an other place. Indeed, the fetishization of French-Sheldon as feminist heroine in the 1920s reveals how germane history and historicism is to modern subjectivities such as that offered by imperial feminist ideology, and how bound up with colonialist desire such acts of historicization are.[1] The distance French-Sheldon's presentations in the 1920s established between herself and a historicized image of herself as a White Queen in Africa stretched across a barrier of time/space, imagined as that which separates a modern, feminist age from a non-modern, pre-feminist one, to create a story of how feminism came to be.[2] The personal history French-Sheldon constructed was also a story of imperial power and racial privilege potent enough to inspire longing in her female audiences for the figure of the White Queen and the pacified Africa she conjured.

THE WHITE QUEEN
AS COLONIAL NOSTALGIA

The artificial nostalgia French-Sheldon evoked in audiences for Africa distanced Africa and Africans chronologically as much as spatially, thereby facilitating the very alterity that permitted French-Sheldon and her auditors to occupy the space of the modern. Homi Bhabha's work can help us think through the operations of power in such narrations. He explains the discursive power of history as a location in time/space by pointing out that "the sign of history does not consist in the essence of the event itself,

> nor exclusively in the immediate consciousness of its agents and actors, but in its form as a spectacle; spectacle that signifies because of the distanciation and displacement between the event and those who are its spectators. . . . Modernity . . . is about the historical construction of a specific position of historical enunciation and address. It privileges those who 'bear witness,' those who are 'subjected,' or in the Fanonian sense . . . historically displaced. It gives them a representative position through the spatial distance, or the time-lag between the Great Event and its circulation as a historical sign of the 'people' or an 'epoch,' that constitutes the memory and the moral of the event as a narrative, a disposition to cultural communality, a form of social and psychic identification.[3]

In French-Sheldon's presentations to audiences in the 1920s, she marked her return from her expedition as the moment between the past and the present, pre-modernity and modernity, pre-feminism and post-feminism. French-Sheldon's public persona comprised a story, the crux of which was a narrative progression culminating in woman's emancipation. Before her expedition "to show what a woman could do" white, middle-class women suffered a subordination akin to that of inferior races and nations. Subsequent to her expedition, modern American women suffer no institutional or cultural restrictions beyond a bit of atavistic and fading "prejudice" from distinctly less "advanced" corners of the social fabric. French-Sheldon echoes other voices that posit a similar history of the present. Feminism is always/already constituted in this view, and "modern" nations can only be imagined as post-feminist. Thus we see a repetitive pattern in the late nineteenth and throughout the twentieth century. The phenomenon of the new woman emerges every second or third decade as each generation of American women claims for itself the ideological inauguration of modern female subjecthood. In the logic of this history, Africa and colonized or post-colonial spaces generally remain perpetually unevolved and unsubjectified inasmuch as they fall on the same side of a line as America does before its evolution to a modern/feminist state. Africa continues to exist in the past, along with female subjugation—the two cannot be separated conceptually as both become symbols of The Past and That Which Is Not American, Modern, White, Western, or even Civilized. Part of the attraction of this graphing of feminism, modernism, history, and colonized peoples can be explained in terms of the psychological constitution of a feminist subject position and the emergence of the female/feminist fetish in the mass media of a century ago.

French-Sheldon created a female self that could be looked at, represented, spoken about—a historical self. White women in the 1920s loved French-Sheldon's performances and loved thinking of themselves as liberated, modern women who no longer faced systematic subjugation in part because to do so put a subjectifying temporal distance between them and Others. On one level of alterity, these Others were Africans; on another level they were the "pioneering" women of French-Sheldon's own generation, whose achievements had brought about the distinction between (a subjugated) past and (a liberated) present. History, then, provided the distance necessary to create (several, various) female fetishes. By desiring such fetishes, young women in the 1920s could re-imagine themselves as desiring subjects, as women who could see mirror images of themselves in the past, making them representable in History.

Many feminist philosophers, among them Luce Irigaray, argue that Woman's representation in History is antithetical to her designation as female. Irigaray demonstrates how the "masculine can partly look at itself, speculate about itself, represent itself and describe itself for what it is, whilst the feminine can try to speak to itself through a new language, but cannot describe itself from outside or in formal terms, except by identifying itself with the masculine, thus by losing itself."[4] Yet French-Sheldon's hyper-realized self as *Bebe Bwana* or the White Queen *was* a real self—that is, a self imagined as having a historical dimension rather than presented as purely fictional. Her masquerade of Woman allowed her to put Woman as lack behind her in history, at once to distance that part of herself enough to own that (Othered) self, and to own the desire for that (Othered) self. Becoming a desiring subject was a central component of the new feminist identity that emerged as a fully subjectified ideal during the 1910s and 1920s.

I have shown why it was crucial that French-Sheldon insisted upon her womanliness at all times, mocking those who imagined her as "unsexed" in Africa, for it was Woman that French-Sheldon intended to hyperbolize in order to distance. Coming across as mannish to her audiences would not have put the subjectifying mechanism of the fetish at her disposal. It is not incidental that French-Sheldon's feminist achievement, that which permits a line to be drawn between the past (in which Woman remains wholly unsubjectified) and a present (in which modern women are liberated from nothing more nor less than the past itself) takes place in a context over-determined as the Past—Africa. Such a contextualization permits French-Sheldon and audience members who identified with her to displace castrated womanliness onto that other time/place with all things imagined as defiled and Other. By imagining that her castrated self only exists in history, French-Sheldon and her audiences could maintain that feminist liberation had always/already occurred in the modern West. The White Queen could be adored as a fetish symbolizing the end to exclusion from subjective existence and the public sphere of History. The poem written by an adoring fan expressing love for French-Sheldon or the "jewelled door" that had swung wide allowing entry to a banquet hall filled with men who had "grown into a collossal size" (discussed in chapters 8 and 9) can be read as one fan's articulation of French-Sheldon as "post-feminist" fetish or the metaphorical distancing mechanism ("the door disclosing all") that has permitted a female fetish allowing those young women to see/desire/own/inhabit that room and the vision of themselves in it. In projecting an image of her historical self, French-Sheldon activated a fetishism that is at once modern and historicist, feminist and post-feminist, humanist and imperialist.

"Post-feminism" may be a neologism that belongs properly to the generation that came of age in the 1980s and 1990s, but as the shadowy underside of feminist narratives and interventions in popular culture, the ideas it conveys have a near century-long existence and should not be considered apart from feminism's more official political and academic discourses of empowerment for women. Like French-Sheldon's one-woman representation of feminist history, the very practice of women's history by academics and the popularization of depictions of women in history inevitably are interpreted as feminist gestures, often in disregard of particular political message or content. The same distancing mechanisms I have outlined here are often employed by popular renditions of women's history to achieve the establishment of woman's subjecthood with similar rhetorical moves. Putting Woman in the past, in effect creating a pantheon of feminist fetishes, establishes the distance between subject and object required to position women as speaking/desiring subjects-of-history. However, when "liberation" means little beyond liberation from an unspecified but abjured Past, the function of women's history is reduced to nothing more than a mechanism of temporal distancing which only serves some women imagined as modern ones by virtue of their national, racial, and class-specific affiliations. This study has been an attempt to split open a confluence of the discourses of history, evolution, modernism, feminism, science, racism, and imperialism by exposing the operations of the imperial feminist fetish at the moment of the

White Queen's successful incorporation into the narratives of American popular culture.

DISENTANGLING IMPERIALISM AND FEMINISM IN POPULAR CULTURE

> You've got yourself a PARTNER!
> —Marion to Indiana Jones in
> *Raiders of the Lost Ark* (1981)

The effacement of Africa and Africans in twentieth-century popular narratives featuring "plucky" and empowered white heroines, such as the character of Marion in the popular 1980s action film, *Raiders of the Lost Ark,* perpetuates the ideological interdependence between Western imperialism and public notions of white American or Western feminism. Such narratives have provided a cultural framework that continues to shape the meaning of any self-identified feminist representation—white and Western-authored or otherwise—in ways that continue to counterpose Western modernity and feminism with non-Western "traditionalism" and patriarchy. The interventions of May French-Sheldon and other figures like her helped make this ideological configuration central to the development of American national identity as well as to myriad global struggles that have arranged themselves around an opposition between Western imperialist/modern/feminist and anti-imperialist/traditional/patriarchal. French-Sheldon's public persona reveals many of the most salient characteristics of the interface between cultural imperialism and feminism as it has commonly appeared in the mass media of the last century. While this study recognizes that academic and activist feminists' access to mass media in the late twentieth century is not unknown, my focus on the construction of mass ideals of feminism stems from the belief that a popular understanding of feminism in the United States has followed more from the vaguely defined but unmistakable stamp of feminism that the popular press and entertainment media have put on particular American female characters and celebrities. Even if white middle-class women (for whom, I would argue, a feminist identity as defined in mass culture is most open) often disclaim knowing precisely what the tenets of feminism might include, they readily recognize and often identify with the signifying elements of the feminist as archetype when encountering her in a narrative text. Meryl Streep as the genteel but determined plantation mistress in East Africa (*Out of Africa,* 1985), Sigourney Weaver as the pioneer gorilla scientist in Central Africa (*Gorillas in the Mist,* 1988), and Holly Hunter as a defiantly mute mail-order bride in colonial New Zealand (*The Piano,* 1993), to choose three latter-day cinematic examples of celebrated imperial feminist heroines or White Queens, communicate the qualities popularly assigned to feminists in the minds of audiences with nary a mention of feminism. Explicitly identifying these figures as feminists in the script is unnecessary. Inevitably popular heroines are overdetermined as feminists through an association between them and colonial penetration (imagining them as frontier women, settlers, or adventurers), Western technology (think of Beryl Markham's and Amelia Earhart's airplanes), or scientific knowledge (especially anthropological knowledge of the "Primitive" or biological expertise such as primatology). The heroines of these stories are imagined as feminists by audiences, not as a result of any specific political position they espouse but by virtue of their ability to demonstrate their racial and national identity. It is no coincidence that so many of these narratives take place principally in Africa or other locales imagined as non-white, non-Western, and non-modern. Such narratives tie popular ideas of feminists to racist, nationalist, and class-specific ideologies by presenting feminism as if it were merely a sign of Western/white/bourgeois superiority. Though non-white and non-middle-class members of audiences may forge some identification with imperial feminist characters, or White Queens as I think of these figures, and subvert those representations in the process, white middle-class women specifically are "hailed" or interpellated by the character of the White Queen. White middle-class women are invited to experience the thrill of full subjecthood by identifying with female characters who have been elevated to the status of Western representatives and permitted to occupy a position next to their elite male counterparts as the Universal Human through an emphasis on their colonialist status. Such figures invite identification with them on the basis of an exclusive relationship to modernity that, as members of a nation imagined as superlatively modern, American white women enjoy collectively (even if unevenly). With this biographical study, I have tried to unpack the persistent image of the White Queen not by pointing out the obvious imperial features of its contemporary manifestations but by hunting down its genealogical traces. The point has been to convey the historical significance of imperial feminism as well as to demonstrate the imperative of dismantling its apparatuses.

The bane of the historicist is the tendency to reconstruct that which we desire to deconstruct. Like other cautionary voices in this post-colonial world, Judith Butler calls upon feminist scholars to heed the criticism launched against the Subject as "an instrument of Western imperialist hegemony." She warns us not to "adopt the very models of domination, not realizing that one way in which domination works is through the regulation and production of subjects."[5] My focus on May French-Sheldon is an attempt to deconstruct feminism as a discourse that produces subjectified and subjected positions. However much I have striven for coherence, I have tried hard to prevent the reader from settling back to absorb this history of feminism and of French-Sheldon as if it were a straightforward biography or narrativized life history. I do not wish to reproduce French-Sheldon as the auteur or originator of imperial feminist discourse. My intention is to contribute to a deconstruction of the discourse that in part produced the French-Sheldon that emerges from these pages. Following Gayatri Chakravorty Spivak's Foucauldian perspective on deconstruction, I maintain that "to describe a formulation qua statement does not consist in analyzing the relations between the author and what she was (or wanted to say, or said without wanting to); but in determining what position can and must be occupied by any individual if she is to be the subject of it."[6] I see French-Sheldon's public self as a primary example of a subject position assigned by the emerging imperial feminist discourse at the turn of the century. By concentrating on one figure at a particularly dynamic moment in the construction of a problematic popular understanding of feminism, I have tried not just to reposition the spotlight back onto a White Queen—to re-fetishize her for the identificatory pleasure of the reader. Instead I have attempted to shine light on her feminine audiences, those subjects-in-the-making, and to dispel the shadows surrounding her Others confined in the wings and backstage, that is those who became *subject to* a maternalist (at best) white, American, feminist imaginary a century ago. The overarching question that has shaped this study of French-Sheldon is best phrased, again, by Judith Butler, who asks, "Through what exclusions has the feminist subject been constructed, and how do those excluded domains return to haunt the 'integrity' and 'unity' of the feminist 'we'?"[7]

I have focused on the set of imperial images that surrounded and constructed French-Sheldon as a feminist heroine to illuminate the Othering practices which have become embedded in everyday, seemingly harmless or relatively insignificant, celebrations of "Woman's" spirit. I would like to cast doubt on the preliminary celebration implicit within the post-modern discovery of "gender-b(l)ending" subjectivities that "exist in the margins of hegemonic discourses" and are "inscribed in micropolitical practices . . . [whose] effects are at the 'local' level of resistances, in subjectivity and self-representation."[8] This work has been an attempt to explain how the construction of subjectivities in the contradictions (the "chinks and cracks") endemic to patriarchal ideologies are not necessarily subversive or are not only subversive: such construction acts to subvert one hierarchical relationship but, in so doing, perpetuates (and reconfigures) others. Space in the margin is no less a site of contestatory power relations than is the space at the center and cannot be assumed to inspire purely "democratic" or "liberating" subjectivites that are not constructed at the expense of (other) Others. This is true of feminist "resistant" subjectivities and empowering historical narra-

tives as well. In the United States, women's studies scholarship often rein-
states class, race, and national hierarchies. This is not simply a ramification
of the overwhelming homogeneity of women's studies in terms of race and
class, though such homogeneity contributes to the problem. White feminist
scholars, for the most part, believe class, race, gender domination is connected, but their work often neglects to explain how this is so. Such a conclusion is defended without being understood by white feminists because
their identity as subjects are at stake. This study means to direct our attention to the ways in which white feminists have experienced and achieved
their subjectivity through White Queen representations (as well as other
problematic cultural constructions) that have been rife within the popular
culture of the last century. White middle-class feminism, as it was histori-
cally permitted by the Enlightenment and then catapulted into a position of
hegemony in the United States by Progressive Era ideologies and events, has
relied on race, class, and national hierarchies to construct itself and to promote the interests of the women to whom it refers. White middle-class feminists do not often threaten these hierarchies not (just) because they lack the
power to do so, but because the serious reconfiguration of these power
structures destabilizes feminist subjectivity as much as it unsettles the hegemony of contemporary liberal humanist ones generally. So why am I, a
white-identified feminist scholar, so concerned about a popular archetype
like the White Queen, seeing as, if I am right, it is just such subjectifying
ideals that have produced my very identity, the class-specific feminine subject position that allows/compels me to speak? Three caveats to the assertions regarding imperial feminism I have made so far in this conclusion
point to the reasons.

First, imperial feminism is not all of feminism. I have tracked one strain
of popular feminist images that at times (like the 1920s) successfully overwhelmed the public understanding of what women's political resistance to
normative femininity was all about. However, if all of twentieth-century
feminism were eclipsed entirely by the figure of the White Queen in mass
cultural narratives, it would be difficult to explain why all or at least most
white middle-class women in the United States have not always resonated to
its representation or been tempted to represent themselves in such a manner. In addition, though white middle-class feminists in the twentieth century have relied heavily on imperial feminist imagery, this does not mean
the hegemonic ideology lacks its own "chinks and interstices" within which
subjectivities might have/be formed that subvert such a set of representations; it is an ideology after all. As with any ideological formulation, the
White Queen is internally contradicted and unstable. My explanations of
the paradoxes in French-Sheldon's texts hopefully reveal to the reader the

gaping holes and contradictoriness of the imperial feminist even in its classic form.

Second, the contradictions and slippages within imperial feminism are related to the caveat that imperial feminism exceeds itself. Not only is it true that *feminist* can and often has prompted something other than or more than imperial feminist meanings, the figure of the White Queen, like any other ideological phenomenon, accomplishes more and less than its purveyors and personifiers intend. Though I have focused on presenting imperial feminism as a coherent discourse to underscore its effective operations, I do not intend to imply that this discourse is static or univocal. The readings given to imperial feminist characters are multiple, as are the uses to which they are put and the contexts in which they are deployed. For example, the hegemonic position of imperial feminism has produced a distinct discourse, the "white woman's burden," giving rise to inter- and intra-national conflicts that take on their own trajectories as anti-feminism becomes a rallying cry for anti-Western, post-colonial nationalists.

Third, imperial feminism efficiently helps to perpetuate the hierarchies that benefit elite women, but it certainly does not succeed in dismantling the category of Woman, nor does it make good on its promise to establish unequivocal subjecthood for even those women most privileged by its discursive power. The same contradiction that keeps the White Queen as somehow similar to the very Othered women she seeks to differentiate herself from poses a persistent danger threatening to render her imperial subjectivity moot. In other words, imperial feminism sows the seeds of the dismantling of its own subject position. Its unreliability points back to the critique of non-white or otherwise marginalized feminists that dominant feminists cannot afford to ignore issues of class, race, and imperialism in their work without endangering the efficacy of their own analyses, even for themselves. It is important to make explicit exactly why this is true.

It is not that the gender oppression elite feminists experience cannot be eradicated because all hierarchies must fall at once for gender to fall. Or, that is not exactly it. It is more true that one can not dissolve Woman for oneself without dissolving it for others, too. Gender is often posed as a binarism inherent to the human condition such that if there is no such thing as Woman here, there can be no such thing as Woman there, at least as we know Woman to be.[9] Since what the White Queen does is deploy Woman as an Othering strategy in her attempt to displace feminine subjugation away from herself and onto colonized women, she cannot relinquish the ontological category or even her own (ambivalent) relationship to it. In other words, though her subjectivity is that granted to her by men as an exception of her sex, she nevertheless remains of her sex. As long as the White

Queen needs Other women (who are definitely not subjectified, not liberated or feminist; everybody cannot be an exception to a rule without collapsing the category) to demonstrate that she is a renegade from the category to which she would otherwise seem confined, paradoxically she remains linked with Woman whenever considered apart from a colonized context. As May French-Sheldon once explained to a fawning reporter, "It is only in the West that my sex really matters."

In the early twentieth-century, the White Queen as a cultural maneuver proved to be one of the most powerful cultural strategies of elite women on their own behalf, not incidentally supporting the United States in defense of its hegemonic status. Imperial feminist narratives have served in part to explain the United States's rise to world power and to justify white middle-class dominance within the United States in the twentieth century. Further, imperial feminist ideology has helped pilot domestic and international gender politicking throughout the twentieth century and into the twenty-first. However attractive and empowering, the representation in the mass media of the strong-minded Western/white woman—necessarily more liberated than her miserably oppressed and often compliant Eastern/non-white sister—succeeded in anchoring a popular notion of feminism to a set of colonial relations. The resonating image of the White Queen has operated at many levels of mainstream American culture to produce a public understanding of feminism that is more than Eurocentric; it is imperialist. My work on May French-Sheldon has led me to believe that a feminism that could succeed in truly freeing me from the ontological subjection of Womanhood would necessarily entail an abandonment of the colonizing strategy of displacing Woman onto Others. Robbing the White Queen of cultural power will require a commitment to the construction of organizational and intellectual weapons aimed at destroying the forces that enact imperial feminism in the name of and in place of feminist liberation. It is my hope that this piece of scholarship contributes to that feminist struggle.

NOTES

INTRODUCTION

1. Patricia Romero, in *Women's Voices on Africa* (New York: Marcus Wiener, 1992), identifies Florence Ninian Von Sass Baker as the first white female explorer of Africa for her travels with her husband, Sir Samuel Baker, who was credited with discovering Lake Albert in east-central Africa in 1861. There were certainly other women whose exploratory travel in Africa predated French-Sheldon's as well; French-Sheldon's claim to the title rested on the fact that she traveled without a husband or European companion (see also note 3 in this chapter).

2. Women did compete with men for authority in colonial East Africa in other ways, particularly in the organization of German hospital services and infrastructure. See Lora Wildenthal, *German Women for Empire, 1884–1945* (Durham, N.C.: Duke University Press, 2001).

3. Arguably, Annie Hore represents French-Sheldon's closest female competitor in sub-Saharan African exploration. Hore traveled, as the title of her travelogue *To Lake Tanganyika in a Bath Chair* (1886) attests, in order to join her husband, a surveyor sent by the British to Ujiji to map the shores of the lake and to study the nations surrounding it. Her purpose in joining him was to help establish a mission on Kavala Island, but she also took advantage of her 830-mile journey from the coast to attempt to show that the route could support wheeled transport. (The porters, who were forced to carry her and her son in a bath chair nearly the entire way, proved that the route could not.) Hore's expedition preceded French-Sheldon's by more than five years, did not include white male chaperonage, was at least as hazardous and scientific, and was recorded in a published account. Nonetheless, French-Sheldon discounted Hore and the few other female missionaries and wives of male missionaries or colonial officers from earlier in the century as not having traveled to Africa purely for the purposes of exploration. The British and American publics simply overlooked Hore's less grandiose and less widely publicized travel completely in their acceptance of French-Sheldon's claim to being the first. Jane Robinson, *Wayward Women: A Guide to Women Travellers* (Oxford: Oxford University Press, 1990), 162–163.

4. In Kiswahili, *bebe* is a term of respect akin to *madame* and is applied to women who have reached middle age or are aged. *Bwana* is a term like *sir*. Though it is used to address supervisors and superiors, it can be applied to males generally without regard to familiarity or to rank (even a young boy might be hailed as *bwana*). There is no such term as *Bebe Bwana*, and it is impossible to tell whether French-Sheldon made up this term herself or if Africans, in fact, ever used it to address her.

5. Ellen Jordan argues in "The Christening of the New Woman," *Victorian Newsletter* 63 (Spring 1983), 19–21, that the phrase *new woman* first appeared in 1894 in the British press in a review of an essay authored by Sarah Grand, "The New Aspect of the Woman Question." A play authored by Sydney Grundy later that same year, "The New Woman," popularized the term further. See Ann Ardis, *New Women, New Novels* (New Brunswick,

N.J.: Rutgers University Press, 1990), p. 10–11, n. 179. For a discussion of the continuities and disparities between the uses of the term *new woman* in the 1890s compared with its use in the 1920s, see Ellen Wiley Todd, "Art, the 'New Woman,' and Consumer Culture," in *Gender and American History since 1890,* ed. Barbara Melosh (London: Routledge, 1993), 127–154; Estelle Freedman, "The New Woman: Changing Views of Women in the 1920s," *Journal of American History* (September 1974): 372–393.

6. Valerie Amos and Pratibha Parmar may have been the first scholars to utilize the phrase *imperial feminist* in their essay "Challenging Imperial Feminism," *Feminist Review* 17 (Autumn 1984): 3–17. My use of the phrase is in accordance with their work and several other scholars researching the problematics of imperial ideologies as they relate to the development of feminism. Antoinette M. Burton identifies a "British Imperial Feminism" at work in Josephine Butler's crusade against the Contagious Diseases Acts in India (1886–1915) in her article "The White Woman's Burden: British Feminists and 'The Indian Woman,' 1865–1915," in *Western Women and Imperialism: Complicity and Resistance,* ed. Nupur Chaudhuri and Margaret Strobel (Bloomington: Indiana University Press, 1992), 137–157 (the term appears on pp. 139, 151); in the same collection Barbara N. Ramusack refers to this same set of impulses as "maternal feminism" in her article, "Cultural Missionaries, Maternal Imperialists, Feminist Allies," 119–136. While I am chary about applying the term *feminist* to historical phenomena that predate the term's inception in language, I agree that colonialist imaginings of gender among mid-nineteenth-century reformers and colonialists prefigured the feminist trope I am attempting to historicize here. For other studies that situate feminism within the context of empire, see Aihwa Ong, "Colonialism and Modernity: Feminist Re-Presentations of Women in Non-Western Societies," *Inscriptions: Groups for the Critical Study of Colonial Discourse* 3/4 (1989): 79–93; Vron Ware, *Beyond the Pale: White Women, Racism, and History* (London: Verso, 1992); Laura E. Donaldson, *Decolonizing Feminisms: Race, Gender, and Empire Building* (Chapel Hill: University of North Carolina Press, 1992); Sidonie Smith, "The Other Woman and the Racial Politics of Gender," in *De/Colonizing the Subject: The Politics of Gender in Women's Autobiography,* ed. Sidonie Smith and Julia Watson (Minneapolis: University of Minnesota Press, 1992), 410–435; Mrinalini Sinha, "Gender and Imperialism: Colonial Policy and the Ideology of Moral imperialism in Late Nineteenth-Century Bengal," in *Changing Men,* ed. Michael Kimmel (London: Sage, 1987), 217–231; Marnia Lazreg, "Feminism and Difference: The Perils of Writing as a Woman on Women in Algeria," *Feminist Studies* 14, no. 1 (Spring 1988): 81–107; Devoney Looser, "Scolding Lady Mary Wortley Montagu? The Problematics of Sisterhood in Feminist Criticism," in *Feminist Nightmares, Women at Odds: Feminism and the Problem of Sisterhood,* ed. Susan Ostrov Weisser and Jennifer Fleischner (New York: New York University Press, 1994), 44–61; Caren Kaplan, "Getting to Know You: Travel, Gender, and the Politics of Representation in *Anna and the King of Siam* and *The King and I,"* in *Late Imperial Culture,* ed. Roman de la Campa, E. Ann Kaplan, and Michael Sprinker (London: Verso, 1995).

7. For an in-depth analysis of French-Sheldon's performance and participation in the fair, see my article "White Queens at the Chicago World's Fair, 1893: New Womanhood in the Service of Class, Race, and Nation," *Gender and History* 12, no. 1 (April 2000): 33–81. See also Jeanne Madeline Weimann, *The Fair Women* (Chicago: Academy Press, 1981), 439–442.

8. Fannie C. Williams, "A 'White Queen' at the World's Fair," *Chautauquan* 18 (1893): 342.

9. See also T. J. Boisseau, "White Queens at the World's Fair, 1893."

10. Ann Heilmann offers an excellent articulation of just how heterogeneous, and internally conflicted at times, the discourse of new womanhood was in *New Woman Fiction: Women Writing First-Wave Feminism* (New York: Macmillan/St. Martin's Press, 2000).

11. Rita Felski, *The Gender of Modernity* (Cambridge, Mass.: Harvard University Press, 1995); Ann Hermann, *The Queering of the Moderns* (New York: Palgrave, 2000).

12. For more on this period, see Nancy Cott, *The Grounding of Modern Feminism* (New Haven, Conn.: Yale University Press, 1987).

13. My utilization of the phrase *civilizing mission* is meant to invoke more than merely the mindset of Christian missionaries in the nineteenth and early twentieth century who believed that their evangelical efforts around the globe benefited "savage" or "barbarian" non-Christians by extending the precepts of civilization as well as spiritual salvation to them. Because even Americans who rejected religious proselytizing and opposed missionary interventions in colonial settings, such as French-Sheldon, embraced a secular "mission" to civilize others, this phrase should be viewed as referring to the idea held generally by Anglo-Americans that Anglo-Saxon culture represented the culmination of human evolution and that, as a consequence of that fact, Anglo-Saxons were duty-bound to "save the world by imposing their own culture on it." See Leslie A. Flemming, "A New Humanity: American Missionaries' Ideals for Women in North India, 1870–1930," in *Women and Imperialism,* ed. Nupur Chaudhuri and Margaret Strobel, 191–206 (quote appears on p. 191). For a thorough discussion of the tendency of white Americans to perceive civilization as a trait of Anglo-Saxon culture, see George W. Stocking Jr., *Race, Culture, and Evolution* (New York: Free Press, 1968).

14. Ladelle Rice, "Lions, Savages, White Eagles, Nothing before Woman Who Faces African Trials Alone," *Daily Lariat,* February 6, 1925. The *Daily Lariat* was the college newspaper for Baylor University in Waco, Texas, where French-Sheldon lectured to enthusiastic audiences in the mid-1920s.

15. See Jill Lapore, "Historians Who Love Too Much: Reflections on Microhistory and Biography," *Journal of American History* 88, no. 1 (June 2001): 129–144.

16. See note 6 in this introduction for the many studies that recognize this dimension and problematize this notion comprising a relatively new subfield of scholarship on "western women and imperialism," as the title of one of the most important of these works signals.

17. Jeanne Madeleine Moore, "Bibi Bwana," *American History Illustrated* 21 (1986): 36–42.

18. Ibid.

19. Eli Lemon Sheldon and May French-Sheldon, trans., *Japan in Art and Industry: With a Glance at Japanese Manners and Customs,* by Félix Régamey (New York: Putnam and Sons, 1893).

20. French-Sheldon, *Herbert Severance: A Novel* (Chicago: Rand, McNally, 1889).

21. Henry Morton Stanley to Eli Sheldon, 6 October 1885, cat. #4/1/7, H. M. Stanley Collection, Archives of the Royal Geographical Society of London.

22. T. J. Boisseau, "White Queens at the World's Fair, 1893."

23. Eli Sheldon reportedly died of complications arising from treatment for "pleurisy"—a common euphemism used at the time to explain or cover up a host of probable illnesses, most scandalous of which would have been venereal disease or syphilis.

24. Circumstances such as the charge of failure to consummate made by his wife who divorced him after two years of marriage point to the possibility that Wellcome was part of a homosexual circle of friends that included Eli Sheldon. See also note 3 in chapter 1 for further discussion of the rumors that circulated around this group of men.

25. "True womanhood" as an early- to mid-nineteenth-century ideal was first identified by Barbara Welter. She lists purity, piety, submissiveness, and domesticity as its cardinal features in her groundbreaking article "The Cult of True Womanhood, 1820–1860," *American Quarterly* 18 (Summer 1966): 151–174.

26. Karen Offen, in "Defining Feminism: A Comparative Historical Approach," *Signs* (Autumn 1988): 119–157, and in "On the French Origins of the Words *Feminism* and

Feminist," Feminist Issues 8, no. 2 (Fall 1988): 45–51, discusses the introduction of these terms into European and American vocabularies in this period. She locates the first appearance of the term in the American press in 1913.

27. A good example is Juliet Flower MacCannell, "Things to Come: A Hysteric's Guide to the Future Female Subject," in *Supposing the Subject,* ed. Joan Copjec (London: Verso, 1994). For a discussion of the Lacanian and Althusserian subjects in conjunction, see Stephen Heath, "The Turn of the Subject," *Cine-Tracts* 8 (Summer–Fall 1979): 32–48. Catherine Belsey explains Althusser's subject in ideology in her work *Critical Practice* (London: Methuen, 1980), 56–65.

28. Joan Scott, "Gender: A Useful Category of Analysis," in *Gender and the Politics of History* (1988; reprint, New York: Columbia University Press, 1999), 42.

29. For an expanded discussion of the opportunities that commodity capitalism provides for women to shape their identity and transform their social relations, see Sarah Berry, *Screen Style* (Minneapolis: University of Minnesota Press, 2000).

30. Susan Ware, *Still Missing: The Search for Modern American Feminism* (New York: W. W. Norton, 1993), 24–25.

31. Much of postmodern feminist cultural theory, in the words of Teresa Ebert, "theorizes culture as an ensemble of conflicting discourses that aim at producing and maintaining subjectivities." "The Romance of Patriarchy: Ideology, Subjectivity, and Postmodern Feminist Cultural Theory," *Cultural Critique* 10 (Fall 1988): 19–57 (quote appears on p. 22).

32. Anne McClintock, *Imperial Leather: Race, Gender, and Sexuality in the Colonial Contest* (New York: Routledge, 1995), 72.

1. THE CARAVAN TREK
TO KILIMANJARO

1. French-Sheldon included this epigraph to the rough draft of an unpublished manuscript entitled "Belgium: Little Mother of a Giant," box 7, M. French-Sheldon Papers, Manuscript Division, Library of Congress.

2. "Ho! For East Africa" is the title of the first chapter in *Sultan to Sultan* (Boston: Arena Press, 1892). For the sake of brevity, *SS* followed by page numbers will be used to identify evidence drawn from this text; page numbers refer to Manchester University Press's recent republication in 1999.

3. Henry Solomon Wellcome, born in Wisconsin in 1853 into a poor farming family, started as a pharmacist's assistant and made his fortune with the help of the wealthier Silas Burroughs with whom he founded Burroughs-Wellcome in 1881. Wellcome ran the British side of the business in London, where he met the Sheldons in the early 1880s. Wellcome's friendship with Henry Stanley, whom he met in the Sheldons' home, led to a passionate interest in medical anthropology and the collection of a vast store of travelers' artifacts, especially from Africa. Wellcome enhanced his own social standing and business contacts by founding the American Society in London, at which he entertained American VIPs and wrote letters of introduction for British capitalists planning trips to the United States. Like Henry Stanley and Eli Sheldon, he was a member of the Savage Club and was an avid philanthropist. The Sheldons were his best friends in London during this period; he stayed in their home during the winter of 1885–1886, recuperating from an illness, and resided with Eli again during the spring of 1891 while May was away in Africa. His close friendship with the Sheldons caused tongues to wag enough that Eli felt compelled to make public statements concerning the platonic nature of Wellcome's relationship with his wife. Wellcome eventually married (unhappily—within a couple of years following the wedding his wife sued for divorce on the grounds that Wellcome refused to consummate the marriage). Al-

though Wellcome's friendship with May deepened following the death of Eli in 1892, and despite the fact that he aided May financially from time to time, there is no evidence that he felt romantically about her. Indeed, there is more reason to speculate that he was homosexual and that he and Eli Sheldon had been lovers. See Robert Rhodes James, *Henry Wellcome* (London: Hodder and Stoughton, 1994).

4. "From Darkest Africa," *Punch, or the London Charivari,* September 5, 1891, 119. This was not the only time *Punch* lampooned French-Sheldon. An interview with French-Sheldon published in *Womanhood* in the next decade regarding African women and polygamous marriages prompted a vicious reverie from the weekly on African men entitled "The White Man's Burden" (reprinted in *Womanhood,* March 1901).

5. French-Sheldon took along the second such kit; Wellcome had sent the first travel kit with Stanley on his recent expedition to find the Emin Pasha (see note 15). Wellcome proceeded to donate kits to all of the high-profile travelers in that period, including Theodore Roosevelt, Richard Byrd, Robert Perry, and Robert Scott. By the first decade of the twentieth century, most professional explorers considered the kit an indispensable item.

6. Traveling in second class was the maid French-Sheldon had brought with her. French-Sheldon does not reveal in *Sultan to Sultan* the fact that she brought a maidservant with her beyond an obscure reference to "the helpless illness of one I took to serve me," in *SS,* 213.

7. See introduction and note 5, for an expanded discussion of "new womanhood."

8. See press release, Arena Press, M. French-Sheldon Papers, box 7.

9. Henry Morton Stanley, *How I Found Livingstone* (1872; reprint, New York: Scribner, Armstrong, and Co., 1972). See also *In Darkest Africa* (New York: Scribner's, 1890).

10. This debate raged in other national contexts as well. See, for example, Lora Wildenthal's discussion of masculinity, violence, and colonialism in *German Women for Empire, 1884–1945* (Durham, N.C.: Duke University Press, 2001).

11. French-Sheldon claimed to have been conversant with many of the most illustrious of nineteenth-century novelists, including George Eliot; Maupassant; Daudet; Zola; and especially Flaubert, whose *Salammbô* French-Sheldon was the first to translate into English in 1885 (followed within months by several other English versions). She claimed that it was her personal relationship with the Flaubert family that facilitated her winning the right to translate Flaubert's most famous orientalist novel. Next to her African travels, and despite the atrocious reviews of her translation, French-Sheldon was most proud of this accomplishment and the fact that her version of *Salammbô* was placed in Flaubert's tomb by order of the French government. French-Sheldon published the translation of *Salammbô* herself, at her and Eli's recently acquired and personally owned printing house, Saxon and Company, in 1886.

12. Although American admiration for Stanley would not wane even in the 1890s, the debate over his methods was to heat up in the context of the American acquisition of Hawaii and other territories in the 1890s. For an expanded discussion of imperialist versus anti-imperialist discussions rife within this decade, see William Appleman Williams, *The Tragedy of American Diplomacy* (New York: Dell, 1959).

13. See letters between Henry Stanley and Eli Sheldon, 17 June 1885, cat. #4/1/4, and 6 October 1885, cat. #4/1/7, in the H. M. Stanley Collection at the Archives of the Royal Geographical Society in London.

14. Leopold had founded the African International Association eight years earlier with the ostensible purpose of discouraging the slave trade in Africa by encouraging exploration and generally opening up the interior to Western influence. In reality, Leopold hoped to secure in the form of a personal possession as much of Africa as he could. Between 1877 and 1885, Leopold launched four major expeditions from the east coast of Africa to Lake Tanganyika, all with vaguely scientific aims. At the Berlin Congress in 1884–1885, Leopold

capitalized on the groundwork these expeditions and other machinations had established to persuade the other European powers to grant him a large degree of control over an area of central Africa thirty times the size of Belgium.

15. Emin Pasha was the title of a German-born physician named Eduard Schnitzer. Schnitzer converted to Islam and moved to Khartoum in 1875 where he began a private practice. After a short time in Khartoum, Schnitzer (then known as Emin Effendi) traveled further up the Nile River to Lado where he met the British governor of the Sudan, Charles Gordon. "Pasha" Gordon engaged Schnitzer/Emin Effendi as his medical officer and within two years appointed the doctor as governor in his stead. Emin Pasha (as Schwitzer then became known) evacuated Lado in 1885 in response to the Mahdist successful uprising against the British/Egyptian government. Emin Pasha, one of only two governors not killed or imprisoned by the Mahdi, established a last-stand capital at Wadelai. He and his camp of about ten thousand were blocked from reaching the east coast by the residents of the intervening land who recognized that the Pasha and his followers would completely deplete the land of crops if allowed to pass through. Both the British and the Germans had an interest in locating the Emin Pasha. They both intended to use expeditions to rescue him as excuses to secure the surrounding territory. Sir William MacKinnon organized the British expedition and chose Stanley to lead it. Though Stanley was supposedly working for the British, the route he chose (he sailed all the way around the southern tip of Africa to the mouth of the Congo River to sail or march upriver towards Emin Pasha) revealed that an important objective of this rescue mission was to help consolidate Leopold's claim to the Congo region.

16. Henry Stanley to Eli Sheldon, 1 May 1891, cat. #4/1/13, H. M. Stanley Collection.

17. Henry Stanley to George S. Mackenzie, 15 January 1891, and to Sir Francis de Winton, 16 January 1891, M. French-Sheldon Papers, box 1.

18. Stanley's concern in cautioning French-Sheldon to be circumspect may refer to the plans he and Eli Sheldon had been making regarding an East African railway. Stanley may also be referring to the personal and possibly sexual relationship he shared with Sheldon.

19. Sir William MacKinnon's British India Steam Navigation Company brought the first scheduled passenger, mail, and cargo service to Zanzibar and had the cable extended to the island from Aden. MacKinnon later formed the Imperial British East Africa Company, which managed British interests in the area from 1888 to 1893. The "Plumed Knight," as James G. Blaine was known in his native Maine, supported French-Sheldon, the "White Queen," principally because they had an associate in common in William E. Curtis, an influential New York lawyer and businessman. More generally, Blaine's foreign policy objectives (though focused primarily on Latin America) aligned with French-Sheldon's intentions to scout out the possibilities for commercial relationships with East Africans. For more on Blaine's influence on U.S. extracontinental ambitions, see Walter LaFeber, *The New Empire: An Interpretation of American Expansion, 1860–1898* (Ithaca, N.Y.: Cornell University Press, 1963), 46–47, 102–105.

20. The phrase suggests an author's gathering of background material for the setting of a novel. Rider Haggard had recently visited the area around Mombasa and used his knowledge of the area to illustrate his best-selling novel *She: A History of Adventure* (1887). Likely this, French-Sheldon's lack of any previous geographical or scientific training, and French-Sheldon's prior publishing success (her novel *Herbert Severance* was published by Rand McNally and won the Bookman Prize in 1889) lent credence to the idea that conducting research for a novel was her aim.

21. See also chapter 4 in this book for an expanded discussion of this meeting.

22. *Posho* is more commonly known as *ugali* in the region today.

23. Donald Simpson, *Dark Companions: The African Contribution to the European Exploration of East Africa* (New York: Barnes and Noble Books, 1976), 5.

24. In *Sultan to Sultan,* French-Sheldon complained woefully about the fact that the (possibly French) maidservant she brought with her from Europe was incapacitated by illness for the entire trek, thus preoccupying the female African servants that French-Sheldon had hired and "depriving" her of their attentions and labor. *SS,* 213.

25. *Wa* is a Swahili prefix indicating *the people of* an area or language group.

26. German women likely staffed the military hospital that treated French-Sheldon. The women's groups active in establishing and supporting such hospitals were actively engaged in the same sorts of debates over women's role in colonization and relations to the primitive, and although French-Sheldon maintained an active dislike for Germans and German culture her entire life, contact with such women may have contributed to her ideas. See, for example, parallels between my reading of French-Sheldon and Lora Wildenthal's analysis of Frieda Von Bulow in *German Women for Empire.*

2. SELF-DISCOVERY

1. French-Sheldon often bragged that the expedition had cost her $50,000.

2. J. S. Pond to M. French-Sheldon, November 16, 1889, cat. #4/4/3, H. M. Stanley Collection, Archives of the Royal Geographical Society, London.

3. Arena Press, press release, box 7, M. French-Sheldon Papers, Manuscript Division, Library of Congress.

4. M. French-Sheldon Papers, box 7.

5. Advertising flyer, M. French-Sheldon Papers, box 7.

6. Ibid.

7. M. French-Sheldon Papers, box 7.

8. Emile Benveniste defines *subjectivity* as "the capacity of the speaker to posit himself as 'subject,' the psychic unity that transcends the totality of the actual experiences it assembles and that makes the permanence of the consciousness" in *Problems in General Linguistics,* trans. Mary Elizabeth Meek (Coral Gables, Fla.: University of Miami Press, 1971), 224–226. My use of the term here is meant to imply both an unspecified subject's emergence through language and the imperialist mastery over self and Others that the Enlightenment subject of Humanism specifically entails.

9. For more on the new-woman novel of the 1890s, see Ann Heilmann, *New Woman Fiction: Women Writing First-Wave Feminism* (New York: Macmillan/ St. Martin's Press, 2000); Sally Ledger, *The New Woman: Fiction and Feminism at the Fin de Siècle* (Manchester: Manchester University Press, 1997); Ann Ardis, *New Women, New Novels* (New Brunswick, N.J.: Rutgers University Press, 1990); and Rita Felski, *The Gender of Modernity* (Cambridge, Mass.: Harvard University Press, 1995).

10. Even apart from the lingering effects of a Victorian "cult of true womanhood," some feminist literary theorists, such as Sidonie Smith, view autobiography as inherently problematic for female authors. According to Smith, the "doubled subjectivity" of an autobiographical account (the autobiographer as protagonist as well as narrator) emphasizes the "maleness" of autobiography by "privileging the autonomous or metaphysical self as the agent of its own achievement and in frequently situating that self in an adversarial stance toward the world, autobiography promotes a conception of the human being that valorizes individual integrity and separateness and devalues personal and communal interdependency." Smith, *A Poetics of Women's Autobiography: Marginality and the Fictions of Self-Representation* (Bloomington: Indiana University Press, 1987), 7, 39–40.

11. This aspect of my study benefits from the extensive groundwork laid by historians regarding the politics of African-American women's racial uplift at the turn of the century, including Bonnie Thornton Dill, "The Dialectics of Black Womanhood," *Signs* 4, no. 3

(1979): 543–555; Tullia K. Brown Hamilton, "The National Association of Colored Women, 1896–1920" (Ph.D. dissertation, Emory University, 1989); and Hazel V. Carby, *Reconstructing Black Womanhood: The Emergence of the Afro-American Woman Novelist* (New York: Oxford University Press, 1987). Important primary documents that can attest to the significance of uplift as a concept in African-American women's culture in this period include Fannie Barrier Williams, "The Club Movement among Colored Women of America," in *A New Negro for a New Century: An Accurate and Up-to-Date Record of the Upward Struggles of the Negro Race,* ed. Booker T. Washington (Chicago: American Publishing House, 1900), and Mary Church Terrell, "What Role Is the Educated Negro Woman to Play in the Uplifting of Her Race?" in *Twentieth-Century Negro Literature,* ed. D. W. Culp (Naperville, Ill.: J. L. Nichols and Co., 1902, 1912), 170–176. Michele Mitchell's research on black men's utilization of imperialist imagery in their visions of the realization of black manhood likewise reveals racial uplift as open to multiple and contradictory uses. See Mitchell's unpublished paper, "The 'Black Man's Burden': African-Americans, Imperialism, and Competing Racial Masculinities, 1890–1910" (paper presented at the annual meeting of the African Studies Association, Orlando, Fla., November 5, 1995).

12. Louise Newman disentangles some of the knots in this complicated ideology in *White Women's Rights: The Racial Origins of Feminism in the United States* (New York: Oxford University Press, 1999). See especially pp. 10–12. She cites Kevin Gaines's work *Uplifting the Race: Black Leadership, Politics, and Culture in the Twentieth Century* (Chapel Hill: University of North Carolina Press, 1996) to explain how middle-class African-American women took up the challenge of "civilizing" other black Americans.

13. For more on French-Sheldon's deployment of the term *uplift* in her attempts to manipulate public opinion regarding colonial strategies in Africa and in her negotiations with the Liberian legislature regarding her purchase of twelve hundred square miles of Liberian property, see chapter 7.

14. See introduction, note 16.

15. Mary Kingsley is probably the best-known example of this phenomenon, with her emphasis on the benefits of a "good, thick skirt" and her objections to opening membership to exclusive men's clubs, such as the Royal Geographical Association, to women even though she more than qualified for such membership. See Mary Russell, *The Blessings of a Good Thick Skirt* (London: Collins, 1986).

16. "Girls' Gossip," *Truth* (London), February 1891, 448.

17. For a discussion of the translation of these Swahili terms, see introduction, note 9.

18. See introduction, note 4.

19. Mary Louise Pratt refers in *Imperial Eyes: Travel Writing and Transculturation* (London: Routledge, 1992) to the process by which colonized people ("the periphery") "determines the metropolis" and vice versa as "transculturation" and is concerned that scholars consider the reverse impact that the experiences of colonization has on metropole culture.

20. This insight belongs to Lisa Bloom, *Gender on Ice* (Minneapolis: University of Minnesota Press, 1993).

21. Pratt, *Imperial Eyes,* 39.

22. The term *anti-conquest* is Mary Louise Pratt's (*Imperial Eyes*), who uses it to describe the unaggressive pose assumed by scientists and adventurers who saw themselves as counterposed to the violence of colonial relations in the nineteenth century. The term is particularly useful in the U.S. context where a debate over formal annexation of overseas colonies raged at the turn of the twentieth century. Like *anti-imperialist, anti-conquest* is a label that discloses the limits of the discourse on international relations at the time, rather than one which demarks wholesale opposition to imperialism in any form.

23. Pratt, *Imperial Eyes,* 78.

24. As quoted in advertising flyer, M. French-Sheldon Papers, box 7.

25. Jacob Riis, author of *How the Other Half Lives,* was a contemporary of French-Sheldon's. Like her, he was a favorite of the progressive and reform-minded on the lecture circuit. Both speakers were popular lecturers at meetings of the Chautauquan Society, for instance.

26. At this time, the British were enjoined in building a railroad through the territory under their control, and American businessmen were building one on the island of Zanzibar. See Charles Miller, *The Lunatic Express: An Entertainment in Imperialism* (New York: Macmillan Co., 1971). Most explorers of East Africa, missionaries, and European colonial officers considered the construction of railroads crucial to the destruction of the slave trade.

27. "What She Saw in Africa," *New York Times,* March 22, 1892, 8.

28. Tuskegee Institute was founded by Booker T. Washington in Alabama in 1881. A vocational school for blacks, Tuskegee came to represent Washington's philosophy that blacks' hopes for class mobility lay in acquiring technical skills and, eventually, property rather than political agitation and erudition. As Houston A. Baker Jr. argues in *Modernism and the Harlem Renaissance* (Chicago: University of Chicago Press, 1987), Washington's philosophy of social change and Tuskegee's industrial training methods were interpreted differently and held varying significance for black and white Americans. French-Sheldon approved of Washington and his vocational emphasis in black education and cites an acquaintance with him in a compendium of documents she gathered entitled "To Whom It May Concern," box 4, M. French-Sheldon Papers, also present in Records of the Department of State, M170, R14, Record Group #59, Case #3523, National Archives and Records Services, Washington, D.C. Commitment to restricting Africans' educational possibilities to those equipping them for lives as low-level workers was central to French-Sheldon's imperial vision. In January 1895 French-Sheldon demonstrated her support for industrial vocational training for blacks by attending the welcoming ceremonies at Wilberforce University in Ohio on January 17, 1895—the day the first set of African students arrived at Wilberforce. *Xenia Gazette,* January 18, 1895 (cited in James T. Campbell, *Songs of Zion: The African Methodist Episcopal Church in the United States and South Africa* [New York: Oxford University Press, 1995]). See also part 2 of this work for more on French-Sheldon's utilization of the rhetoric of black racial uplift to support her own professional and entrepreneurial agendas.

29. Pratt, *Imperial Eyes,* 155–164. The term is Marie-Claire Hoock-Demarle's; see her essay "Le Langage Littéraire des Femmes Enquetrices" in *Un fabuleux destin: Flora Tristan,* ed. Stephane Michaud (Dijon, France: Editions Universitaires, 1985).

30. Mary P. Ryan in her groundbreaking study *Womanhood in America: From Colonial Times to the Present* (New York: W. W. Norton, 1975), 142–147, 226–235, characterized "social housekeeping" as the nineteenth-century argument that women's domestic expertise and character should be brought to bear on the public sphere to improve it. Other studies that discussion this same phenomenon include Nancy Cott, *The Bonds of Womanhood: Women's Sphere in New England, 1790–1835* (New Haven, Conn.: Yale University Press, 1977); Linda Gordon, *Women's Body, Women's Right: A Social History of Birth Control* (New York: Penguin, 1974); Kathryn Kish Sklar, *Catherine Beecher: A Study in American Domesticity* (New Haven, Conn.: Yale University Press, 1973), 80–89, 135–137, 151–167, 221–222, 264–265; and Paula Baker, "Women and American Political Society, 1780–1920," *American Historical Review* 89 (June 1984): 620–647.

3. FORGING A FEMININE COLONIAL METHOD

1. "A Lady in Africa," review of *Sultan to Sultan,* by May French-Sheldon, *Critic,* April 1, 1893, 193.

2. Hugh Robert Mill quotes G. N. Curzon in the *London Times* in *The Record of the Royal Geographical Society, 1830–1930* (Kensington Gore, London: RGS, 1930), 110–111 (no precise date or issue given). It cannot be verified that Curzon was referring to French-Sheldon, but in the absence of any other American woman receiving membership in the Royal Geographical Society at the time, we can assume that readers of the *London Times* presumed she was his target.

3. "A Lady in Africa," *Critic,* April 1, 1893, 193–194; Review of *Sultan to Sultan,* by May French-Sheldon, *Nation* 56, no. 1437 (January 12, 1893): 36; "What She Saw in Africa," *New York Times,* March 22, 1892, 8; "A White Lady Visits the Masai," *New York Times,* December 11, 1892, 19.

4. French-Sheldon attributes this quote to the *Philadelphia Times* in her promotional flyer. M. French-Sheldon Papers, box 7, Manuscript Division, Library of Congress.

5. "The Lady Errant," *Spectator,* August 29, 1891, 285–287.

6. Ibid.

7. Ibid. French-Sheldon met this challenge among others in *Sultan to Sultan;* see her explanation of her encounter with "native" nudity in which she parenthetically refers to this comment in the *Spectator*'s review by stressing, "this I wish to explain more fully because I have been very much misquoted on the subject." *SS:* 179–180.

8. Ibid.

9. Like the phrase *true womanhood,* this term was widely utilized in the nineteenth century and refers to middle-class women's domesticity and alienation from the marketplace.

10. "What She Saw in Africa," *New York Times,* March 22, 1892, 8.

11. "A White Lady Visits the Masai," *New York Times,* December 11, 1892, 19.

12. The phrase *social housekeeping* is often used by historians to refer to the argument that women were needed in the public sphere and that their particular talents and traits could be effectively transferred to that sphere to establish order and bring the virtues associated with true womanhood to the larger society. A seminal work that relates this issue to the emergence of feminist ideology in the period is Rosalind Rosenberg's *Beyond Separate Spheres* (New Haven, Conn.: Yale University Press, 1982). Mary P. Ryan uses this term to describe arguments proposed by women suffrage activists earlier in the nineteenth century in *Womanhood in America: From Colonial Times to the Present* (New York: W. W Norton, 1975), 142–147, 226–235. "Bringing domesticity outward" was the way nineteenth-century female social workers and teachers viewed their vocations, according to Linda Nicholson in *Gender and History: The Limits of Social Theory in the Age of the Family* (New York: Columbia University Press, 1986), 54; Paula Baker uses the term *public motherhood* to indicate similar arguments being made in the early twentieth century. See "The Domestication of Politics: Women and American Political Society, 1780–1920," *American Historical Review* 89 (June 1984): 635.

13. Review of *Sultan to Sultan,* 36.

14. Alison Blunt discusses this incident in the context of Mary Kingsley's opposition to women's membership in the Royal Geographical Society in *Travel, Gender, and Imperialism: Mary Kingsley and West Africa* (New York: Guilford Press, 1994), 148–154.

15. The term is R. W. Frantz's. See *The English Traveller and the Movement of Ideas, 1660–1732* (1934; reprint, New York, Octagon Books, 1968), 31.

16. Gretchen Kidd Fallon, "British Travel-Books from the Middle-East, 1890–1914: Conventions of the Genre and Three Unconventional Examples" (Ph.D. dissertation, University of Maryland, 1981), 67.

17. For more on this development, see George W. Stocking Jr., *Victorian Anthropology* (New York: Macmillan, 1987), 250–257.

18. This is not to deny that there was little opportunity for women in the Victorian era to demonstrate these skills. Even by the turn of the twentieth century, few women had engaged in ethnographic graduate work. My point in this passage is that women shaped social science discourse in ways that resulted in a re-valuation of traits imagined as typically feminine. Paula Baker argues similarly that "social science tied science to traditional concerns of women" and notes that social science was imagined as the "feminine gender of Political Economy" in the mid-nineteenth century in her article "The Domestication of Politics," 620–647.

19. M. French-Sheldon, "Customs among the Natives of East Africa, from Teita to Kilimegalia with Special Reference to their Women and Children," *Journal of the Anthropological Institute* (May 1892): 368. This passage, like all of the material in this article, appears almost verbatim in *Sultan to Sultan* (on pp. 152–153).

20. "What She Saw in Africa," *New York Times*, March 22, 1892, 8.

21. Much of my thinking about French-Sheldon's literary strategies as I describe them in this chapter has been shaped by Mary Louise Pratt's analysis of what she terms the "anti-conquest" in her seminal study, *Imperial Eyes: Travel Writing and Transculturation* (London: Routledge, 1992).

22. Advertising flyer, M. French-Sheldon Papers, box 7.

23. Fannie C. Williams, "A 'White Queen' at the World's Fair," Chautauquan 18 (1893): 343. See Tim Young, *Travellers in Africa: British Travelogues, 1850–1900* (Manchester: Manchester University Press, 1994) for an expanded discussion of the meaning of passages such as this.

24. Advertising flyer, M. French-Sheldon Papers, box 7.

25. Pratt, *Imperial Eyes*, 69–85.

26. For an expanded discussion of Mary Kingsley's modest self-presentation, see Katherine Frank, "Voyages Out: Nineteenth-Century Women Travelers in Africa," in *Gender, Ideology, and Action: Historical Perspectives on Women's Public Lives*, ed. Janet Sharistanian (Westport, Conn.: Greenwood Press, 1986), and Pratt, *Imperial Eyes*, 215.

27. Williams, "A White Queen at the World's Fair," 343.

28. M. French-Sheldon, "Customs among the Natives of East Africa," 390.

4. SEX AND THE SULTANS

1. Fannie C. Williams, "A 'White Queen' at the World's Fair," *Chautauquan* 18 (1893): 342–344.

2. It is worth repeating that French-Sheldon was accompanied on her trek by at least one other white person—her European maidservant. Furthermore, French-Sheldon was accompanied by German or British officers she met up with along the trail on several occasions, and her caravan was often joined by Arab caravans for short periods. Finally, of course, French-Sheldon was never "alone" in Africa in the sense that she employed well over one hundred African men as well as several women to aid her on her journey.

3. Advertising flyer, M. French-Sheldon Papers, box 7, Manuscript Division, Library of Congress.

4. I am thinking here particularly of Mary Kingsley, the most immediate (and more widely known) successor to French-Sheldon in terms of women's travel to Africa. For a full discussion of Kingsley's avoidance of sexualization as well as the efforts exerted by other white women travelers to this end in this period, see Dea Birkett, *Spinsters Abroad: Victorian Lady Explorers* (New York: Oxford University Press, 1989).

5. The city's name is usually spelled *Moshi*, but French-Sheldon spells it *Moschi* in *Sultan to Sultan* and elsewhere, probably picking up the habit from Germans in the area.

5. CONFESSIONS OF A WHITE QUEEN

1. For an extended discussion of white women travelers' ambivalent appropriation of the "monarch of all I survey" trope, see Mary Louise Pratt, *Imperial Eyes: Travel Writing and Transculteration* (London: Routledge, 1992), 215.

2. This quote is attributed to Thomas W. Knox, "author and traveler," in 1893 by the Arena Press who designed the press release for *Sultan to Sultan* in which this quote appears. M. French-Sheldon Papers, box 7, Manuscript Division, Library of Congress.

3. My capitalization is meant to remind readers of the paradigmatic rendering of a white queen in Africa, "She Who Must Be Obeyed" as imagined by Rider H. Haggard, the nineteenth-century novelist and author of *She: A History of Adventure* (New York: Harper, 1887).

6. AN IMPERIAL SPY IN THE CONGO

1. Quoted in Howard Wolf and Ralph Wolf, *Rubber: A Story of Glory and Greed* (New York: Covici, Friede Publishers, 1936), 113.

2. The most recent biography of Leopold II, *King Leopold's Ghost* by Adam Hochshild, reiterates the point of view of the members of the Congo Reform Association and others of the time and since that Belgian monopolization and exploitation of the Congo was an "atrocity" of enormous dimension. (New York: Houghton Mifflin, 1998).

3. French-Sheldon's papers at the Library of Congress include several telegrams from W. T. Stead to French-Sheldon requesting her presence at upcoming events or arranging for her to speak publicly on the issue of colonial reform in Central Africa. All the materials relating to French-Sheldon's contract with W. T. Stead discussed in this chapter issue from documents found in M. French-Sheldon's Papers, box 1, Manuscript Division, Library of Congress.

4. W. T. Stead to French-Sheldon September 26, 1903, M. French-Sheldon Papers, box 1.

5. Mary Kingsley became the most famous of Victorian women travelers to Africa in the late 1890s. Her two major publications were *Travels in West Africa* (1897) and *West African Studies* (1899). She also wrote *The Story of West Africa*, published in 1900. French-Sheldon's jealousy of the attention and respect Kingsley's work garnered her is evidenced by the reference French-Sheldon makes to Kingsley in her correspondence with the Liberian legislature. See "To Whom It May Concern" compendium, exhibit letter no. 1, to President Gibson, October 12, 1903, in which French-Sheldon notes that her travels predate Kingsley's, in M. French-Sheldon Papers, box 4, also contained in Records of the Department of State, M170, R14, Record Group #59, Case #3523, National Archives and Records Services, Washington, D.C.

6. S. J. S. Cookey, *Britain and the Congo Question, 1885–1913* (New York: Humanities Press, 1968), 56. The British merchant at the center of this controversy was John Holt who later became a correspondent of French-Sheldon's.

7. W. T. Stead to French-Sheldon, September 22, 1903, M. French-Sheldon Papers, box 1.

8. "Memorandum of Instructions to Mrs. Sheldon" from W. T. Stead, October 2, 1903, M. French-Sheldon Papers, box 1.

9. E. D. Morel, *Red Rubber: The Story of the Rubber Slave Trade Flourishing on the Congo in the Year of Grace 1906* (1906; reprint, New York: Haskell House Publishers, 1970), vii–xvii. Johnston negotiated the Uganda Agreement for the British in 1899.

10. W. T. Stead to French-Sheldon, September 22, 1903, M. French-Sheldon Papers, box 1.

11. Wolf and Wolf paraphrases the decree in *Rubber,* 116.

12. Ibid., 116.

13. Ibid., 115.

14. A flyer French-Sheldon used to advertise her lectures noted that French-Sheldon "is especially interested in the achievements of women and counts her unique experiences chiefly valuable from that point of view." M. French-Sheldon Papers, box 7.

15. The "A.B.C. " code relies on letter to phrase transmutations (matching letters and words for relatively meaningless phrases). The code was developed as a guidebook in 1874, by William Clause-Thue, for commercial telegram senders. See David Kahn, *The Codebreakers: The Story of Secret Writing.* (New York: Macmillan, 1967). I am indebted to W. Madsen for suggesting Kahn's work and for help in understanding this system.

16. Stead to French-Sheldon, October 2, 1903, M. French Sheldon Papers, box 1.

17. Stanley Shaloff, *Reform in Leopold's Congo* (Richmond, Va.: John Knox Press, 1970), p. 98, n. 42.

18. Leopold went to great pains to thwart his opposition, dispatching six agents in 1904, for instance, to suppress the reports of Morel and William Morrison, an American Protestant minister, and to prevent them from testifying against him at the Thirteenth International Peace Congress in Boston. In this regard he did not succeed, though it appears he had the presiding Cardinal Gibbons in his pocket. See Shaloff, *Reform in Leopold's Congo,* 95.

19. William Roger Louis, "Roger Casement and the Congo" *Journal of African History* 5, no. 1 (1964): 102.

20. "Mrs. French Sheldon and Congo Critics," *Journal of Commerce,* January 4, 1905.

21. Telegram from Fuchs to French-Sheldon, January 26, 1904. M. French-Sheldon Papers, box 1.

22. Dozens of letters in the French-Sheldon Papers attest to this as do several documents held in the L'Archives du Palais Royale/Koninklijk Archief Cabinet du Roi, # III BJ 18; #80, #129, Brussels, Belgium.

23. "Mrs. French-Sheldon and Congo Critics," *Journal of Commerce,* January 4, 1905.

24. W. T. Stead uses the Congolese phrase *without fear or favour* in his letter to French-Sheldon explaining the sorts of exposés he hoped she could accomplish. Stead to French-Sheldon, September 26, 1903, M. French-Sheldon Papers, box 1.

25. Louis, "Roger Casement and the Congo," 99.

26. Ibid., 109.

27. Ibid., 108.

28. Casement and Morel's first meeting, which Sir Arthur Conan Doyle would refer to as the most "dramatic scene in modern history," occurred in the home of Herbert Ward (a protégé of Henry Stanley and a good friend of French-Sheldon) according to Louis, "Roger Casement and the Congo," 114; Cookey, *Britain and the Congo Question,* 108.

29. The Congo Reform Association was officially founded on March 23, 1904, by E. D. Morel.

30. Ruth Slade, *King Leopold's Congo: Aspects of the Development of Race Relations in the Congo Independent State* (London: Oxford University Press, 1962). This report was not released until November 1905, however, and only after a softening by the Belgian monarch who feared its power to incite the public against him.

31. M. French-Sheldon Papers, box 1.

32. "Mrs. French-Sheldon and Congo Critics," *Journal of Commerce,* January 4, 1905.

33. Apparently, French-Sheldon was unswayed by Mary Kingsley's persuasive appeals on behalf of Liverpool merchants which she read in the two books by Kingsley that W. T. Stead had lent her for her journey. The far more famous and influential Kingsley made un-

restricted trade in West Africa a central theme in the works she produced about her travels in West Africa. For more on Kingsley's advocation of British merchant's interests in West and Central Africa, see J. E. Flint, "Mary Kingsley—A Reassessment," *Journal of African History* 4 (1963): 95–104.

34. *Times* (London), February 3, 1905, 8.

35. "Mrs. French Sheldon and Congo Critics," *Journal of Commerce,* January 4, 1905.

36. Ibid.

37. *Times* (London), February 3, 1905, 8.

38. Ibid.

39. Ibid.

40. Ibid.

41. "Mrs. French Sheldon and the Congo Critics," *Journal of Commerce,* January 4, 1905.

42. *Times* (London), February 3, 1905, 8.

43. Ibid.

44. "Mrs. French Sheldon and the Congo Critics," *Journal of Commerce,* January 4, 1905.

45. Note or letter fragment, M. French-Sheldon Papers, box 4.

46. Charles Miller, *The Lunatic Express: An Entertainment in Imperialism* (New York: Macmillan, 1971), 262.

47. See newspaper clipping, "Anti-Congo Calumnies: Instructive Lecture by Mrs. French Sheldon," M. French-Sheldon Papers, box 1.

48. Neither Stead nor French-Sheldon ever chose to reveal their connection to the public.

49. Stanley's widow, Lady Dorothy Tennant, encouraged French-Sheldon to see her defense of Leopold and the Congo Free State as a defense of Stanley's personal legacy in a letter, dated February 9, 1905, written to French-Sheldon to congratulate her on her letter to the *Times.* Other cohorts of Henry Stanley, such as Herbert Ward, had less trouble voicing criticisms of the Congo Free State. Ward, a close friend of French-Sheldon's, urged her to de-personalize their disagreement concerning the Congo in a letter to her, dated June 2, 1905. See M. French-Sheldon Papers, box 1.

50. Joseph Conrad, *Heart of Darkness,* ed. Robert Kimbrough, Norton Critical Edition (New York: Norton, 1988).

7. A PLANTATION MISTRESS IN LIBERIA

1. Several letters which testify to her business relations with plantation owners and district managers in the Congo are extant. See Ian Hogg to French-Sheldon, May 1, 1904; M. Cherrout to French-Sheldon, October 28, 190? (year unclear); and G. Renard to French-Sheldon, December 30, 1904. French-Sheldon's contacts extend back as far as 1895, when she visited friends in Liberia. See M. French-Sheldon Papers, box 1, Manuscript Division, Library of Congress.

2. French-Sheldon to Gibson, October 12, 1903, pamphlet "To Whom It May Concern, exhibit letter no. 1, located in M. French-Sheldon Papers, box 4, and Records of the Department of State, M170, R14, Record Group #59, Case #3523, National Archives and Records Services, Washington, D.C.

3. Ibid.

4. Ibid.

5. Rubber was not the only raw material French-Sheldon and other colonialists in the region were interested in harvesting. Ivory was still a big draw, although its collection was

waning due to supply limitations and the interruption in the ivory-slave trade. French-Sheldon was interested in all sorts of timber products and minerals. In fact, her interest in West African radium deposits continued long after all hopes of a colonization company were dashed. In the 1920s French-Sheldon attempted to obtain information from the Belgian embassy in Washington concerning new caches of radium discovered in Africa. See E. R. Cartier (Belgian ambassador in Washington, D.C.) to French-Sheldon, November 29, 1922, M. French-Sheldon Papers, box 1.

6. French-Sheldon to Gibson, October 12, 1903, in pamphlet "To Whom It May Concern," exhibit letter no. 1.

7. Edward W. Chester, *Clash of Titans: Africa and U.S. Foreign Policy* (Maryknoll, N.Y.: Orbis Books, 1974), 130.

8. Suzanne Miers and Richard Roberts, eds., *The End of Slavery in Africa* (Madison: University of Wisconsin Press, 1988), 16–17.

9. Sir Harry S. Johnston, a future member of the Congo Reform Association negotiated the deal for the British.

10. Lyon to Elihu Root, November 27, 1906, General Records of the Department of State, M170, R14, Record Group #59, Case #3523, National Archives and Records Services, Washington, D.C.

11. Copy of contract between French-Sheldon and Liberian legislature, in pamphlet "To Whom It May Concern," exhibit no. 6. In a letter from French-Sheldon to the president of Liberia, Arthur Barclay, dated October 3, 1906, French-Sheldon sweetly entreated him as to "whether the 1000 acres granted to me can be located near to Dr. Blyden's 600 acres? This would be my wish." French-Sheldon may have been trying to normalize what had become, by this point, a tense and conflict-ridden situation.

12. "To Whom It May Concern," exhibit no. 22.

13. "To Whom It May Concern," exhibit no. 6.

14. Ibid.

15. Lyon to Root, November 27, 1906, General Records of the Department of State, M170, R14, Record Group #59, Case #3523. This file contains several dozen documents pertaining to French-Sheldon's negotiation with the Liberian government including many appeals to the Roosevelt administration tendered by French-Sheldon and lawyers on her behalf.

16. Howard Wolf and Ralph Wolf, *Rubber: A Story of Glory and Greed* (New York: Covici, Friede Publishers, 1936), 253.

17. This is French-Sheldon's spelling. Possibly she deliberately misspelled *Rockefeller* to refer to the power of that family without committing legally to having obtained that family's support for the scheme.

18. S. J. S. Cookey, *Britain and the Congo Question, 1885–1913* (New York: Humanities Press, 1968), 175.

19. Wolf and Wolf, *Rubber,* 170.

20. Quoted in ibid., 171.

21. Lyon to Root, November 27, 1906, General Records of the Department of State, M170, R14, Record Group #59, Case #3523.

22. Lonny Ward Fendall discusses French-Sheldon's failed attempts to convince the Roosevelt administration to support her in her conflict with the Liberian government in "Theodore Roosevelt and Africa: Deliberate Non-involvement in the Scramble for Territory and Influence" (Ph.D. dissertation, University of Oregon, 1972).

23. French-Sheldon to Barclay, May 9, 1906, "To Whom It May Concern." (A few months later French-Sheldon attempted the opposite strategy, writing to President Barclay: "The more I think over the management of African affairs on all sides and the iron heel the Whites thrust upon the Blacks, the more I am convinced your policy of working the confi-

dence and cooperation of the Natives, is the only sure and righteous political and human policy. Liberia as I have always said I feel is in the position to teach the world the greatest lesson ever taught re African affairs." French-Sheldon signed this letter, "Ever your loving friend," and included the postscript: "Love to Mrs. Barclay—wish she would write." Letter dated July 12, 1906, "To Whom It May Concern."

24. Introduction to compendium, "To Whom It May Concern," 3.

25. French-Sheldon to Barclay, October 3, 1906, "To Whom It May Concern."

26. My reference to her desire to own a farm in Africa is meant to invoke the famous first line of Karen Blixen's (Isak Dinesen's) autobiographical work *Out of Africa*, "I had a farm in Africa . . ." (1938; reprint, New York: Penguin Books, 1984), 13.

27. Quoted in Philip C. Jessup, *Elihu Root* (New York: Dodd, Mead and Company, 1938), ii.

28. Stanley Shaloff, *Reform in Leopold's Congo* (Richmond, Va.: John Knox Press, 1970), 84–106.

29. Ibid., 97. See also *New York Tribune,* June 15, 1904. The *Tribune* was, nevertheless, one of the first U.S. newspapers to call for an international scrutiny of the Congo.

30. For more on Ida B. Wells-Barnett's anti-lynching campaign, see Gail Bederman, *Manliness and Civilization* (Chicago: University of Chicago Press, 1995), and for the connections between lynching and white women, see Vron Ware, *Beyond the Pale: White Women, Racism, and History* (London: Verso, 1992).

31. Quoted in Shaloff, *Reform in Leopold's Congo,* 90.

32. Elihu Root, before taking office as secretary of state, had acted as an attorney for Tom Ryan, the multi-millionaire who sat at the helm of the American Congo Company (and whose affiliation Leopold had assiduously courted for some time). Senator Nelson W. Aldritch was also a founding member.

33. Cookey, *Britain and the Congo Question,* 107; Wolf and Wolf, *Rubber,* 126–127.

34. In an odd twist, in the foreword of her manuscript, French-Sheldon opened this history of Belgium with the following phrase: "The author aspires to pay tribute to the Belge since her 'Birth as a Nation.'" French-Sheldon capitalized *Birth* and *Nation,* perhaps in reminiscence of that infamous film title *Birth of a Nation* (1913). Whatever her intention, in the context of French-Sheldon's position in the Congo scandal, and in light of the domestic race riots which greeted the opening of this film in the United States in 1913, her choice of words suggest the politics of white solidarity which this chapter seeks to illuminate.

35. May 30, 1921, M. French-Sheldon Papers, box 1.

36. M. French-Sheldon Papers, box 1. The granting of this honor to individuals in an attempt to reward or to gain their help during the years of the Congo controversy was a practice Leopold engaged in freely. For example, Leopold in 1905 granted the award to a confidante of Theodore Roosevelt, Maurice Low, in the hope that it might sway Roosevelt to Leopold's side. (It did not.) See Cookey, *Britain and the Congo Question,* p. 170, n. 2.

37. Annie Coombs analyzes how material culture "functioned metonymically" to "preserve" an invented Africa in artifact collections and museum displays in her brilliant study, *Reinventing Africa* (New Haven, Conn.: Yale University Press, 1994), 3–4. See also Arjun Appadurai, *The Social Life of Things: Commodities in Cultural Perspective* (Cambridge, Mass.: Harvard University Press, 1986).

38. "Mrs. Eli French-Sheldon," *New York Times,* February 11, 1936.

39. Here Hammond is quoting the *New York Tribune,* March 22, 1892. His unquestioning repetition of this paper's obituary demonstrates the point I am trying to make here concerning the snowball effect of public representations of French-Sheldon as a great humanitarian founded upon an uncritical assessment of the rhetoric of philanthropy and reform with which French-Sheldon successfully surrounded herself.

40. Hammond. "American Interest in the Exploration of the Dark Continent," 228–229.

8. TAKING FEMINISM ON THE ROAD

1. Advertisement, April 7, 1924, M. French-Sheldon Papers, Manuscript Division, Library of Congress, box 7.

2. See Florence G. McKibben to French-Sheldon, April 28, 1924, and May 7, 1924; Harold L. Bruce to French-Sheldon, April 21, 1924. M. French-Sheldon Papers, box 2.

3. Ladelle Rice, "Lions, Savages, White Eagles, Nothing before Woman Who Faces African Trials Alone," *Daily Lariat,* February 6, 1925.

4. "Real Life Sheik Adventure," *Los Angeles Daily Times,* March 11, 1923.

5. "Distinguished World Explorer Guest of Berkeley Pen Women at Luncheon," *Wasp,* August 30, 1924 (newsletter of the League of American Pen Women, Berkeley, California, branch).

6. Ibid.

7. The evidence is incontrovertible. Newspaper treatments separated by hundreds of miles and months or even years of time mirror each other almost exactly. See, for example, Rice, "Lions, Savages, White Eagles," *Daily Lariat* (Texas), February 6, 1925, and the *Carmel Pine Cone* (California), February 16, 1924. Furthermore, French-Sheldon's papers include a handwritten draft of an article that appeared word for word in a London newspaper except for one mistake on the part of the reporter (or was it French-Sheldon's verbal slip?) who credited Leopold instead of Albert with sending French-Sheldon a brass button from his coat. See "Congo Heroine's Proud Relics," *Sunday Chronicle,* February 15, 1927. Other evidence provided by her scrapbook corroborates my conclusion. One of her news clippings ("Real Life 'Sheik' Adventure," *Los Angeles Daily Times,* March 11, 1923) has French-Sheldon's handwritten note pasted over a section relating the tale of her meeting with the Sultan of Zanzibar and her impressions of the sultana. The note consists of the phrase, "N. B. Replacement of this part" alongside a paraphrased excerpt from *Sultan to Sultan* noting the "sullen envy" of all of the Sultan's wives, indicating French-Sheldon's detailed engagement with the press's reiteration of her public storytelling.

8. "Around the Lobbies," *San Francisco Chronicle,* April 9, 1924; "Distinguished World Explorer Guest of Berkeley Pen Women at Luncheon," *Wasp,* August 30, 1924.

9. News clipping fragment, March 12, 1910, describing lecture to the Polyglot Club, London. See French-Sheldon Papers, box 7.

10. See scrapbook, M. French-Sheldon Papers, box 7.

11. "Real Life 'Sheik' Adventure," *Los Angeles Sunday Daily Times,* March 11, 1923.

12. Up to 1921, French-Sheldon received very little public recognition from the Belgian monarchy other than obtaining a brass button off Albert I's coat during an audience with him soon after his ascendance to the throne. (The button is in M. French-Sheldon's Papers, box 1.) Ostensibly, the Belgian award was due to her much earlier defense of Leopold II (French-Sheldon's "enormous assistance in helping Belgium solve her Congo Trouble in 1903 and 1904," as the *London Chronicle* tactfully phrased it, May 15, 1927). The long-awaited award was also probably the result of French-Sheldon's virulent anti-German diatribes during World War I, her support of the Belgian Red Cross, and her beatification of Belgium in her unpublished history of that country, entitled "Belgium: Little Mother of a Giant," which she enthusiastically dedicated to King Albert I.

13. Louis Franck (Belgian minister of colonies) to French-Sheldon, January 8, 1920, M. French-Sheldon Papers, box 1.

14. The "Bookerism" French-Sheldon espoused should not be assumed to be the same as the philosophies Booker T. Washington promoted, or African-American followers of

Washington heard and supported. As Houston A. Baker Jr. points out in his elegant essays on the subject of minstrelsy and masking, whites and blacks interpreted the speeches and writings of Washington in very different ways. See *Modernism and the Harlem Renaissance* (Chicago: University of Chicago Press, 1987), 25–47.

15. See chapter 1, note 12.

16. Mary Poovey, *Uneven Developments: The Ideological Work of Gender in Mid-Victorian England* (Chicago: University of Chicago Press, 1988), 198.

17. Curiously, French-Sheldon also found herself in the position of having to refute rumors of her death, following a series of ill-informed obituaries on her that appeared in the first few years of the new century.

18. "She Just Keeps on the Go," *San Francisco Chronicle,* February 20, 1924.

19. "Around the Lobbies," *San Francisco Examiner,* April 19, 1924.

20. "Baylor Beauty Fails to Land Kiss from World-Famous Explorer at Reception," *Daily Lariat,* February 24, 1925.

21. "Distinguished World Explorer Guest of Berkeley Pen Women at Luncheon," *Wasp,* August 30, 1924.

22. Karen Offen, "On the French Origins of the Word *Feminism* and *Feminist,*" *Feminist Issues* 8, no. 2 (Summer 1988): 45–51. Susan Ware argues in *Still Missing: Amelia Earhart and the Search for Modern Feminism* (New York: W. W. Norton, 1993) that the National Woman's Party "had appropriated this term" such that "social reformers went out of their way not to use it to describe themselves" (p. 126). Whether or not this is an accurate assessment of why female reformers often evaded or rejected the term, the difficulty or impossibility that female activists, careerists, or adventurers had in repudiating the label is more significant to this study than the attempts the NWP may have purposefully made to restrict it to their supporters.

23. Nancy Cott's work on this period, and her careful insistence on the historicity of the term *feminism,* forms the foundation for my thinking. See *The Grounding of Modern Feminism* (New Haven, Conn.: Yale University Press, 1987).

24. Ibid., 53.

25. Feminism's power to interpellate its subjects (i.e., grant them a subject position within a field of its own making) is quite evident in this statement. In the case of interpellation, according to Louis Althusser, one is hailed by the identity whether one chooses to be or not based on outward behaviors or characteristics that mark one as such. This does not always work against the power of an interpellated subject to speak; in fact it enables one to speak by granting subjectivity and providing rhetorical tools even as it constrains what one might wish to say. This may be the root of the frustration of women who are subjectified enough to speak by virtue of feminism but do not wish to be pigeonholed or persecuted as feminists or even forced to "mean" the same thing that "feminists" do. See Louis Althusser, *Lenin and Philosophy and Other Essays* (New York: Monthly Review Press, 1971).

26. Dorothy Dunbar Bromley, "Feminist—New Style," *Harper's Monthly Magazine* 155 (October 1927): 552–560.

27. Ibid., 552.

28. Ibid (emphasis added).

29. "With the Gayest Parisian Clothes She Travelled Alone through African Jungles with No Greater Damage than a Thorn in Her Eye," *Evening Sun,* February 15, 1915.

30. The chalk drawing of Anthony and the unnamed woman is held in the French-Sheldon Papers, box 6. It is more than likely that French-Sheldon met Susan B. Anthony, since they often traveled in the same circles. They both attended and spoke at the Congress of Women at the Columbian Exposition in 1893, for instance, and the *New York Times* reported on March 22, 1892, that French-Sheldon attended a lecture at the Sorosis Club, where she was seated near Elizabeth Cady Stanton, a fellow activist and good friend of Anthony's.

31. "Interview with Eagle Reports She Notes the Change in Attitude of the Public toward Her Work since She Made Her First Trip," *Brooklyn Daily Eagle,* April 10, 1915.

32. "Woman Explorer Finds Sex Has Achieved Economic Independence in Jungle," *New York Press,* April 4, 1915.

33. "Congratulatory Message of Mme. M. French-Sheldon," *Baylor Towers,* vol. 2, no. 3 (March 1925): 4.

34. Rice, "Lions, Savages, White Eagles, "*Daily Lariat,* February 6, 1925. I discuss the implications of likening French-Sheldon to a father in this passage, as well as other psychosexual components of audience reactions in the 1920s in chapters 9 and 10.

35. "Lone Woman Who Quelled Rebel Caravan in Heart of Africa Holds Baylor Audience Spellbound," *Waco News-Tribune,* February 8, 1925, 16. Scrapbook, M. French-Sheldon Papers, box 7.

36. "Women's Number," *Baylor Towers: A Magazine of University Life* 2, no. 3 (March 1925): 3–4. I analyze the erotic aspects of this poem further in chapter 10.

37. Ibid.

38. This poem can be found in M. French-Sheldon Papers, box 2.

39. I discuss audience's erotic reactions to French-Sheldon in more depth in chapters 9 and 10.

40. Valerie F. Rochen to French-Sheldon (n.d.), M. French-Sheldon Papers, box 2.

41. Cobby de Stivers to French-Sheldon (n.d.), M. French-Sheldon Papers, box 2.

42. Bird Clayes to French-Sheldon, December 1, 1924, M. French-Sheldon Papers, box 2.

43. Letter fragment, M. French-Sheldon Papers, box 2.

9. MASQUERADING AS
THE SUBJECT OF FEMINISM

1. The phrase was first used by Jane Marcus to describe the phallic iconography constructed by British suffragists prior to World War I. See Jane Marcus, "The Asylums of Antaeus: Women, War, and Madness: Is There a Feminist Fetishism?" in *The Difference Within: Feminism and Critical Theory,* eds. Elizabeth A. Meese and Alice Parker (Amsterdam: John Benjamins Publishing Co., 1989), 49–83. Lisa Ticknor analyses a different set of feminist iconographic images in Britain during this period in her demonstration of the nationalist and patriarchal uses to which feminist imagery may be put. See *The Spectacle of Women: Imagery of the Suffrage Campaign, 1907–14* (London: Chatto and Windus, 1987).

2. Joan Riviere's early essay, "Womanliness as a Masquerade" (1929), reprinted in *Formations of Fantasy,* ed. Victor Burgin, James Donald, and Cora Kaplan (London: Routledge, 1986), 35–44, and Sarah Kofman's work on female psychological development in *The Enigma of Woman,* trans. Catherine Porter (1980; reprint, Ithaca, N.Y.: Cornell University Press, 1985), provide a theoretical framework as do those of Naomi Schor, "Female Fetishism: The Case of George Sand," in *The Female Body in Western Culture,* ed. Susan Rubin Suleiman (Cambridge, Mass.: Harvard University Press, 1986), 363–372, and Laura Mulvey, "Visual Pleasure and Narrative Cinema," *Screen* 16 (Autumn 1975): 6–18. See also Linda Williams, *Hard Core: Power, Pleasure, and the Frenzy of the Visible* (Berkeley: University of California Press, 1989); Kaja Silverman, *The Acoustic Mirror: The Female Voice in Psychoanalysis and Cinema* (Bloomington: Indiana University Press, 1988); Marjorie Garber, *Vested Interests: Cross-Dressing and Cultural Anxiety* (New York: Routledge, 1992), especially chapter 5: "Fetish Envy," 118–127; and Anne McClintock, *Imperial Leather: Race, Gender and Sexuality in the Colonial Contest* (New York: Routledge, 1995).

3. Certainly, this is more than an insight produced by historians; debates over seeming violations of true womanhood by female noteworthies or the quality of "unwomanliness" exhibited by "modern" women are rife within the mass media of the period. For a contemporary discussion of the power of the press in this regard, see Louisa Themson-Price, "The Womanly Woman," *The Vote* (October 8, 1910): 286. The substance of Themson-Price's article echoes the point I make here that the late-nineteenth-century ideals of true womanhood and new womanhood were being successfully merged by the 1910s.

4. Billie Melman, *Women and the Popular Imagination in the Twenties: Flappers and Nymphs* (New York: St. Martin's Press, 1988), 147.

5. This is the basis for the analysis of mass culture's relationship to "the feminine" offered by Andreas Huyssen, "Mass Culture as Woman: Modernism's Other," in *Studies in Entertainment,* ed. Tania Modleski (Bloomington: Indiana University Press, 1986), 188–207.

6. While fears of the "mannish" woman span this period, by the 1920s she had achieved the status of a psychoanalytic neurosis: "the mannish lesbian." See Esther Newton, "The Mythic Mannish Lesbian: Radclyffe Hall and the New Woman," *Signs* 9, no. 4 (Summer 1984): 557–575.

7. Stephen Heath, "Joan Riviere and the Masquerade," in *Formations of Fantasy,* ed. Victor Burgin, James Donald, and Cora Kaplan. (London: Routledge, 1986), 48–49.

8. Such an interpretation of the operations of the "masquerade" has endured. As recently as 1990, Judith Butler characterized the dominant interpretation of the "masquerading woman" to be a woman who "wishes for masculinity in order to engage in public discourse with men and as a man as part of a male homoerotic exchange." Judith Butler, *Gender Trouble: Feminism and the Subversion of Identity* (New York: Routledge, 1990), 52.

9. French-Sheldon's self-presentation was noted for its "drag" quality by a scholar as early as Katherine Frank's "Voyages Out: Nineteenth-Century Women Travelers in Africa," in *Gender, Ideology, and Action: Historical Perspectives on Women's Public Lives,* ed. Janet Sharistanian (New York: Greenwood Press, 1986), 82.

10. Alisa Solomon, "It's Never Too Late to Switch," in *Crossing the Stage: Controversies on Cross-Dressing,* ed. Lesley Ferris (London: Routledge, 1993), 145.

11. Garber, *Vested Interests,* 39–55. Garber's nineteenth-century example of the ridicule encountered by women who were accused of trying to wear trousers is Dr. Mary Walker, the founder of the mid-nineteenth-century Mutual Dress Reform and Equal Rights Association. For more on Walker and the politics of dress reform in the nineteenth-century, see Charles McCool Snyder, *Dr. Mary Walker* (New York: Arno Press, 1974).

12. Cartoon, *Punch, or the London Charivari,* September 26, 1891, 147.

13. Mary Russo, "Female Grotesques: Carnival and Theory," in *Feminist Studies/ Critical Studies,* ed. Teresa de Lauretis (Bloomington: Indiana University Press, 1985), 224.

14. Alisa Solomon, "It's Never Too Late to Switch," 145; see also Peggy Phelan on the validation of male authority that cross-dressing affords men who demonstrate how fully they can "wear" or master the figure of woman, "Crisscrossing Cultures," in *Crossing the Stage: Controversies on Cross-Dressing,* ed. Lesley Ferris (New York: Routledge), 161.

15. Luce Irigaray, *This Sex Which Is Not One,* trans. Catherine Porter (Ithaca, N.Y.: Cornell University Press, 1985); Nancy Miller, "Emphasis Added: Plots and Plausibilities in Women's Fiction," *PMLA* 96 (1981): 36–48; Mary Ann Doane, "Film and the Masquerade—Theorizing the Female Spectator," *Screen* 23, no. 3/4 (September/October 1982): 74–87; Mary Russo, "Female Grotesques"; Linda Kauffman, *Discourses of Desire: Gender, Genre, and Epistolary Fictions* (Ithaca, N.Y.: Cornell University Press, 1986). See also scholars of queer theory such as Jack Babuscio, "Camp and the Gay Sensibility," in *Gays and Film,* ed. Richard Dyer (New York: New York Zoetrope, 1984), and Vito Russo, "Camp,"

in *Gay Men: The Sociology of Male Homosexuality,* ed. Martin Levine (New York: Harper and Row, 1979).

16. From French-Sheldon's promotional flyer. She attributes the quote to the *Times,* St. Thomas, Ontario.

17. "Noted Woman Explorer, 78, Here, Wants to Fly to Africa," *San Francisco Call and Post,* February 20, 1924.

18. News clipping fragment, probably from Ladelle Rice, "Lions, Savages, White Eagles, Nothing before Woman Who Faces African Trials Alone," *Daily Lariat,* February 6, 1925.

19. "Interview with Eagle Reports She Notes the Change in Attitude of the Public toward Her Work since She Made Her First Trip," *Brooklyn Daily Eagle,* April 10, 1915.

20. Carroll Smith-Rosenberg, "Discourses of Sex and Sexuality: The New Woman, 1870–1936," in *Disorderly Conduct: Visions of Gender in Victorian America* (New York: Knopf, 1985). See also Martha Vicinus's discussion of the "female celibate pedagogue" in her essay "Distance and Desire: English Boarding School Friendships, 1870–1920," in *Hidden From History: Reclaiming the Gay and Lesbian Past,* ed. Martin Duberman, Martha Vicinus, and George Chauncey Jr. (New York: Meridian, 1989), 212–229. Interestingly enough, French-Sheldon never received any criticism that I know of concerning her sexual orientation, despite her childlessness and long-term relationship with Nellie Butler. Instead, apparently, rumors did exist which questioned the platonic nature of her friendship with Henry S. Wellcome in London. See communication from Ann Butler accompanying the bequeathing of French-Sheldon's African collection to the Henry S. Wellcome Museum, Contemporary Medical Archives Centre, London, England. See also Miss E. Butler to Captain Johnston-Saint, October 23, 1932, HSW/Sheldon File, "Sheldon, Ethnographie," Henry S. Wellcome Museum.

21. See Janet Staiger, *Bad Women: Regulating Sexuality in Early American Cinema* (Minneapolis: University of Minnesota Press, 1995), on the centrality of sexual freedom and expressiveness to 1910s and 1920s new womanhood, and Sarah Berry, *Screen Style* (Minneapolis: University of Minnesota Press, 2000), for interesting perspectives on the power of consumer capitalism to create the conditions for self-transformation.

22. "Paris Film Scene Stirs Writer," *Los Angeles Daily Times,* fragment found in scrapbook, M. French-Sheldon Papers.

23. "Woman Explorer Finds Sex Has Achieved Economic Independence in Jungle," *New York Press,* April 4, 1915.

24. "Baylor Beauty Fails to Land Kiss from World-Famous Explorer at Reception," *Daily Lariat,* February 24, 1925.

25. Rice, "Lions, Savages, White Eagles," *Daily Lariat,* February 6, 1925.

26. Garber, *Vested Interests,* 356.

27. Ibid., 354–356.

28. Many dominatrix characters in popular culture exhibit cross-dressed magnetism, including the pop singer Madonna, of whom much has been written. See especially Shelagh Young, "Feminism and the Politics of Power," in *The Female Gaze: Women as Viewers of Popular Culture* ed. Lorraine Gammen and Margaret Marshment (Seattle: The Real Comet Press, 1989), 173–188, and Lisa Frank and Paul Smith, eds., *Madonnarama* (New York: Cleis Press, 1993). The character of Alexis in the 1980s television show *Dynasty* represents another recent example of a character who because rather than in spite of her excessive "wearing" of femininity seems more virile. See Mark Finch, "Sex and Address in 'Dynasty,'" *Screen* 27, no. 6 (1986): 24–42. While I see significant commonalities, I would, however, caution against viewing the "femme fatale" and the White Queen as entirely coterminous, since the doomed quality of the cinematic vamp in the 1920s was so distinctly a function of her inability to convey white racial purity.

29. Esther Newton, *Mother Camp: Female Impersonators in America* (Chicago: University of Chicago Press, 1972), 3. Jacques Lacan focuses on the significance of the dualism inside/outside in the constitution of the sexed subject in "The Mirror Stage," in *Ecrits: A Selection,* trans. Alan Sheridan (New York: W. W. Norton and Company, 1977), 1–7.

30. Garber, *Vested Interests,* 356; Jacques Lacan, "The Signification of the Phallus," in *Ecrits: A Selection,* trans. Alan Sheridan, 289. The classic essay on transvestism is Otto Fenichel, "The Psychology of Transvestism," in *Psychoanalysis and Male Sexuality,* ed. Hendrik M. Ruitenbeek (1930; reprint, New Haven, Conn.: College and University Press, 1966). See also Jacques Lacan and Wladimir Granoff, "Fetishism: The Symbolic, the Imaginary, and the Real," in *Perversions,* ed. Sandor Lorand (New York: Gramercy Publishing, 1956), 265–276.

31. Ella Sterling Mighels to French-Sheldon, July 21, 1924; Florence G. McKibben to French-Sheldon, April 28, 1924; Valerie F. Rochon to French-Sheldon, March 26, 1924; "Baylor Beauty Fails to Land Kiss from World-Famous Explorer at Reception," *Daily Lariat,* February 24, 1925. The letters in this note all appear in M. French-Sheldon Papers, box 2.

32. "Women's Number," *Baylor Towers: A Magazine of University Life* 2, no. 3 (March 1925): 3–4. In *The Madwoman in the Attic: The Woman Writer and the Nineteenth-Century Imagination* (New Haven, Conn.: Yale University Press, 1979), Sandra Gilbert and Susan Gubar document the phallicism associated with pens even in pre-Freudian Victorian literature; indeed, the question they pose at the outset of that volume, "Is a pen a metaphorical penis?" (p. 3) could be viewed as the central question posed by the authors in their work on women as writers.

33. Judith Mayne in writing about the films of Dorothy Arzner in the early 1930s, contends that Arzner's films "cite the [lesbian] persona, and are therefore informed by lesbian desire." Like Mayne, I am not implying that French-Sheldon and Butler's relationship was or was not "lesbian" in the sense that they had sexual relations with one another; nevertheless as I document, French-Sheldon's public persona "cited" lesbianism in small part as a result of the fact that her primary relationship was with a woman rather than a man. Judith Mayne, "Lesbian Looks: Dorothy Arzner and Female Authorship," in *How Do I Look? Queer Film and Video,* ed. Bad-Object Choices (Seattle: Bay Press, 1991), 114. For a good discussion of the dangers of inferring lesbianism from stereotypical elements associated with a lesbian lifestyle, see Esther Newton and Shirley Walton, "The Misunderstanding: Toward a More Precise Sexual Vocabulary," in *Pleasure and Danger,* ed. Carole Vance (Boston: Routledge, 1984), 242–250, and Sarah Halprin's review of E. Ann Kaplan's *Women and Film: Both Sides of the Camera,* "Writing in the Margins," *Jump Cut* 29 (February 1984): 32.

34. The psychoanalytic literature on fetishism is extensive. My sources include Alasdair Pettinger, "Why Fetish?" *New Formations* 19 (Spring 1993): 83–93; David L. Raphling, "Fetishism in a Woman" *Journal of the American Psychoanalytic Association* 37, no. 2 (1989): 469–491; William Pietz, "The Problem of the Fetish, I," *Res* 9 (Spring 1985): 5–17; William Pietz, "The Problem of the Fetish, II," *Res* 13 (Spring 1987): 23–46; William Pietz, "The Problem of the Fetish, III," *Res* 16 (Autumn 1988): 105–24; G. Zavitzianos, "The Perversion of Fetishism in Women" *Psychoanalysis Q* 51 (1982): 405–425; G. Dudley, "A Rare Case of Female Fetishism," *International Journal of Sexology* 8 (1954): 32–34. Sigmund Freud discusses fetishism in his essay, "Fetishism," in *Sexuality and the Psychology of Love* ed. Philip Reiff (1920; reprint, New York: Collier Books, 1963), 214–219.

35. This is Garber's paraphrasing of Lacan on the subject, *Vested Interests,* 119. Also see Lacan, "The Signification of the Phallus."

36. Garber, *Vested Interests,* 120.

37. Kofman, *Enigma of Women.*

38. Ibid. Sigmund Freud, "Fetishism," in *The Standard Edition of the Complete Psychological Works,* vol. 21, trans. James Strachey (London: Hogarth Press, 1963), 152–153.

39. Bird Clayes to French-Sheldon, December 1, 1924, M. French-Sheldon Papers, box 2.

40. M. French-Sheldon Papers, box 2.

41. I am indebted to Elsa Barkley Brown for my understanding of this concept and to Patricia Hill Collins, *The Politics of Black Feminist Thought* (Cambridge, Mass.: Unwin Hyman, 1990).

42. "Interview with Eagle Reports She Notes the Change in Attitude of the Public toward Her Work since She Made Her First Trip," *Brooklyn Daily Eagle,* April 12, 1915.

43. Ella Sterling Mighels to French-Sheldon, July 21, 1924, M. French-Sheldon Papers, box 2.

44. Garber, *Vested Interests,* 121.

45. Fannie C. Williams, "A 'White Queen' at the World's Fair," *Chautauquan* 18 (1893), 342.

46. "With the Gayest Parisian Clothes She Travelled Alone through African Jungles with No Greater Damage than a Thorn in Her Eye," *Evening Sun,* February 15, 1915. See small scrapbook in French-Sheldon's Papers, box 7.

47. Quoted in Naomi Schor, "Female Fetishism: The Case of George Sand," in *The Female Body in Western Culture,* ed. Susan Rubin Suleiman (Cambridge, Mass.: Harvard University Press, 1986), 363–372.

48. This is Naomi Schor's translation of Kofman, "Female Fetishism," 368–369.

49. Schor, "Female Fetishism," 369.

50. For more on the proscription of women's same-sex relationships and a prescription of heterosexuality, see Christina Simmons, "'Living Happily Ever After in Heterosexual Matehood': Fear of Lesbianism in the Ideology of Companionate Marriage," *Frontiers* 4, no. 3 (Fall 1979): 54–59; Lewis Erenberg, *Steppin' Out: New York Nightlife and the Transformation of American Culture, 1890–1930* (Westport, Conn.: Greenwood Press, 1981). See also Newton, "The Mythic Mannish Lesbian."

51. Elizabeth Berg, "The Third Woman," *Diacritics* 12 (1982): 11–20. Quote appears on 13.

52. Ibid., 19.

53. Marcus, "The Asylums of Antaeus," 71.

54. Ibid. Marcus draws much of her material for this article from the work of W. J. T. Mitchell, *Iconology: Image, Text, Ideology* (Chicago: University of Chicago Press, 1986). See also Lisa Ticknor, *The Spectacle of Women: Imagery of the Suffrage Campaign, 1907–1914* (London: Chatto and Windus, 1987). One caveat that I have to Marcus's work is that she may be oversimplifying the concept of fetishization in her equating a feminist iconography with feminist fetishization. For this reason, her work may not speak to the same psychodynamics of fetishism to which Berg likely would wish to confine her analysis.

55. Marcus, "The Asylums of Antaeus," 76.

56. Marjorie Garber makes the argument that an audience always experiences a transvestite's boundary crossing on multiple levels simultaneously, by which Garber means to refer to both the real/not real boundary as well as to class and race boundaries. Still, Garber rarely interrogates this latter set of boundary crossings except to indicate that all meaning (all difference) derives from the theatrical space created by cross-dressing in violation of them.

57. Marcus, "The Asylums of Antaeus," 75–76.

58. This is a phrase that appears at the bottom of a flyer advertising French-Sheldon's lectures. M. French-Sheldon Papers, box 1.

59. This is Carole-Anne Tyler's paraphrasing of Irigaray in "Boys Will Be Girls: The Politics of Gay Drag," in *Inside/Out: Lesbian Theories, Gay Theories,* ed. Diana Fuss (New York: Routledge, 1991), 52. See also Irigaray, *This Sex Which Is Not One.*

60. Homi Bhabha, "The Other Question: Stereotype, Discrimination and the Discourse of Colonialism," reprinted in *The Location of Culture* (London: Routledge, 1994), 75.

61. Tyler, "Boys Will Be Girls," 60.

62. Berg, *The Third Woman,* 19.

63. Mary Ann Doane, *Femmes Fatales: Feminism, Film Theory, Psychoanalysis* (New York: Routledge, 1991), 38.

64. French-Sheldon was born in Pennsylvania in 1847, and her mother's family connections were all in Philadelphia, New York, and Boston. But her father's family was Southern, and his affluence stemmed from his family's ownership of cotton and indigo plantations. See Jeanne Madeleine Moore, "Bibi Bwana," *American History Illustrated* 21 (October 1986): 36–42.

65. Riviere, "Womanliness as a Masquerade," 42.

66. See, for example, *I'm No Angel* (1933) and *She Done Him Wrong* (1933).

67. According to Mary Ann Doane, Riviere's patient's fantasy life "obsessively turns around and reinscribes her sexuality, born as it is of power and its effects, within another field of power relations—that of race." Doane, *Femmes Fatales,* 38.

10. THE QUEEN, THE SHEIK, THE SULTANA, AND THE FEMALE SPECTATOR

1. This view does not originate in the twentieth century, as Ann Douglas has documented. The view that mass culture appeals to women more than men and has a passive, less intellectual, and less morally pulchritudinous quality accompanied the rise of the novel in the early nineteenth century. Ann Douglas, *The Feminization of American Culture* (New York: Doubleday, 1977). Scholarship associated with the Frankfurt School presents a variation of this thesis stemming from a concern regarding the increasingly central role that consumerist cultural production had assumed in the popular culture of the United States in the 1930s.

2. Mary P. Ryan, "The Projection of a New Womanhood: The Movie Moderns in the 1920s," in *Our American Sisters: Women in American Life and Thought,* ed. Jean E. Friedman and William G. Shade (Boston: Allyn and Bacon, 1976), 367–371.

3. Ibid., 367.

4. See Janet Staiger's discussion of the modern girl's flaunting of sexuality in *Bad Women: Regulating Sexuality in Early American Cinema* (Minneapolis: University of Minnesota Press, 1995).

5. Stanley Cavell, *The World Viewed: Reflections on the Ontology of Film* (New York: Viking Press, 1971), 33.

6. See Diane Negra's discussion of the racial and ethnic specific contours of women's identification with cinema idols in *Off-white Hollywood: American Culture and Ethnic Female Stardom* (New York: Routledge, 2001).

7. "Distinguished World Explorer Guest of Berkeley Pen Women at Luncheon," *Wasp,* August 30, 1924.

8. Annette Kuhn, *The Power of the Image: Essays on Representation and Sexuality* (London: Routledge, 1985), 64.

9. "With the Gayest Parisian Clothes She Travelled Alone through African Jungles with No Greater Damage than a Thorn in Her Eye," *Evening Sun,* February 15, 1915.

10. Kenneth Cameron, *Africa on Film: Beyond Black and White* (New York: Continuum, 1994), 17.

11. On the significance of Rider Haggard's *She* as a colonialist text, see Sandra M. Gilbert and Susan Gubar, *No Man's Land: The Place of the Woman Writer in the Twentieth Century,* vol. 2: *Sexchanges* (New Haven, Conn.: Yale University Press, 1989), 5–25; the critique of Gilbert and Gubar by Laura Chrisman, "The Imperial Unconscious? Representations of Imperial Discourse," in *Colonial Discourse and Post-Colonial Theory,* eds. Patrick Williams and Laura Chrisman (New York: Columbia University Press, 1994), 498–516; and T. J. Boisseau, "White Queens in the Dark Mirror: The Construction of White Female Subjectivity in the Othering of Africa," (paper presented at the annual meeting of the African Studies Association, Orlando, Fla., November 7, 1995.

12. See Anne McClintock"s reading of Haggard's stories, *Imperial Leather: Race, Gender, and Sexuality in the Colonial Context* (New York: Routledge, 1995).

13. Cameron, *Africa on Film,* 17 (emphasis added).

14. Ibid., 190.

15. Ibid.

16. Laura Mulvey, "Visual Pleasure and Narrative Cinema," *Screen* 16 (Autumn 1975): 6–18.

17. Laura Mulvey, "Afterthoughts on 'Visual Pleasure and Narrative Cinema,' Inspired by *Duel in the Sun,*" *Framework* 15/16/17 (1981): 12–15.

18. Naomi Schor, "Female Fetishism: The Case of George Sand," in *The Female Body in Western Culture,* ed. Susan Rubin Suleiman (Cambridge, Mass.: Harvard University Press, 1986), 369.

19. Janet Walker, "Psychoanalysis and Feminist Film Theory: The Problem of Sexual Difference and Identity," in *Multiple Voices in Feminist Film Criticism,* ed. Diane Carson, Linda Dittmar, and Janice R. Welsch (Minneapolis: University of Minnesota Press, 1994), 86.

20. Mulvey, "Afterthoughts," 15.

21. Following Mulvey's lead, the concept of the female spectator as masochist is further elaborated in the works of Raymond Bellour, "Psychosis, Neurosis, Perversion," *Camera Obscura* 3, no. 4 (1979), 66–91, and "Hitchcock the Enunciator," *Camera Obscura* 2 (1977), 74–87.

22. Mary Ann Doane is perhaps the most prominent of feminist film theorists who have engaged in vigorous debate over Mulvey's model. Doane rejects the notion that women's pleasure operates via fetishistic or voyeuristic drives which imperfectly mirror men's. See Mary Ann Doane, "Film and the Masquerade: Theorising the Female Spectator," *Screen* 23, no. 3/4 (September/October 1982). Doane, in turn, has been accused of imagining women as outside or at least "marginal" to the operations of patriarchy that produce sexual difference in the first place. For an excellent discussion of these theoretical positions, see Jackie Stacey, "Desperately Seeking Difference" in *The Female Gaze: Women as Viewers of Popular Culture,* ed. Lorraine Gamman and Margaret Marshment (Seattle: The Real Comet Press, 1989), 112–129.

23. Rudolph Valentino acted in several films prior to *The Sheik* (between 1918 and 1920 he appeared in seventeen films, and fourteen more between 1921 and 1926). Miriam Hansen's discussion of Valentino as the preeminent male "sex-god" of twenties cinema has formed much of my thinking about the relationship between French-Sheldon and Valentino's films. See Hansen, "Pleasure, Ambivalence, Identification: Valentino and Female Spectatorship," *Cinema Journal* 25, no. 4 (Summer 1986): 6–32, and *Babel and Babylon: Spectatorship in American Silent Film* (Cambridge, Mass.: Harvard University Press, 1991).

24. Hansen, "Pleasure, Ambivalence, Identification," 6.

25. Billie Melman differentiates between subgenres within this genre which correlate with each of these three areas and differ slightly in their features in *Women and the Popular Imagination: Flappers and Nymphs* (New York: St. Martin's Press, 1988), 95.

26. Melman, *Women and the Popular Imagination,* 90.

27. Hansen's discussion of the popularity of silent travelogue films featuring the presence of a live lecturer in the 1910s and 1920s supports my argument that cinematic and extra-cinematic practices in this period would have prepared audiences to form psychological relationships with French-Sheldon that parallel their identification with cinematic idols. See *Babel and Babylon,* 96–98.

28. The collection *Haunted Bells and Other Stories* includes three other fictional short stories unrelated to French-Sheldon's expedition in Africa. *Haunted Bells and Other Stories* (London: Saxon and Co., n.d.). (To identify quotations from this text, *HB,* followed by page numbers will appear in parenthetical citations in the text.) The only copy of this text in existence that I know of is held at the Bibliothèque Royale Albert Iᵉʳ in Brussels, Belgium. Though written in the third person, and grouped as they are with three other stories not related to French-Sheldon's travels or personal history, "Pearl" and "Peril" are thinly veiled autobiographical sketches of French-Sheldon's experiences in East Africa in 1891. In light of French-Sheldon's later decision to present these stories as actual episodes and herself as the protagonist, it is interesting that the word "true" appears in the title on the title page of this collection, whereas "true" does not appear in the title on the frontispiece. The "inside-story" title, *Haunted Bells and Other True Stories,* suggests that a "confusion" over the truthfulness of these stories and a conflation between these "stories" and her "ethnography" was present in French-Sheldon's mind even in the 1890s when she first published *Haunted Bells.*

29. See, for instance, "Lone Woman Who Quelled Revolt," *Waco News-Tribune,* February 8, 1925.

30. Melman, *Women and the Popular Imagination,* 89–106, 134–144.

31. "Real Life 'Sheik' Adventure," *Los Angeles Times,* Sunday, March 11, 1923. See also "Noted Woman Explorer, 78, Here, Wants to Fly to Africa," *San Francisco Call and Post,* February 20, 1924, for a similar version of the same story.

32. Miriam Hansen makes note of the fantasy that female fans engaged in that they might be beaten by Valentino's hands in *Babel and Babylon,* 283. French-Sheldon's story reverses the punishment.

33. Miriam Hansen notes that some contemporary observers believed that female fans' desire for Valentino was that of the incestuous mother for the sexually available son. *Babel and Babylon,* 262.

34. Perhaps this is French-Sheldon's fantasy of Valentino, since she bore little regard herself for the adored Italian-American celebrity. "Noted Woman Explorer, 78, Here, Wants to Fly to Africa," *San Francisco Call and Post,* February 20, 1924, included a comment which reveals French-Sheldon's racist disgust for "real," "dirty" Arabs who do not, according to French-Sheldon, resemble the "American boy who is called a sheik." In full, the quote reads: "If the Americans really knew these Arabs they would realize what a misnomer the term is for the beau ideal of America. The sheik is dirty and complex. The American boy who is called a sheik is much given to care of his personal appearance. And he certainly is not complex." Miriam Hansen notes that Valentino's publicists toyed with the image of him as "Immigrant Boy Who Made Good" in an effort to undo the decadence associated with his foreignness. See *Babel and Babylon,* 259.

35. Marjorie Garber, *Vested Interests: Cross-Dressing and Cultural Anxiety* (New York: Routledge, 1992), 310.

36. Miriam Hansen discusses some of these same issues in the context of the 1920s at greater length and complexity in her article "Pleasure, Ambivalence, Identification.

37. Foucault develops the idea of power as productive rather than restraining and modern sexuality as produced rather than repressed by discourse. Michel Foucault, *The History of Sexuality, Volume I: An Introduction,* trans. Robert Hurley (New York: Random House, 1980).

38. Rachel du Plessis, *Writing Beyond the Ending* (Bloomington: Indiana University Press, 1985).

39. According to Judith Mayne, in instances when gender hierarchy is being denied "the racial stereotype affirms the distinction between white subject and black object just when the distinction between male subject and female object is being put into question." "Lesbian Looks: Dorothy Arzner and Female Authorship, " in *How Do I Look? Queer Film and Video,* ed. Bad-Object Choices (Seattle: Bay Press, 1991), 125.

40. Much of the work of both Claude Lévi-Strauss and Jacques Lacan takes as a premise the idea that human society is created and a subject position is secured within it by way of an "exchange of women." Gayle Rubin noted long ago the dire ramifications of these theories for "real" women. While I concede to neither the universality that the "exchange of women" assumes, nor the inevitability of this as an underlying structure of Western, white, bourgeois culture, I do believe such a notion informs French-Sheldon's texts and other popularly constructed feminist imagery in this period; hence my decision to re-deploy this model of "culture" and "language" as a framework for examining the operations of patriarchy in this text and the functions of Imperial Feminism generally. Gayle Rubin, "The Traffic in Women: Notes on the Political Economy of Sex," in *Towards an Anthropology of Women,* ed. Rayna R. Reiter (New York: Monthly Review Press, 1975), 157–210.

41. For more on how museums functioned metonymically to represent Africa, see Annie Coombs, *Reinventing Africa* (New Haven, Conn.: Yale University Press, 1994).

42. According to Mary Ann Doane, Sigmund Freud first referred to "the sexual life of adult women" as the "dark continent" in his article "The Question of Lay Analysis: Conversations with an Impartial Person," reprinted in *The Standard Edition of the Complete Psychological Works of Sigmund Freud,* vol. 20, ed. James Strachey (London: Hogarth, 1963): 212. Doane quotes and analyzes this passage of Freud's in Doane, "Dark Continents: Epistemologies of Racial and Sexual Difference in Psychoanalysis and the Cinema," in *Femmes Fatales: Feminism, Film Theory, Psychoanalysis* (New York: Routledge, 1991), 209–248.

43. Susan Ware, *Still Missing: Amelia Earhart and the Search for Modern American Feminism* (New York: W. W. Norton, 1993), 177.

44. T. J. Boisseau, review of *Still Missing,* by Susan Ware, *Journal of Popular Culture* 29, no. 3 (Winter 1995): 237–243.

45. Garber, *Vested Interests,* 118.

CONCLUSION

1. My own historical study of French-Sheldon does not avoid entirely the ontological pitfalls of historicism, of course. My attempt to make the issues at stake in historical representations of women, and feminism explicit, however, hopefully contributes to the undermining of such effects by refusing to deny or repress them. As Mimi White, following de Certeau's insights into the effects of historical representation, has observed in reference to the making of a feminist historical documentary, feminist history does a disservice to its own cause by often "repress[ing]" the construction of historical "distance as an active principle informing its structure." "Rehearsing Feminism: Women/History in *The Life and Times of Rosie the Riveter* and *Swing Shift,*" in *Multiple Voices in Feminist Film Criticism,* ed. Diane Carson, Linda Dittmar, and Janice R. Welsch (Minneapolis: University of Minnesota Press, 1994), 321.

2. This distance, according to Irigaray, negates Woman's usual "sameness" or, what Mary Ann Doane thinks of as a tendency towards "over-identification" with (an objectified) image, and thereby permits feminine audiences to experience desire for a fetishized object. See Luce Irigaray, "When the Goods Get Together," in *New French Feminisms,* eds. Elaine Marks and Isabelle de Courtivon (New York: Schocken Books, 1981); Mary Ann Doane, "Film and the Masquerade: Theorising the Female Spectator," *Screen* 23, no. 3/4 (September/October 1982).

3. Homi Bhabha, *The Location of Culture* (London: Routledge, 1994), 243.

4. Luce Irigaray, "Women's Exile," *Ideology and Consciousness* 1 (May 1977): 74.

5. Judith Butler, "Contingent Foundations: Feminism and the Question of 'Postmodernism,'" in *Feminists Theorize the Political,* ed. Judith Butler and Joan W. Scott (New York: Routledge, 1992), 14.

6. Gayatri Chakravorty Spivak, "A Response to 'The Difference Within: Feminism and Critical Theory,'" in *The Difference Within: Feminism and Critical Theory,* ed. Elizabeth Meese and Alice Parker (Amsterdam: John Benjamins Publishing Co., 1989), 207–220 (quote appears on pp. 208–209).

7. Butler, "Contingent Foundations," 14.

8. Teresa de Lauretis, *Technologies of Gender: Essays on Theory, Film and Fiction* (Bloomington: Indiana University Press, 1987), 18.

9. For more on the function of gender as that which designates the human from the non-human, see Anita Levy, *Other Women: The Writing of Class, Race, and Gender, 1832–1898* (Princeton, N.J.: Princeton University Press, 1991), 7, 57–59. Mimi White's translation of de Certeau's work on historical representation has helped me see how the assertion of difference sustains the ontological links I refer to here. White translates Michel de Certeau: "If on the one hand history functions by expressing the position of one generation in relation to previous ones by saying: 'I am not that,' it always affects this affirmation with a no less dangerous complement which makes a society avow: 'I am other than I want and determined by that which I deny.'" White, "Rehearsing Feminism," 321.

BIBLIOGRAPHY

PRIMARY SOURCES

Blixen, Karen (Isak Dinesen). *Out of Africa*. 1938. Reprint, New York: Penguin, 1984.

Bromley, Dorothy Dunbar. "Feminist—New Style." *Harper's Monthly Magazine* 155 (October 1927): 552–560.

"Distinguished Woman Explorer Guest of Berkeley Pen Women at Luncheon," *Wasp*, August 30, 1924.

French-Sheldon, May. "Customs among the Natives of East Africa from Teita to Kilimegalia with Special Reference to their Women and Children." *Journal of the Anthropological Institute* (May 1892): 358–390.

———. *Haunted Bells and Other Stories*. London: Saxon and Co., n.d.

———. *Herbert Severance: A Novel*. Chicago: Rand, McNally and Company, 1889.

———. Papers. Manuscripts Division, Library of Congress.

———. *Sultan to Sultan: Adventures among the Masai and Other Tribes of East Africa*. Boston: Arena Press, 1892.

General Records of the Department of State. M170, R14, Record Group #59, Case #3523, National Archives and Records Services, Washington, D.C.

"Girls' Gossip." *Truth* (London). February 1891, 448.

Grand, Sarah. "The New Aspect of the Woman Question." *North American Review* 158, no. 448 (March 1894): 270–277.

Grundy, Sydney. *The New Woman*. London: Chiswick Press, 1894.

Haggard, Rider H. *She: A History of Adventure*. New York: Harper, 1887.

Hore, Annie. *To Lake Tanganyika in a Bath Chair*. London: Sampson Low, Marston, Searle, and Rivington, 1886.

"A Lady in Africa." Review of *Sultan to Sultan*, by May French-Sheldon. *Critic*, April 1, 1893, 193–194.

Morel, E. D. *Red Rubber: The Story of the Rubber Slave Trade Flourishing on the Congo in the Year of Grace 1906*. 1906. Reprint, New York: Haskell House Publishers, 1970.

Régamey, Félix. *Japan in Art and Industry: With a Glance at Japanese Manners and Customs*. Trans. Eli Lemon Sheldon and May French-Sheldon. New York: Putnam and Sons, 1893.

Review of *Sultan to Sultan*, by May French-Sheldon, *Nation* 56, no. 1437 (January 12, 1893): 36.

Riis, Jacob. *How the Other Half Lives: Studies among the Tenements of New York*. New York: Charles Scribner's Sons, 1890.

Riviere, Joan. "Womanliness as a Masquerade." 1929. Reprinted in *Formations of Fantasy*, ed. Victor Burgin, James Donald, and Cora Kaplan, 35–44. London: Routledge, 1986.

Stanley, Henry Morton. Collection. Archives of the Royal Geographical Society of London.

———. *How I Found Livingstone*. 1872. Reprint, New York: Scribner, Armstrong, and Co., 1972.

———. *In Darkest Africa.* New York: Scribner's, 1890.

Terrell, Mary Church. "What Role Is the Educated Negro Woman to Play in the Uplifting of Her Race?" In *Twentieth-Century Negro Literature,* ed. D. W. Culp, 172–176. Naperville, Ill.: J. L. Nichols and Co., 1902, 1912.

Themson-Price, Louisa. "The Womanly Woman." *The Vote* (October 8, 1910): 286.

Williams, Fannie Barrier. "The Club Movement among Colored Women of America." In *A New Negro for a New Century: An Accurate and Up-to-Date Record of the Upward Struggles of the Negro Race,* ed. Booker T. Washington, 379–405. Chicago: American Publishing House, 1900.

Williams, Fannie C. "A 'White Queen' at the World's Fair." *Chautauquan* 18 (1893): 342–344.

"Women's Number," *Baylor Towers: A Magazine of University Life* 2, no. 3 (March 1925): 3–4.

SECONDARY SOURCES

Althusser, Louis. *Lenin and Philosophy and Other Essays.* New York: Monthly Review Press, 1971.

Amos, Valerie, and Pratibha Parmar. "Challenging Imperial Feminism." *Feminist Review* 17 (Autumn 1984): 3–17.

Appadurai, Arjun. *The Social Life of Things: Commodities in Cultural Perspective.* Cambridge, Mass.: Harvard University Press, 1986.

Ardis, Ann. *New Women, New Novels.* New Brunswick, N.J.: Rutgers University Press, 1990.

Babuscio, Jack. "Camp and the Gay Sensibility." In *Gays and Film,* ed. Richard Dyer, 40–57. New York: New York Zoetrope, 1984.

Baker, Houston A., Jr. *Modernism and the Harlem Renaissance.* Chicago: University of Chicago Press, 1987.

Baker, Paula. "The Domestication of Politics: Women and American Political Society, 1780–1920." *American Historical Review* 89 (June 1984): 620–647.

Bederman, Gail. *Manliness and Civilization.* Chicago: University of Chicago Press, 1995.

Bellour, Raymond. "Hitchcock the Enunciator," *Camera Obscura* 2 (1977): 66–91.

———. "Psychosis, Neurosis, Perversion." *Camera Obscura* 3, no. 4 (1979): 104–132.

Belsey, Catherine. *Critical Practice.* London: Methuen, 1980.

Benveniste, Emile. In *Problems in General Linguistics,* trans. Mary Elizabeth Meek. Coral Gables, Fla.: University of Miami Press, 1971.

Berg, Elizabeth. "The Third Woman." *Diacritics* 12 (1982): 11–20.

Berry, Sarah. *Screen Style.* Minneapolis: University of Minnesota Press, 2000.

Bhabha, Homi. *The Location of Culture.* London: Routledge, 1994.

Birkett, Dea. *Spinsters Abroad: Victorian Lady Explorers.* Oxford: Oxford University Press, 1989.

Bloom, Lisa. *Gender on Ice.* Minneapolis: University of Minnesota Press, 1993.

Blunt, Alison. *Travel, Gender, and Imperialism: Mary Kingsley and West Africa.* New York: Guilford Press, 1994.

Boisseau, T. J. Review of *Still Missing* by Susan Ware. *Journal of Popular Culture* 29, no. 3 (Winter 1995): 237–243.

———. "White Queens at the Chicago World's Fair, 1893: New Womanhood in the Service of Class, Race, and Nation." *Gender and History* 12, no. 1 (April 2000): 33–81.

———. "White Queens in the Dark Mirror: The Construction of White Female Subjectivity in the Othering of Africa." Paper presented at the annual meeting of the African Studies Association, Orlando, Fla., November 1995.

Burton, Antoinette M. "The White Woman's Burden: British Feminists and 'The Indian Woman,' 1865–1915." In *Western Women and Imperialism: Complicity and Resistance,* ed. Nupur Chaudhuri and Margaret Strobel, 137–157. Bloomington: Indiana University Press, 1992.

Butler, Judith. "Contingent Foundations: Feminism and the Question of 'Postmodernism.'" In *Feminists Theorize the Political,* ed. Judith Butler and Joan W. Scott, 3–21. New York: Routledge, 1992.

————. *Gender Trouble: Feminism and the Subversion of Identity.* New York: Routledge, 1990.

Cameron, Kenneth. *Africa on Film: Beyond Black and White.* New York: Continuum, 1994.

Campbell, James T. *Songs of Zion: The African Methodist Episcopal Church in the United States and South Africa.* New York: Oxford University Press, 1995.

Carby, Hazel V. *Reconstructing Black Womanhood: The Emergence of the Afro-American Woman Novelist.* New York: Oxford University Press, 1987.

Cavell, Stanley. *The World Viewed: Reflections on the Ontology of Film.* New York: Viking Press, 1971.

Chester, Edward W. *Clash of Titans: Africa and U. S. Foreign Policy.* Maryknoll, N.Y.: Orbis Books, 1974.

Chrisman, Laura. "The Imperial Unconscious? Representations of Imperial Discourse." In *Colonial Discourse and Post-Colonial Theory,* ed. Patrick Williams and Laura Chrisman, 498–516. New York: Columbia University Press, 1994.

Collins, Patricia Hill. *The Politics of Black Feminist Thought.* Cambridge, Mass.: Unwin Hyman, 1990.

Conrad, Joseph. *Heart of Darkness.* Ed. Robert Kimbrough. Norton Critical Edition. New York, W. W. Norton, 1988.

Cookey, S. J. S. *Britain and the Congo Question, 1885–1913.* New York: Humanities Press, 1968.

Coombs, Annie. *Reinventing Africa.* New Haven, Conn.: Yale University Press, 1994.

Cott, Nancy. *The Bonds of Womanhood: Women's Sphere in New England, 1790–1835.* New Haven, Conn.: Yale University Press, 1977.

————. *The Grounding of Modern Feminism.* New Haven, Conn.: Yale University Press, 1987.

de Lauretis, Teresa. *Technologies of Gender: Essays on Theory, Film, and Fiction.* Bloomington: Indiana University Press, 1987.

Dill, Bonnie Thornton. "The Dialectics of Black Womanhood." *Signs* 4, no. 3 (1979): 543–555.

Doane, Mary Ann. *Femmes Fatales: Feminism, Film Theory, Psychoanalysis.* New York: Routledge, 1991.

————. "Film and the Masquerade: Theorizing the Female Spectator." *Screen* 23, no. 3/4 (September/October 1982): 74–87.

Donaldson, Laura E. *Decolonizing Feminisms: Race, Gender, and Empire Building.* Chapel Hill: University of North Carolina Press, 1992.

Douglas, Ann. *The Feminization of American Culture.* New York: Doubleday, 1977.

Dudley, G. "A Rare Case of Female Fetishism." *International Journal of Sexology* 8 (1954): 32–34.

du Plessis, Rachel. *Writing Beyond the Ending.* Bloomington: Indiana University Press, 1985.

Ebert, Teresa. "The Romance of Patriarchy: Ideology, Subjectivity, and Postmodern Feminist Cultural Theory." *Cultural Critique* 10 (Fall 1988): 19–57.

Erenberg, Lewis. *Steppin' Out: New York Nightlife and the Transformation of American Culture, 1890–1930.* Westport, Conn.: Greenwood Press, 1981.

Fallon, Gretchen Kidd. "British Travel-Books from the Middle-East, 1890–1914: Conventions of the Genre and Three Unconventional Examples." Ph.D. dissertation, University of Maryland, 1981.

Felski, Rita. *The Gender of Modernity.* Cambridge, Mass.: Harvard University Press, 1995.

Fendall, Lonny Ward. "Theodore Roosevelt and Africa: Deliberate Non-involvement in the Scramble for Territory and Influence." Ph.D. dissertation, University of Oregon, 1972.

Fenichel, Otto. "The Psychology of Transvestism." In *Psychoanalysis and Male Sexuality,* ed. Hendrik M. Ruitenbeek, 203–220. 1930. Reprint, New Haven, Conn.: College and University Press, 1966.

Finch, Mark. "Sex and Address in 'Dynasty.'" *Screen* 27, no. 6 (1986): 24–42.

Flemming, Leslie A. "A New Humanity: American Missionaries' Ideals for Women in North India, 1870–1930." In *Western Women and Imperialism: Complicity and Resistance* ed. Nupur Chaudhuri and Margaret Strobel, 191–206. Bloomington: Indiana University Press, 1992.

Flint, J. E. "Mary Kingsley—A Reassessment." *Journal of African History* 4 (1963): 95–104.

Foucault, Michel. *The History of Sexuality, Volume I: An Introduction.* Trans. Robert Hurley. New York: Random House, 1980.

Frank, Katherine. "Voyages Out: Nineteenth-Century Women Travelers in Africa." In *Gender, Ideology and Action: Historical Perspectives on Women's Public Lives,* ed. Janet Sharistanian, 67–93. Westport, Conn.: Greenwood Press, 1986.

Frank, Lisa, and Paul Smith, eds. *Madonnarama.* New York: Cleis Press, 1993.

Frantz, R. W. *The English Traveller and the Movement of Ideas, 1660–1730.* 1934. Reprint, New York: Octagon Press, 1968.

Freedman, Estelle. "The New Woman: Changing Views of Women in the 1920s." *Journal of American History* 61, no. 2 (September 1974): 372–393.

Freud, Sigmund. "Fetishism." In *Sexuality and the Psychology of Love,* ed. Philip Reiff, 214–219. 1920. Reprint, New York: Collier Books, 1963.

———. "Fetishism." In *The Standard Edition of the Complete Psychological Works.* Vol. 21. Trans. James Strachey, 152–153. London: Hogarth Press, 1963.

Gaines, Kevin. *Uplifting the Race: Black Leadership, Politics, and Culture in the Twentieth Century.* Chapel Hill: University of North Carolina Press, 1996.

Garber, Marjorie. *Vested Interests: Cross-Dressing and Cultural Anxiety.* New York: Routledge, 1992.

Gilbert, Sandra, and Susan Gubar. *The Madwoman in the Attic: The Woman Writer and the Nineteenth-Century Imagination.* New Haven, Conn.: Yale University Press, 1979.

———. *No Man's Land: The Place of the Woman Writer in the Twentieth Century.* Vol. 2: *Sexchanges.* New Haven, Conn.: Yale University Press, 1989.

Gordon, Linda. *Women's Body, Women's Right: A Social History of Birth Control.* New York: Penguin, 1974.

Halprin, Sarah. "Writing in the Margins." *Jump Cut* 29 (February 1984): 32.

Hamilton, Tullia K. Brown. "The National Association of Colored Women, 1896–1920." Ph.D. dissertation, Emory University, 1989.

Hammond, Harold E. "American Interest in the Exploration of the Dark Continent." *Historian: A Journal of History* 18, no. 2 (Spring 1956): 202–229.

Hansen, Miriam. *Babel and Babylon: Spectatorship in American Silent Film.* Cambridge, Mass.: Harvard University Press, 1991.

———. "Pleasure, Ambivalence, Identification: Valentino and Female Spectatorship." *Cinema Journal* 25, no. 4 (Summer 1986): 6–32.

Heath, Stephen. "Joan Riviere and the Masquerade." In *Formations of Fantasy,* ed. Victor Burgin, James Donald, and Cora Kaplan, 48–49. London: Routledge, 1986.

———. "The Turn of the Subject." *Cine-Tracts* 8 (Summer–Fall 1979): 32–48.

Heilmann, Ann. *New Woman Fiction.* New York: Macmillan/St. Martin's Press, 2000.

Hermann, Ann. *The Queering of the Moderns.* New York: Palgrave, 2000.

Hochshild, Adam. *King Leopold's Ghost.* New York: Houghton Mifflin, 1998.

Hoock-Demarle, Marie-Claire. "Le Langage Litteraire des Femmes Enquetrices." In *Un fabuleux destin: Flora Tristan,* ed. Stephane Michaud. Dijon, France: Editions Universitaires, 1985.

Huyssen, Andreas. "Mass Culture as Woman: Modernism's Other." In *Studies in Entertainment,* ed. Tania Modleski, 188–207. Bloomington: Indiana University Press, 1986.

Irigaray, Luce. *This Sex Which Is Not One.* Trans. Catherine Porter. Ithaca, N.Y.: Cornell University Press, 1985.

———. "When the Goods Get Together." In *New French Feminisms,* ed. Elaine Marks and Isabelle de Courtivon, 107–110. New York: Schocken Books, 1981.

———. "Women's Exile." *Ideology and Consciousness* 1 (May 1977): 62–67.

James, Robert Rhodes. *Henry Wellcome.* London: Hodder and Stoughton, 1994.

Jessup, Philip C. *Elihu Root.* New York: Dodd, Mead and Company, 1938.

Jordan, Ellen. "The Christening of the New Woman." *Victorian Newsletter* 63 (Spring 1983): 19–21.

Kahn, David. *The Codebreakers: The Story of Secret Writing.* New York: Macmillan, 1967.

Kaplan, Caren. "Getting to Know You: Travel, Gender, and the Politics of Representation in *Anna and the King of Siam* and *The King and I.*" In *Late Imperial Culture,* ed. Roman de la Campa, E. Ann Kaplan, and Michael Sprinker, 33–52. London: Verso, 1995.

Kauffman, Linda. *Discourses of Desire: Gender, Genre, and Epistolary Fictions.* Ithaca, N.Y.: Cornell University Press, 1986.

Kofman, Sarah. *The Enigma of Woman.* Trans. Catherine Porter. 1980. Reprint, Ithaca, N.Y.: Cornell University Press, 1985.

Kuhn, Annette. *The Power of the Image: Essays on Representation and Sexuality.* London: Routledge, 1985.

Lacan, Jacques. *Ecrits: A Selection.* Trans. Alan Sheridan. New York: W. W. Norton, 1977.

Lacan, Jacques, and Wladimir Granoff. "Fetishism: The Symbolic, the Imaginary, and the Real." In *Perversions,* ed. Sandor Lorand, 265–276. New York: Gramercy Publishing, 1956.

LaFeber, Walter. *The New Empire: An Interpretation of American Expansion, 1860–1898.* Ithaca, N.Y.: Cornell University Press, 1963.

Lapore, Jill. "Historians Who Love Too Much: Reflections on Microhistory and Biography." *Journal of American History* 88, no. 1 (June 2001): 129–144.

Lazreg, Marnia. "Feminism and Difference: The Perils of Writing as a Woman on Women in Algeria." *Feminist Studies* (Spring 1988): 81–107.

Ledger, Sally. *The New Woman: Fiction and Feminism at the Fin de Siècle.* Manchester: Manchester University Press, 1997.

Levy, Anita. *Other Women: The Writing of Class, Race, and Gender, 1832–1898.* Princeton, N.J.: Princeton University Press, 1991.

Looser, Devoney. "Scolding Lady Mary Wortley Montagu? The Problematics of Sisterhood in Feminist Criticism." In *Feminist Nightmares, Women at Odds: Feminism and the Problem of Sisterhood,* ed. Susan Ostrov Weisser and Jennifer Fleischner, 44–61. New York: New York University Press, 1994.

Louis, William Roger. "Roger Casement and the Congo." *Journal of African History* 5, no. 1 (1964): 99–120.

MacCannell, Juliet Flower. "Things to Come: A Hysteric's Guide to the Future Female Subject." In *Supposing the Subject,* ed. Joan Copjec, 106–132. London: Verso, 1994.

Marcus, Jane. "The Asylums of Antaeus: Women, War and Madness—Is There a Feminist Fetishism?" In *The Difference Within: Feminism and Critical Theory,* 49–83. Amsterdam: John Benjamins Publishing Co., 1989.

Mayne, Judith. "Lesbian Looks: Dorothy Arzner and Female Authorship." In *How Do I Look? Queer Film and Video,* ed. Bad-Object Choices, 103–135. Seattle: Bay Press, 1991.

McClintock, Anne. *Imperial Leather: Race, Gender, and Sexuality in the Colonial Contest.* New York: Routledge, 1995.

Melman, Billie. *Women and the Popular Imagination in the Twenties: Flappers and Nymphs.* New York: St. Martin's Press, 1988.

Miers, Suzanne, and Richard Roberts, eds. *The End of Slavery in Africa,* Madison: University of Wisconsin Press, 1988.

Mill, Hugh Robert, ed. *The Record of the Royal Geographical Society, 1830–1930.* Kensington Gore, London: RGS, 1930.

Miller, Charles. *The Lunatic Express: An Entertainment in Imperialism.* New York: Macmillan Co., 1971.

Miller, Nancy K. "Emphasis Added: Plots and Plausibilities in Women's Fiction." *PMLA* 96, no. 1 (January 1981): 36–48.

Mitchell, Michele. "The 'Black Man's Burden': African-Americans, Imperialism, and Competing Racial Masculinities, 1890–1910." Paper presented at the Annual Meeting of the African Studies Association, Orlando, Fla., November 5, 1995.

Mitchell, W. J. T. *Iconology: Image, Text, Ideology.* Chicago: University of Chicago Press, 1986.

Moore, Jeanne Madeleine. "Bibi Bwana." *American History Illustrated* 21 (October 1986): 36–42.

Mulvey, Laura. "Afterthoughts on 'Visual Pleasure and Narrative Cinema,' Inspired by *Duel in the Sun*." *Framework* 15/16/17 (1981): 12–15.

———. "Visual Pleasure and Narrative Cinema." *Screen* 16 (Autumn 1975): 6–18.

Negra, Diane. *Off-white Hollywood: American Culture and Ethnic Female Stardom.* New York: Routledge, 2001.

Newman, Louise. *White Women's Rights: The Racial Origins of Feminism in the United States.* New York: Oxford University Press, 1999.

Newton, Esther. *Mother Camp: Female Impersonators in America.* Chicago: University of Chicago Press, 1972.

———. "The Mythic Mannish Lesbian: Radclyffe Hall and the New Woman." *Signs* 9, no. 4 (Summer 1984): 557–575.

Newton, Esther, and Shirley Walton. "The Misunderstanding: Toward a More Precise Sexual Vocabulary." In *Pleasure and Danger,* ed. Carole Vance, 242–250. Boston: Routledge, 1984.

Nicholson, Linda. *Gender and History: The Limits of Social Theory in the Age of the Family.* New York: Columbia University Press, 1986.

Offen, Karen. "Defining Feminism: A Comparative Historical Approach." *Signs* 14, no. 1 (Autumn 1988): 119–157.

———. "On the French Origins of the Word *Feminism* and *Feminist*." *Feminist Issues* 8, no. 2 (Summer 1988): 45–51.

Ong, Aihwa. "Colonialism and Modernity: Feminist Re-Presentations of Women in Non-Western Societies" *Inscriptions: Groups for the Critical Study of Colonial Discourse* 3/4 (1989): 79–93.

Pettinger, Alasdair. "Why Fetish?" *New Formations* 19 (Spring 1993): 83–93.

Phelan, Peggy. "Crisscrossing Cultures." In *Crossing the Stage: Controversies on Cross-Dressing,* ed. Lesley Ferris, 155–170. New York: Routledge, 1993.

Pietz, William. "The Problem of the Fetish, I." *Res* 9 (Spring 1985): 5–17.

———. "The Problem of the Fetish, II." *Res* 13 (Spring 1987): 23–46.

————. "The Problem of the Fetish, III." *Res* 16 (Autumn 1988): 105–124.

Poovey, Mary. *Uneven Developments: The Ideological Work of Gender in Mid-Victorian England.* Chicago: University of Chicago Press, 1988.

Pratt, Mary Louise. *Imperial Eyes: Travel Writing and Transculturation.* London: Routledge, 1992.

Ramusack, Barbara N. "Cultural Missionaries, Maternal Imperialists, Feminist Allies." In *Western Women and Imperialism: Complicity and Resistance,* ed. Nupur Chaudhuri and Margaret Strobel, 119–136. Bloomington: Indiana University Press, 1992.

Raphling, David L. "Fetishism in a Woman." *Journal of the American Psychoanalytic Association* 37, no. 2 (1989): 469–491.

Robinson, Jane. *Wayward Women: A Guide to Women Travellers.* Oxford: Oxford University Press, 1990.

Romero, Patricia. *Women's Voices on Africa.* New York: Marcus Wiener, 1992.

Rosenberg, Rosalind. *Beyond Separate Spheres.* New Haven, Conn.: Yale University Press, 1982.

Rubin, Gayle. "The Traffic in Women: Notes on the Political Economy of Sex." In *Towards an Anthropology of Women,* ed. Rayna R. Reiter, 157–210. New York: Monthly Review Press, 1975.

Russell, Mary. *The Blessings of a Good Thick Skirt.* London: Collins, 1986.

Russo, Mary. "Female Grotesques: Carnival and Theory." In *Feminist Studies/Critical Studies,* ed. Teresa de Lauretis, 213–229. Bloomington: Indiana University Press, 1985.

Russo, Vito. "Camp." In *Gay Men: The Sociology of Male Homosexuality,* ed. Martin Levine. New York: Harper and Row, 1979.

Ryan, Mary P. "The Projection of a New Womanhood: The Movie Moderns in the 1920s." In *Our American Sisters: Women in American Life and Thought,* ed. Jean E. Friedman and William G. Shade, 367–371. Boston: Allyn and Bacon, 1976.

————. *Womanhood in America: From Colonial Times to the Present.* New York: W. W. Norton, 1975.

Schor, Naomi. "Female Fetishism: The Case of George Sand." In *The Female Body in Western Culture,* ed. Susan Rubin Suleiman, 363–372. Cambridge, Mass.: Harvard University Press, 1986.

Scott, Joan. *Gender and the Politics of History.* 1988. Reprint, New York: Columbia University Press, 1999.

Shaloff, Stanley. *Reform in Leopold's Congo.* Richmond, Va.: John Knox Press, 1970.

Silverman, Kaja. *The Acoustic Mirror: The Female Voice in Psychoanalysis and Cinema.* Bloomington: Indiana University Press, 1988.

Simmons, Christina. "'Living Happily Ever After in Heterosexual Matehood': Fear of Lesbianism in the Ideology of Companionate Marriage." *Frontiers* 4, no. 3 (Fall 1979): 54–59.

Simpson, Donald. *Dark Companions: The African Contribution to the European Exploration of East Africa.* New York: Barnes and Noble Books, 1976.

Sinha, Mrinalini. "Gender and Imperialism: Colonial Policy and the Ideology of Moral Imperialism in Late Nineteenth-Century Bengal." In *Changing Men,* ed. Michael Kimmel, 217–231. London: Sage, 1987.

Sklar, Kathryn Kish. *Catherine Beecher: A Study in American Domesticity.* New Haven, Conn.: Yale University Press, 1973.

Slade, Ruth. *King Leopold's Congo: Aspects of the Development of Race Relations in the Congo Independent State.* London: Oxford University Press, 1962.

Smith, Sidonie. "The Other Woman and the Racial Politics of Gender." In *De/Colonizing the Subject: The Politics of Gender in Women's Autobiography,* ed. Sidonie Smith and Julia Watson, 410–435. Minneapolis: University of Minnesota Press, 1992.

———. *A Poetics of Women's Autobiography: Marginality and the Fictions of Self-Representation.* Bloomington: Indiana University Press, 1987.

Smith-Rosenberg, Carroll. *Disorderly Conduct: Visions of Gender in Victorian America.* New York: Knopf, 1985.

Snyder, Charles McCool. *Dr. Mary Walker.* New York: Arno Press, 1974.

Solomon, Alisa. "It's Never Too Late to Switch." In *Crossing the Stage: Controversies on Cross-Dressing,* ed. Lesley Ferris, 144–154. London: Routledge, 1993.

Spivak, Gayatri Chakravorty. "A Reponse to 'The Difference Within: Feminism and Critical Theory.'" In *The Difference Within: Feminism and Critical Theory,* ed. Elizabeth Meese and Alice Parker, 207–220. Amsterdam: John Benjamins Publishing Co., 1989.

Stacey, Jackie. "Desperately Seeking Difference." In *The Female Gaze: Women as Viewers of Popular Culture,* ed. Lorraine Gamman and Margaret Marshment, 112–129. Seattle: The Real Comet Press, 1989.

Staiger, Janet. *Bad Women: Regulating Sexuality in Early American Cinema.* Minneapolis: University of Minnesota Press, 1995.

Stocking, George W., Jr. *Race, Culture, and Evolution.* New York: Free Press, 1968.

———. *Victorian Anthropology.* New York: Macmillan, 1987.

Ticknor, Lisa. *The Spectacle of Women: Imagery of the Suffrage Campaign, 1907–1914.* London: Chatto and Windus, 1987.

Todd, Ellen Wiley. "Art, the 'New Woman,' and Consumer Culture." In *Gender and American History since 1890,* ed. Barbara Melosh, 127–154. London: Routledge, 1993.

Tyler, Carole-Anne. "Boys Will Be Girls: The Politics of Gay Drag." In *Inside/Out: Lesbian Theories, Gay Theories,* ed. Diana Fuss, 32–70. New York: Routledge, 1991.

Vicinus, Martha. "Distance and Desire: English Boarding School Friendships, 1870–1920." In *Hidden From History: Reclaiming the Gay and Lesbian Past,* ed. Martin Duberman, Martha Vicinus, and George Chauncey Jr., 212–229. New York: Meridian, 1989.

Walker, Janet. "Psychoanalysis and Feminist Film Theory: The Problem of Sexual Difference and Identity." In *Multiple Voices in Feminist Film Criticism,* ed. Diane Carson, Linda Dittmar, and Janice R. Welsch. Minneapolis: University of Minnesota Press, 1994.

Ware, Susan. *Still Missing: Amelia Earhart and the Search for Modern American Feminism.* New York: W. W. Norton, 1993.

Ware, Vron. *Beyond the Pale: White Women, Racism, and History.* London: Verso, 1992.

Weimann, Jeanne Madeline. *The Fair Women.* Chicago: Academy Press, 1981.

Welter, Barbara Welter. "The Cult of True Womanhood, 1820–1860." *American Quarterly* 18 (Summer 1966): 151–174.

White, Mimi. "Rehearsing Feminism: Women/History in *The Life and Times of Rosie the Riveter* and *Swing Shift.*" In *Multiple Voices in Feminist Film Criticism,* ed. Diane Carson, Linda Dittmar, and Janice R. Welsch, 318–329. Minneapolis: University of Minnesota Press, 1994.

Wildenthal, Lora. *German Women for Empire, 1884–1945.* Durham, N.C.: Duke University Press, 2001.

Williams, Linda. *Hard Core: Power, Pleasure, and the Frenzy of the Visible.* Berkeley: University of California Press, 1989.

Williams, William Appleman. *The Tragedy of American Diplomacy.* New York: Dell, 1959.

Wolf, Howard, and Ralph Wolf. *Rubber: A Story of Glory and Greed.* New York: Covici, Friede Publishers, 1936.

Young, Shelagh. "Feminism and the Politics of Power." In *The Female Gaze: Women as Viewers of Popular Culture,* ed. Lorraine Gammen and Margaret Marshment, 173–188. Seattle: The Real Comet Press, 1989.

Young, Tim. *Travellers in Africa: British Travelogues, 1850–1900.* Manchester: Manchester University Press, 1994.

Zavitzianos, G. "The Perversion of Fetishism in Women." *Psychoanalysis Q* 51 (1982): 405–425.

INDEX

Page numbers in italics refer to illustrations.

TRACEY JEAN BOISSEAU is Assistant Professor of cultural and women's history in the Department of History at the University of Akron. She has published articles on May French-Sheldon in *Signs and Gender and History* and recently edited a new edition of *Sultan to Sultan* (first published in 1892 by May French-Sheldon).